SIBLING RELATIONSHIPS

SIBLING RELATIONSHIPS

Editor

PROPHECY COLES

KARNAC

LONDON   NEW YORK

First published in 2006 by
H. Karnac (Books) Ltd.
6 Pembroke Buildings, London NW10 6RE

British Library Cataloguing in Publication Data

A C.I.P. for this book is available from the British Library

ISBN 1 85575 323 5

Edited, typeset and produced by The Studio Publishing Services Ltd,
www.publishingservicesuk.co.uk
E-mail: studio@publishingservicesuk.co.uk

Printed in Great Britain

www.karnacbooks.com

CONTENTS

Prophecy Coles is a psychoanalytic psychotherapist. She has published several papers on siblings, and is the author of *The Importance of Sibling Relationships in Psychoanalysis* (Karnac, 2003).

Leonore Davidoff is a Research Professor in the Department of Sociology, University of Essex. Her books include (with Catherine Hall) *Family Fortunes: Men & Women of the English Middle Class, 1780–1850* (revised edition, 2002); *Worlds Between: Historical Perspectives on Gender and Class* (1995); *The Family Story: Blood Contract & Intimacy 1830–1960* (with M. Doolittle, J. Fink, and K. Holden, 1999). She is the founder editor of the journal *Gender & History*.

Robert Hinshelwood is Fellow of the Royal College of Psychiatry and of the Institute of Psychoanalysis. He is currently Professor in the Centre for Psychoanalytic Studies, University of Essex; and previously Director of The Cassel Hospital. He has written widely on Kleinian psychoanalysis, including *The Dictionary of Kleinian Thought* (1989) and *Clinical Klein* (1994); and on a psychoanalytic approach to social and political processes in *Observing*

Organisations (with Wilhem Skogstad, 2000) and *Thinking about Institutions* (2001).

Vivienne Lewin is a psychoanalytic psychotherapist in private practice. She trained at the London Centre for Psychotherapy and is a Training Therapist and Supervisor. Her publications include two papers on twins, "Working with a twin; implications for the transference" (1994) *British Journal of Psychotherapy*, 10(4), and "The twin in the transference" in *Ideas in Practice* (Bishop, Foster, Klein & O'Connell (Eds.), Karnac, 2002). She has also published a book on twins and the twinning process, *The Twin in the Transference* (Whurr, 2004).

Juliet Mitchell is Professor of Psychoanalysis and Gender Studies and a Fellow of Jesus College Cambridge. She is a Full Member of the International Psychoanalytic Society. Her books include: a new edition of *Psychoanalysis and Feminism* (2000); *Selected Melanie Klein* (Penguin, 2000); *Mad Men and Medusas: Reclaiming Hysteria and the Effects of Sibling Relations on the Human Condition* (Penguin, 2000); *Women: the Longest Revolution; Psychoanalysis and Feminism*; and *Women's Estate*. Her latest book, *Siblings: Sex and Violence*, was published by Polity Press in October 2003. Juliet Mitchell is married to the anthropologist Jack Goody and has one daughter and five step-children. She lives in Cambridge.

Elspeth Morley is a full Training Member of the British Association of Psychotherapists and of the Society for Couple Psychoanalytical Psychotherapists. She has a BA from Oxford in PPE and obtained her professional social work qualification at the LSE. She worked as a London Juvenile Court probation officer, followed by becoming Prinicipal Family Social Worker for the Family Welfare Association. In 1994 she gained an MA at the University of Hertfordshire with her thesis, "Using the focus of couple psychotherapy in work with the individual patient". Her full-time private psychoanalytic practice with individuals and with couples includes work with her husband, Dr Robert Morley, as co-therapist. She trains couple counsellors on TCCR Relationships Counselling for London Diploma and Conversion Courses.

Estelle Roith is the author of *The Riddle of Freud* (1987), in which she examines the Jewish influences of Freud's troubled theories of femininity. She has written and lectured on subjects ranging from child abuse to the *fatwa* on Salman Rushdie. Dr Roith is a psychoanalytic psychotherapist in private practice in London. She trained at the London Centre for Psychotherapy. She is currently working on an extension of some of the ideas presented in this book.

Margaret Rustin is a Consultant Child Psychotherapist at the Tavistock Clinic, London, and is Chair of its Professional Committee. She has written widely on child psychotherapeutic practice, co-editing and contributing to *Closely Observed Infants* (1989); *Psychotic States in Children* (1997); and *Assessment in Child Psychotherapy* (2000). She is co-author, with Michael Rustin, of *Narratives of Love and Loss: Studies in Modern Children's Fiction* (1987/2001) and *Mirror to Nature: Drama, Psychoanalysis and Society* (2002).

Michael Rustin is Professor of Sociology at the University of East London, and a Visiting Professor at the Tavistock Clinic. He has written widely on psychoanalytic topics. He is author of *The Good Society and the Inner World* (1991), and *Reason and Unreason: Psychoanalysis, Science and Politics* (2001); and with Margaret Rustin, *Narratives of Love and Loss: Studies in Modern Children's Fiction* (1987/2001) and *Mirror to Nature: Drama Psychoanalysis and Society* (2002).

Jennifer Silverstone is a psychoanalytic psychotherapist working in private practice. She is a Training Therapist and Supervisor. She was a member of the editorial board of the *British Journal of Psychotherapy* and has written several clinical papers, including *An Absence of Mind*, in *Ideas in Practice* (Bishop, Foster, Klein, & O'Connell (Eds.), Karnac, 2002).

Harriet Thistlethwaite studied history at Oxford, then worked as a publishing editor until 1987 before training at The London Centre for Psychotherapy. She took a Masters in Psychoanalytic Studies at the Tavistock, UEL in 2000, and in 2005 qualified in the MA in Creative Writing (Poetry) at Royal Holloway, University of London.

Gary Winship (PhD, MA, Dip Gp Psych, Dip Add, RMN) is a UKCP registered psychotherapist and lecturer at the University of Sheffield, formerly Adult Psychotherapist at the Maudsley, Berkshire and at Broadmoor.

PREFACE

This book has come about due to the encouragement of Karnac, and in particular, Leena Hakkinen. The story goes back some way. I approached Karnac in the mid-1990s with the idea that I should collect some of the seminal papers on siblings, for I was writing a paper on the subject (Coles, 1998) and there seemed to be no reference text that I could turn to. Graham Sleight, who was at Karnac at the time, suggested that I should write the missing book myself, giving the references that I had found useful. This became *The Importance of Sibling Relationships in Psychoanalysis* (Coles, 2003). I approached Karnac again with my first idea about a collection of papers on siblings, but the proposal was turned down for a second time and they suggested instead that I commission an original collection of papers, which has now become this present volume.

I want to thank all the contributors for their patience and cooperation with this project. My special thanks go to Melanie Hart and Ann Scott for their editorial help. Finally, but most importantly, my thanks to Walter, who has supported and encouraged me throughout.

Prophecy Coles
Editor

Introduction

Prophecy Coles

There is no general acceptance that our relationships with our siblings help to structure our psychic world. We are at the early stages of finding a theoretical framework into which to put our clinical or everyday observations about them, and this task is made more difficult because there is not even common agreement about the nature of these relationships. Are they based upon hatred, the wish to murder, and a fear of death? Is the birth of a sibling necessarily traumatic? Can there be strong positive relationships between siblings? Do we learn democratic ideas of equality and fairness from the nursery and the playground, with our siblings and our peers? What about only children?

One of my grandsons (aged seven) was recently asked to write on "My Family" at school. He was given no instruction as to how he should approach the topic. His opening sentences went something like this. "I have a sister who is very beautiful (aged five) and I have another sister (aged two) who has blonde curls around the back of her neck. My mother is covered in freckles." There are many things that we might want to say about this grandson's feelings about "My Family", but for present purposes what is striking is that his siblings are every bit as important in his thinking, at that moment, as his mother is. The papers in this volume help us to see how rich and formative sibling relationships can be.

In my book, *The Importance of Sibling Relationships in Psychoanalysis* (Coles, 2003), I suggested that one reason for the neglect of sibling relationships in our psychological theories was linked to the over-riding importance that Freud gave to the Oedipus complex. Until quite recently it has been accepted that the only relationships central to emotional development were the parental ones. What seems to have changed is that this idea, and others associated with some of the central beliefs of psychoanalysis, are more open to questioning. There is greater freedom to debate whether the conflict model of the human psyche is the essential one, or whether the need for secure attachment is incompatible with the concept of the death drive. Arguments continue about the scientific status of psychoanalytic knowledge, and there is greater interest in the cultural determinates of our psychological theories. Many people agree with Said when he wrote

> No-one has ever devised a method for detaching the scholar from the circumstances of life, from the fact of his involvement (conscious or unconscious) with a class, a set of beliefs, a social position, or from the mere activity of being a member of a society. [Said, 1978]

If the scholar cannot be detached from the "circumstances of life", then the question might be: what is happening in our society at the moment that is contributing to the fresh contemporary interest in the relationships between brothers and sisters? Does the interest come from a freeing of psychoanalytic thinking or is the interest more widespread? And if so, why? To take one example, a recent exhibition at Tate Britain (October 2003) on the art of Augustus John and Gwen John had, as its central theme, the sibling relationship. The question asked by the organizers was whether the sibling relationship was reflected in or illuminated the work of these artists. In a discussion group with Emma Freud, Adam Phillips, and Michael Holroyd, held at the Museum, it was suggested that a psychoanalytic approach to their paintings might see their work as containing and reflecting two sides of the same coin. Augustus John turned away from an inner world of sadness and loneliness—their mother died when they were small children—towards a lively, outward flamboyance. His sister, Gwen John, on the other hand, was able to stay with the pain but at the expense of outward liveliness. Each found a way to contain the mental states that the other could not bear.

Jenny Uglow, in a recent talk[1] on her book *The Lunar Men* (2002), said,

> Ideas are probably not produced by individuals; they are more likely to be produced by the exchange of ideas. It takes you away from a romantic idea of the individual genius. How do we think? Do we always think on our own? Or are we always thinking in relationship to other people.

The idea that we are always thinking in relationship to other people is not new. Fairbairn (1946), Bion (1962), Winnicott (1976), and more recently Peter Hobson (2002), have suggested something similar in emphasizing the primary importance of a mother's interaction with her child for future emotional and intellectual development. However, what is significant in Uglow's view is that our thinking seems to be at its most creative when we are engaged in discussion with our contemporaries. In other words, our peers and our siblings play a crucial part in the development of mind. The isolated genius, battling against the outside world of jealous rivals and attackers, seems to have shifted as a model of the thinker.[2] We more readily agree with the geneticist Professor Howard Trevor Jacobs,[3] who, when interviewed about his recent award, said "One night of crazy brain-storming over a few beers is likely to produce more exciting results than twenty years' solitary study in the laboratory." Our deepening understanding of our dependence upon each other and, in this case, upon our contemporaries, is being reflected in the "widening scope of psychoanalysis" (Loewald, 1980). The analyst is less likely to be idealized as an authority figure. Therapy is conceptualized, by some, as a craft that is learned in interaction with the patient. The greater democracy in the consulting room may allow the horizontal ties of sibling relationships to become more apparent, and as the idea of a sibling transference becomes more familiar it may feel less threatening to the structure of therapy.

There may be another reason for the interest in siblings and their relationships. Many people live in what is now called the "blended" family. The "blended" family describes a unit made up of changing sexual partners and the offspring from these short-lived unions. Marriages, too, are unstable, since divorce statistics suggest half of them will end in this way.[4] Our interest in sibling relationships may reflect the lack of stability in the family and a nostalgia for the support of a large family with many brothers and sisters.

I have been surprised to discover that it was not only in psychoanalytic theory that sibling relationships have been ignored. Sociology, history, literary theory, as well as economic and political theory, have all had a tendency to dismiss the impact of brothers and sisters upon each other. It is for this reason that I have included sociological and literary criticism to try and widen our understanding of this cultural phenomenon. There may be disappointment at the shortage of clinical material, but I need to remind the reader that we are still in the early days of thinking about the relevance of sibling relationships to inner psychic structure in the UK. This is not so in the USA, where there has been a steady interest in the impact of siblings, most notably Bank & Kahn (1997) and Volkan & Ast (1997). There have been a few lone voices over the years in the UK; for instance, in the early 1990s Mander (1991) reminded us of the importance of sibling rivalry in the inner world; later, Mitchell (2000, 2003) continued that theme. There have been therapists who have written about the sibling dynamic in groups (Brunori, 1998; Hopper, 2000), but there are not many therapists, yet, who are writing about the impact of sibling relationships on their clinical work.

Part I. Culture and literature

The book opens with Leonore Davidoff's[5] sociological and historical account of siblings, "The sibling relationship and sibling incest in historical context". This chapter sets the tone for much of what is to follow. ". . . some of [the] most powerful emotional bonds, as well as practical human interactions, still remain between brothers and sisters". And yet, she says "Despite the centrality of this relationship, both historically and in contemporary life, it remains strangely neglected, relegated to a fragmentary footnote of the historical record." Davidoff asks whether a reason for this neglect is because siblings "have no direct effect upon reproduction". Since the nineteenth century the idea that sibling relationships are non-reproductive has leant on a more hotly debated question about the nature of sibling sexual desire. Freud's view was that sibling sexual desire is kept in check only by social taboos, whereas Westermarck believed that there is ". . . an inbuilt aversion to such mating as protection against debasing the gene pool".

Whether it is inbuilt aversion or sexual taboo, Davidoff argues for the significance that brother and sister attachments have held in autobiography and oral history, and shows how these relationships become especially prominent during the period of the Romantic movement. For men of the late eighteenth and early nineteenth centuries "Sisters, less psychically dangerous than mothers, and without the sexuality (with its potential for childbearing) of wives, seem to have embodied the perfect ideal". The exemplar of an intense sibling relationship is the well-documented one of Dorothy and William Wordsworth. The erotic overtones of their relationship and their involvement with each other throughout their lives seems a world away from family life today. The question asked by Davidoff is: why have our economic, political and literary theories ignored the "vivid portraits of actual brothers and sisters", such as the Wordsworths? She points out a gap between the theories that academics and intellectuals use and our everyday experience, and wonders when we will allow ourselves to be informed, intellectually, by what we know intuitively. Davidoff ends by pondering whether a cultural development of the horizontal bonds of sibling relationships "could be a model for a nascent civil society". Davidoff's view that sibling relationships have been ignored in sociological and historical analysis because "they have no effect upon reproduction" might give one reason why they have been ignored in psychoanalysis.

Estelle Roith's paper (Chapter Two), takes up ideas about sibling rivalry that may lie at the heart of a particularly intense religious struggle that is engaging the world today. Her chapter, "Ishmael and Isaac: an enduring conflict", suggests that it is the relationship between the two half brothers, Ishmael and Isaac, and between them and their father, Abraham, that needs to be explored if we are to understand the conflicts between Judaism, Christianity, and Islam. All three faiths are able to say, "We are the children of Abraham". So what divides them? Roith's answer is simple and yet profound. "The fact is that the Abrahamic faiths begin with the rejection and exclusion of one child in favour of another". The two sons of Abraham are pitted against each other from the moment when Sarah becomes so jealous of Ishmael, after the birth of Isaac, that she insists that he and his mother Hagar are expelled into the wilderness. The two sons are also let down by Abraham because he is prepared to sacrifice them. Roith asks the difficult question, "Why should . . . [Judaism and Islam] wish to compete for what seems like the dubious honour of having their founding father offered up for slaughter by a so-called loving father, in unquestioning obedience to a demanding deity?" This leads her into an exploration of the meaning of sacrifice. She concludes that Freud's belief in the "primal horde", in which the brothers unite to kill the father, is contradicted in this tale. It is Abraham's willingness to sacrifice his two sons that lies at the heart of this primordial sibling conflict that is still being fought out between Jews, Christians, and Moslems.

Robert Hinshelwood and Gary Winship, the authors of Chapter Three, "Orestes and democracy", explore the development of democratic ideals from within a psychological theory about the family. Has psychoanalytic theory, they ask, in emphasizing the emotions of rivalry and guilt and the wish to murder, ignored "the bond of devotion" that can exist between siblings? They show how, in Aeschylus's *Oresteia*, and in particular *The Libation Bearers*, we see the presence of this bond between Orestes and Electra as they agree to kill their mother, Clytemnestra, in expiation for the murder of their father Agamemnon. This play, the authors suggest, is not an exploration of the feminine counterpart to Oedipus, for Electra does not slay her mother. Aeschylus's intention was to demonstrate the anarchy that follows upon (sibling) democracy. But, in a telling reading of the drama, from within the tradition of psychoanalytic theory, Hinshelwood and Winship suggest that the murder of Clytemnestra by her son Orestes is at odds with the Freudian belief of the "primal horde" killing off the patriarch. To ignore the difference between the sibling bond of Orestes and Electra and the sibling conflicts in Sophocles' Oedipus trilogy is to turn a blind eye to the role of the parents in these two tragic dramas. Sibling bonds and sibling conflict is nurtured within the family through many generations. The psychoanalytic model of the family that Hinshelwood and Winship propose suggests that democracy can only grow in the context of a benign autocracy. An infant needs protection by someone in authority who can, at the same time, guard the infant's belief that he is "His Majesty" until he gains the maturity to give up this omnipotence. Both parent and child need to change and grow, over time, for democracy to flourish. What these authors add to the more traditional psychoanalytic focus of mother and child is that it is the "bond of devotion" between siblings that must be nurtured within the family if democratic ideals are to spread into the wider social world.

In Chapter Four, "The siblings in *Measure for Measure* and *Twelfth Night*", Margaret and Michael Rustin suggest that sibling relationships have been ignored not only in psychological theories about the family, but also in literary criticism of Western theatre. They redress this lack by looking at Shakespeare's dramatization of sibling relationships in these two plays. Like Aeschylus, Shakespeare places his theatrical dramas against a backdrop of political concerns. The breakdown of sibling relationships in *Measure for Measure* could be read as a metaphor for "a broader moral crisis" besetting late Elizabethan and early Jacobean England. However, Rustin and Rustin argue that Shakespeare's understanding of the complexity of sibling relationships takes us beyond the political arena. Shakespeare understood that there can be creative sibling bonds that sustain and help in adversity, while there can be conflictual sibling relationships that fail in times of difficulty or social breakdown. In *Measure for Measure*, Isabella's brother is about to be hanged for lechery. Claudio appeals to his sister to plead his cause with the Governor. Isabella is about to become a nun. The Governor is prepared to restore Claudio's freedom if Isabella will sleep with him. She refuses. Claudio is furious with her and unable to imagine that, for Isabella, giving up her virginity could be comparable in meaning to his death. They are unable to help each other, for neither can understand the other's sexual predicament. Rustin and Rustin draw the conclusion that "This refusal of thoughts which would give rise to psychic conflict can be seen as the consequence of a mind in which there is no room for siblings". By contrast, they suggest, in *Twelfth Night*, the twin siblings Viola and Sebastian, though they believe they have lost each other, keep each other alive in their minds and are therefore able to live hopeful lives in the present. Their twin-ship offers ". . . [a] family identity and a sense of fundamental safety which family membership represents". Rustin and Rustin stress Shakespeare's insight that the intimacy and trust, and even bisexual identification, that is possible between brother and sister, allows for adult heterosexual coupling. "Siblings being able to maintain mutual interest, concern and respect for each other are thus a metaphor for a state of mind in which thoughts are allowed to come alive in the mind and be given house-room, even if they challenge the comfort of the status-quo."

In Chapter Five, Harriet Thistlethwaite takes us through a harrowing account of some of the psychological consequences of being a replacement baby for an unmourned dead sibling in "The replacement child as writer". Such replacement babies are traumatized before they are born, not by birth but by death. Thistlewaite illustrates her view by looking at the work of two creative geniuses, Eugene O'Neill and Rainer Maria Rilke. "Do not return. If you can bear to, stay / dead with the dead", Rilke writes in a poem *Requiem for a Friend*. Rilke was a replacement baby for a dead sister, Ismene. "[S]tay / dead with the dead' is a powerful indication of the sort of unconscious dialogue these replacement babies have to negotiate with their dead sibling. O'Neill was born two and a half years after the death of an older brother Edmund, who had died of measles when he was two. In one of his last great plays, *A Long Day's Journey into Night* (1956), Eugene O'Neill puts the unconscious dialogue in an equally graphic way. O'Neill actually calls his hero Edmund. In a long soliloquy Edmund says, "That's what I wanted—to be alone with myself in another world where truth is untrue and life can hide from itself" (p. 78). Both O'Neill and Rilke intuitively understood that if they are to have a chance to live then they must find a way in which their dead sibling must be allowed to be dead. For O'Neill this was a difficult task that he struggled against all his life. He was asked one day why he kept looking at himself in the mirror. He replied, "I'm just looking to see if I'm alive".

Part II. Clinical theory

It is in the sixth chapter by Juliet Mitchell, "Sibling trauma: a theoretical consideration", that we turn to some of the hard theoretical thinking that needs to be done if siblings are to find their representation in psychoanalytic theory. What Mitchell proposes here has been elaborated in her two most recent books (2000, 2003), though in this chapter we get a particularly clear understanding of the central place siblings have in her understanding of mental life. Mitchell is formulating a causal theory, or model of explanation, about siblings that borrows from a psychoanalytic model of the parent–child relationship founded on trauma, desire, and the threat of castration. Trauma, for Mitchell, has a strong and a weak sense. Weak trauma can be recovered from. Strong trauma, she believes, "does not change or develop, it is absolute for all time, it cannot be repressed or defended against". For trauma to become strong, in a psychological sense, it has to break through "psychological barriers" that are man-made, such as the threat of castration or the taboo on incest, and then it becomes set as a complex and part of the structure of our unconscious life. At the birth of a sibling Mitchell believes the self is annihilated; one is "not oneself", but is "beside oneself" or "out of one's mind". This is strong, culturally imposed, trauma. Mitchell supports her idea that sibling relationships are based upon this annihilating strong trauma by arguing that parents deny that children are traumatized by the birth of a sibling, and, ". . . [i]f there is denial we are looking at a strong trauma with all that implies". She also makes the point that if there is a compulsion to repeat this is evidence of strong trauma. She uses the case of Sylvia Plath, taken from Earnshaw's (1995) study, to illustrate her case. Plath compulsively repeated, by killing herself, the trauma she had experienced at the birth of her brother when she was nearly three. "When her own live son is born she feels as she did as the little girl when her live baby brother arrived—she experiences herself as doubly dead—dead because Warren has replaced her, dead because she wants to be the Warren she has imaginatively killed. She kills herself." In killing herself she is repeating her "already taken place death". Mitchell ends her chapter with the warning that if we fail to understand that the birth of a sibling is a strong trauma, then we are bound to enact or compulsively repeat the trauma. Wars, violence, rape, and abuse, as well as suicide, are the inevitable consequence of this and "then there can be no ethics in which we respect the other and ourselves as other to that sibling other".

In Chapter Seven, Vivienne Lewin takes us to the heart of one the powerful myths about siblings in "The idealization of the twin relationship". We all believe that if you are a twin you are somehow special, because we have given to the twin relationship the symbolic value of perfect unity. What our idealization of twins ignores, however, is the difficult task they have in maturing emotionally and becoming separate. This problem is compounded in cases where one twin dies at birth. Lewin considers the life of Elvis Presley. A dead twin preceded his birth, and there seems to have been some surprise that there was a second, alive, baby. The emotional trauma for a twin who has a dead twin at birth is substantially different from other birth traumas, such as those that Mitchell and Thistlethwaite each consider. It is not surprising that monozygotic twins feel that they have lost half of themselves at the death of their twin, even if the death takes place at birth, for they were one egg at the beginning of their life. This feeling was certainly true in the case of Presley. His difficulty was compounded, moreover, by the fact that he and his mother then formed a twinning relationship and could not be separated except at her death. The unconscious twinning seems to have continued even beyond death, since Elvis died at forty-two, the age he believed his mother was when she died. Lewin relates our idealization of twins to a Kleinian model of the internalized good mother with her twin breasts. As Lewin puts it, the therapeutic task for a monozygotic twin may be to find a way of giving up being an identical twin and becoming a non-identical one. What is of interest to theoreticians is that the therapist who works with twins is forced to engage with a powerful sibling relationship. Twin siblings cannot be ignored and the parental transferences have to fit in alongside this powerful dynamic. Lewin makes it clear, both in this chapter and in her earlier book (2003), that this is no easy task.

In Chapter Eight, "The influence of sibling relationships on couple choice and development", Elspeth Morley spells out the intricate interweaving of early vertical and horizontal relationships, as they surface in later marital difficulties. Morley has a graphic model for the early parental and sibling structures. "My analogy," she says, ". . . is to a staircase, with each lateral tread being both preceded and followed by the vertical." She argues that in many cases of couple therapy the task is to understand their lateral relationships before they can take the vertical step up to create the next generation. Morley looks particularly at the case of the Wolf Man. She suggests that Freud ignored his patient's lateral relationship with both his sister and, later, his wife, Therese. As a consequence, the Wolf Man was never helped to move into the vertical position that would have allowed him and his wife to become parents.

In the final chapter, "Siblings", Jennifer Silverstone shares her experience of working with the sibling transference in her everyday life as a therapist. She takes the view that one of the important roles siblings can have for each other is to carry the family narrative when the parents have failed to do so. Such failure is especially clear in those cases where the parents have experienced extreme trauma, such as the Holocaust. But Silverstone argues that parents may also fail to carry the family narrative if they are unable to contain their ambivalence towards their children. Silverstone draws upon Parker's (1995) seminal book on maternal ambivalence and on the thinking of Winnicott (1975). Siblings can become important internal objects when maternal ambivalence is denied. She describes three clinical cases of maternal failure and the work that she and her patients had to do to recognize the failure, live with the sibling transference, and move on to a more integrated place.

It has been a moving experience to learn, through reading these chapters, of the different ways in which siblings are being thought about at this moment, within sociological, historical, and literary criticism as well as psychotherapy. It has helped to reinforce my conviction that we need to keep questioning the reasons for our beliefs. Why did we think siblings were unimportant in the structure of our psychic life, and why are we beginning to think that we missed something important? At the very least I hope the reader will be as stimulated as I have been to think further about siblings.

Notes

1. At the Centre for Editing Lives, at Queen Mary College, University of London, reported in The *Independent*, 23 November 2004.
2. Freud (1900a) wrote, "My emotional life has always insisted that I should have an intimate friend and a hated enemy". And he linked this need to the intimate relationship he had had with his nephew,

John, during the first three years of his life. I am suggesting that Freud was at his most intellectually creative when he had an emotionally intimate friend. See Freud's encounter with Fliess (Masson, 1985).

3. The *Observer*, 5 December 2004.

4. There were 306,000 marriages and 167,000 divorces in 2004 (the *Independent*, 22 March 2005).

5. Versions of this chapter have appeared in *Quaderni Storici, 83*(2) (August 1993) and in *World's Between: Historical Perspectives on Gender & Class* (Polity Press, 1995). It also includes material from an article, "'A double singleness': sibling incest in the late 18th and early 19th century English middle class", published in *L'Homme, Zeitschrift fur Feminische Geschichtwissenschaft*, 13(1), 2002 ("'Eins seinzu zweit': Geschwisterinzest in der englischen Mittelschicht des spaten 18. und fruhen 19. Jahrhunderts').

References

Bank, S. P., & Kahn, M. D. (1997). *The Sibling Bond*. New York: Basic Books.

Bion, W. (1962). *Learning from Experience*. London: Karnac.

Brunori, L. (1998). Special edition: Papers from the sibling workshop. *Group Analysis, 31*(3): 305–307.

Coles, P. (1998). The children in the apple tree. *Australian Journal of Psychotherapy, 1–2*: 10–33.

Coles, P. (2003). *The Importance of Sibling Relationships in Psychoanalysis*. London: Karnac.

Earnshaw, A. (1995). *Time will Tell; What was I doing at My Child's Age Now? What Happened to my Parents at this Time in their Lives?* Glebe, Australia: A & K Enterprises. Fast Books.

Fairbairn, W. R. D. (1946). *Psychoanalytic Studies of the Personality*. London: Routledge & Kegan Paul.

Freud, S. (1900a). The interpretation of dreams. *S.E.*, 4–5.

Hobson, P. (2002). *The Cradle of Thought*. London: Pan Macmillan.

Hopper, E. (2000). Sibling relationships in groups. *Psychotherapy, 53*: 267–315.

Loewald, H. (1980). *Papers on Psychoanalysis*. New Haven, NJ: Yale University Press.

Mander, G. (1991). Some thoughts on sibling rivalry and competitiveness. *British Journal of Psychotherapy, 7*(4): 368–380.

Mitchell, J. (2000). Mad Men and Medusa: Reclaiming Hysteria and the Effects of Sibling Relationships on the Human Condition. London: Penguin.

Mitchell, J. (2003). *Siblings: Sex and Violence*. Oxford: Polity.

Parker, R. (1995). *Torn in Two: The Experience of Maternal Ambivalence*. London: Virago.

Said, E. W. (1978). *Orientalism*. London: Random House.

Uglow, J. (2002). *The Lunar Men*. London: Faber & Faber.

Volkan, V. A., & Ast, G. (1997). *Siblings in the Unconscious and Psychopathology*. New York: International Universities Press.

Winnicott, D. W. (1976). *The Maturational Process & the Facilitating Environment*. London: Hogarth Press.

PART I
CULTURE AND LITERATURE

CHAPTER ONE

The sibling relationship and sibling incest in historical context

Leonore Davidoff

"The sibling is the beginning of the stranger"

(Japanese Proverb quoted in Sylvia Yanagisako, *Transforming the Past: Tradition and Kinship among Japanese Americans*, Stanford University Press, 1985, p. 193)

That tender union, all combin'd
Of Nature's holiest sympathies
'Tis Friendship in its loveliest dress
'Tis Love's most perfect tenderness

(Mary Ann Hedge, "Brother and Sister", 1832)

From the thundering majesty of Greek tragedy to the brutal Icelandic sagas, to the sentimentality of such Victorian verses as the above, the relationship of brother and sister has haunted our cultural heritage. And in everyday lives some of the most powerful emotional bonds, as well as practical human interactions, still remain between brothers and sisters.[1] In the rare cases where historians have noticed sibling relationships, their importance has been evident. Sisters and brothers have acted as surrogate parents (and children), informal teachers, adult co-residents, friends, and even, on occasion, lovers.

Despite the centrality of this relationship, both historically and in contemporary life, it remains strangely neglected, relegated to a fragmentary footnote of the historical record. To understand why, it must first be understood as embedded within the seemingly ubiquitous phenomena of kinship and family. However, the concepts *kinship* and *family* are themselves products of Western cultural thought, culled from ideas about religion, nationality, ethnicity, social class, welfare and health provisions, division of property, notions of social honour, of "the person", and all of these framed by perceptions of gender.[2]

All we can claim at the moment is that for modern (and even postmodern) Western societies, family and kinship still provide systematic patterns based on symbols, as well as structures that try to make sense of the basic problems of order and individual identity connected with birth, socialization, and succession. They have been seen, therefore, as the "building blocks" of society as well as a symbolic idiom of political and economic relationships, and, as such, they have both to respond to and make meaningful change and represent that which is stable.

While ultimately rooted in physical reproduction, both kinship and family are centrally organized around an assumed gender order; indeed, it has been argued that the gender and kinship systems are mutually constructed, since kinship is based on the division between politico-jural and domestic domains.[3] In Western societies, this has meant that historically what may appear to be a natural order has been heavily moulded by those power centres of culture and material resources, the church and the state including the legal system.[4]

The power of definition is especially significant in the case of siblings whose social relations are organized along horizontal lines (at least theoretically), as collaterals, rather than through vertical lines of filiation. Unlike spouses, however, siblings have no direct effect on reproduction—in short, the sibling relationship is the structural basis for neither the formation of families nor their continuation. On the contrary, their presence can be potentially divisive, fragmenting material, cultural, and emotional resources.

In this sense, siblings occupy the boundaries between familial and the non-familial, possible strangers.

The analysis of historical change is further complicated by the issue of from whose viewpoint these structures, symbolic orders and organizing principles have been created. In the nineteenth century, when the concept of kinship systems was being formed, it was the central adult "ego", usually male, who was the focus of the grid of kinship. Recently, however, there has been a shift in perspective: family and kinship systems are increasingly regarded as *process*. The lived meaning of kinship ties, as well as non-kin close personal relationships, has begun to override rigidly defined categories. For example even as late as eighteenth-century England, just as the word *family* encompassed non-relatives, *friend* also referred to kin.[5]

At first sight, defining *brother* and *sister* might seem deceptively simple. Since human beings are capable of reproducing more than one offspring over a lifetime, the sharing of at least one common parent would be enough to ensure the categories. But immediately there are gradations implied by the expectation of a two-parent norm, so that we have *half-siblings* who share one physical parent but not the other, and *step-siblings* who share a parent through remarriage but not through physical reproduction.[6] The latter category raises issues about whether it is the "blood" relationship (consanguinity) or social kinship through marriage (affinity)—or both—that should be the defining characteristic of kin relations, including siblingship. The instability and variability of these definitions is to be found both historically and in a wide variety of cross-cultural contemporary studies. For example, in societies with a matrilineal focus, a brother has special interest in his sister's children who, in turn, recognize him, rather than their physical father, as the central masculine figure.[7]

Yet, despite such variance, a common theme seems to run through the notion of brotherhood and sisterhood, one that is related to basic issues of personal identity and the formation of *self*. The myth of Narcissus, searching for himself in his own reflection, is echoed in many beliefs about siblings. But, as with parts of the self, brothers and sisters can represent rejected traits, values, and behaviours; they can repel as well as attract. Because of their shared parentage, all siblings, whether of the same or different sex, seem to possess a special quality of "unity in difference", a mirroring of the self, two parts of one whole "split along the fault lines of ambivalence".[8]

There are several reasons for the inherent tension between identification and repulsion among siblings, a quality captured in George Eliot's phrase "a like, unlike", in her poem "Brother and Sister". One reason for this is the probable sharing of childhood experiences within the household, Eliot's "two flowers growing on one stem".[9] The effects of a mutual infancy and childhood are expressed in a passage written in the 1830s by Alfred Tennyson, whose hero speaks, significantly, about a foster-sister with whom he later fell in love:[10]

> She was my foster-sister: on one arm
> The flaxen ringlets of our infancies
> Wandered, the while we rested: one soft lap
> Pillowed us both: a common light of eyes
> Was on us as we lay: our baby lips
> Kissing one bosom, ever drew from thence
> The stream of life, one stream, one life, one blood.

The shared childhood, the shared name, and the sharing of family resources as well as traditions could also bring out the opposite emotions of envy or disengagement. Precisely because the bonds could be threateningly and smotheringly close, there was often rivalry and the enhancement of difference. From Cain and Abel onwards, in Western culture, the struggle over parental love, resources, and rewards has often meant that brothers and sisters spell trouble. "A rapid shift of 'hot and cold' acceptance and rejection, closeness and distance seems more characteristic of these ties than any other", and—media attention notwithstanding—conflict and violence within families is most common between siblings, although contained within a relatively safe environment and often condoned by adults.[11]

In structural terms, siblings are not always the equals portrayed in the model or the ideal. Given the long period in which a parent is capable of generating children (even for women, well over twenty years), some siblings will be of an age that is more like a parent than peer generation to those born later in the family. And in cultures which emphasize masculine primacy, all brothers, including the younger, start with power and privilege over all sisters, no matter what the age differences.[12] This potential age gap between siblings, large enough to create pseudo-generational differences, muddies the categories and confuses clear authority lines, creating an *intermediate generation* between parents and children. When the eldest siblings married and had young children of their own, their teenage sisters and brothers would often come live with them for various periods of time as mother's helpers or apprentices, as playmates to their young "nieces and nephews" close in age to themselves.[13] Although families with large numbers of offspring would obviously be more likely to exhibit such a pattern, two or three siblings could still be widely spaced. In the centuries before the fall in family size, high infant and child mortality could leave large gaps between siblings and in all periods the likelihood of such wide age differences is increased in step- and half-sibling relationships.[14]

Since a common childhood milieu is usually a large constituent in creating a sibling relationship, one of the most significant qualities of the role is its impact on the moulding of gender identity, in emotional terms as well as behaviour. Particularly in cultures that differentiate sharply between the genders, inculcating appropriate forms of femininity and masculinity into young children is a high priority. Brothers and sisters, in a way not possible in single-sex and only-child families, can rehearse the sexual division of labour, from tasks to emotions. The tension between prescribed gender ideals and the realities of physique, personality, birth order, and relationship to parents and other adults in the household has produced some of the most salient "family dramas".[15]

In modern Western society some of the most vivid memories of what femininity meant to young girls are in relation to their brothers. In some cases this could mean pride in carrying out a womanly role, being "little mother" to others in the family. In others it could be bitterness about curtailment of free time and allocation of fewer family resources.[16] In particular, girls' personal loyalty towards, and involvement with, their brothers' concerns may have been stressed, while the boys in the family took for granted both their right and their duty to turn to external pursuits. A brother acting as instructor, guide, or "window on the world" for sisters was also being initiated into the wider sphere outside the family, an opportunity often denied many girls.[17] This pattern has been widespread but may have differed significantly depending on class, family, and community culture. For example, in many sections of the British working class girls took an active role in gaining employment and might well have acted for their brothers.

For the nineteenth-century bourgeoisie, from which so much of our literary heritage derives, there was an almost compulsive focus on contrasting masculine and feminine categories, at a time when these attributes were integral to bourgeois identity. The way this could be played out through sibling relationships echoes in Victorian texts. Harriet Martineau had helped bring up her younger brother James as well as a sister. But in early adulthood she and James had a violent disagreement over religious beliefs that was never reconciled. The attachment Harriet felt for James was the strongest passion of her life; obsessive love tinged with envy is evident in her statement that "brothers are to sisters what sisters can never be to brothers as objects of engrossing and devoted affection", a sentiment also expressed in numerous diaries, memoirs, and letters of the period.[18] Such attachments could be to a brother's advantage, as in families where the sister contributed to his education and occupational mobility, or where she forwent part of her own patrimony, or worked to provide income for his further training and/or capital for his setting up in a trade, profession, or enterprise.[19]

Between brothers, and between sisters, too, siblings can provide models to be emulated or rejected. Since there is always a range of masculine and feminine behaviours and meanings available, children and young people are acutely aware of same-sex siblings as models, sometimes identifying with one another but sometimes rejecting such identification. In some cases, these patterns take the form of rebellion against parents and authority figures; in others, a sister or brother can become conformist as a form of rejection of a rebellious sib.[20]

Thus, although both same- and opposite-sex siblings provide models, the content and the form may differ according to the general expectations of gender roles. Brothers and sisters represent the comparative reference group *par excellence*, effective kin from birth and, unlike friends, social givens.[21] In their shadow, decisions—subconscious as well as conscious—are made about life choices, even in situations where those choices are severely limited by material and financial deprivation.

The historical picture of siblings is also blurred because kinship relations have so often been used as metaphor. The idea of "a double singleness" has made both same and cross-sex siblings a favourite device for exploring some of the social, moral, and spiritual questions in many cultures. When potential identification is even greater, as in the case of twins, the fascination about individual identity and consciousness is more marked. Twinship confounds the sense that each person must be unique but also plays to the longing for perfect understanding, the myth of twin souls. Many cultures assign special and magical qualities to twins, either good or evil, sometimes to the point where one twin may be deliberately killed at birth.[22] In literature, cross-sex twins have often been used to explore the limits of gender boundaries by switching identities, usually with the girl twin in disguise as her brother, thus providing a variant of cross-dressing transgression, where the brother–sister dyad offers opportunities to escape the restrictive ties involved in being a sibling of either sex.[23]

Creation myths, too, have often used the theme of brother–sister marriage, alliances that were supposed to produce offspring with superhuman powers. Brother–sister incest as an explanation of human origins is found in almost every culture, including the Judaic–Christian tradition. (Adam and Eve were, in a sense, "siblings", and their children, Cain and Abel, each married their sisters).[24] While incestuous brother–sister relationships evoke horror with their implication of familial and social chaos, they also hold strong fascination, being seen as "an attempt by fragmented man to achieve wholeness and immortality", perfect oneness in a somehow purer and spiritual union.[25] For centuries the idea of an incestuous union has evoked ideas of both the sublime and the horrific.

Since the nineteenth century, this attraction, this yearning for wholeness, has usually been debated within a context of concern about the biological consequences of inbreeding. At the present time, however, a great deal of confusion exists over the issue of incest in general. In the first place, there is no longer a consensus that inbreeding between even close relatives, let alone degrees of affinity as distant as cousins, does have negative consequences such as higher infertility, mortality, and morbidity rates in the offspring of such unions. It is possible that co-adapted gene complexes are to some extent actually preserved by inbreeding; alternatively, negative genes are less frequently reproduced because their carriers are themselves infertile.[26]

Furthermore, while it does seem to be the case that almost all known societies have some kind of prohibition on sexual intercourse between brothers and sisters as well as parents and children, the causes and mechanisms of this pattern are widely disputed, from Freudians who claim the natural eroticism of all family relationships to upholders of the "Westermarck effect" which posits an inbuilt aversion to such mating as protection against debasing the gene pool (or those who uphold both positions and distinguish between ultimate and proximate causes).[27]

Partly because of such narrow debates, not enough attention has been paid to the slippage between prohibitions against sexual relationships through marriage as opposed to "blood". Cultural rules banning sexual relations between relatives in general are not the same thing as "inbreeding avoidance". In part, this is because the term *relatives* is ambiguous, since it can refer to cultural rather than genetic categories.[28] These discussions, centred on the negative genetic effects on human populations, are seldom linked to the legal, religious, and moral revisions that have greatly reduced the degrees of kinship forbidden in marriage.[29]

The more the topic of brother–sister incest in particular is investigated in different contexts, the less sure are our conclusions. Even one of the best-known exceptions to sibling incest, brother–sister intermarriage among the Hawaiian and Egyptian Ancient Kingdom royal houses, is under dispute. Modern Egyptologists have found little hard evidence for the commonly held belief in widespread sibling marriage in the Ancient Kingdom, even among ruling families. Of those cases actually documented, many alliances were between "half" sisters and brothers and much confusion has been caused by the use of the word sister as a term for wife.[30]

The shift in the late nineteenth century from incest as a definition of marriage affinities allowed by the church and presented as a moral issue to scientific concerns about the effects of genetic inbreeding on physical and mental health shows how historically embedded our thinking is on the subject.[31] Relatives in many cases do not avoid (all) sexual or incestuous contact, nor do they avoid the same kind of sexual contact from one culture or one historical time to the next, nor is all sexual activity between relatives necessarily considered incestuous. In the mid-1970s, an eminent anthropologist writing on incest claimed: "there does not seem to be any theory or combination of theories which does more than define a part of the problem and worry it vigorously".[32] And a dozen years later, a book length study concludes that the subject remains an "enigma".[33] Here, if nowhere else is a warning that the interpretation of a seemingly "natural" relationship such as that between brothers and sisters is heavily influenced by contemporary views.

* * * * *

It was, perhaps, in the Romantic movement of the late eighteenth and early nineteenth century, with its rejection of Enlightenment individualism, that brother–sister attachments have received most attention. As the individual, freed from the trammels of community and family, became the hero of modernism, men—and it was mainly men in this role—felt a hunger for human bonds. Women, as mothers, sisters, and wives or idealized as Muses, might provide one such refuge. Sisters, less psychically dangerous than mothers, and without the sexuality (with its potential for childbearing) of wives, seem to have embodied the perfect ideal. Nineteenth-century life and literature overflow with accounts of the centrality of sisters to spiritual values, as in the case of William Gladstone whose "sainted sister", Anne, seven years his senior, in her fervent religious belief and faith that he was God's instrument in the world, underpinned both his own Christian beliefs and his remarkable self-confidence.[34]

Again and again, European writers around this period, turned to the story of Sophocles' *Antigone*, a play that has usually been interpreted as exemplifying the state in opposition to private conscience, but that can also be seen as being centrally about kinship, the bonds of "common blood" and in particular the ties between brother and sister. In *Antigone*, the insistence that the sister be allowed to bury her brother in direct contradiction to the laws of the city is part of the assumption that, in death, males pass from the domain of the polis back to that of the family, for it is there that ritual burial, the ultimate holy duty surpassing man-made law, will be performed. Implicitly, this interpretation equates the family with women, the polis with men, and uses the brother–sister bond as their symbolic expression. In this they follow Hegel, who also was inspired by the "Antigone" theme, but explicitly rejected any hint of incestuous attachment and claimed that it was precisely the asexuality of brothers and sisters that allowed them to encapture most perfectly the elements of essential masculinity and femininity.[35] This theme is ubiquitous among nineteenth century writers and artists; for example, Charles Dickens often used brother–sister relations to illustrate the moral (feminine, natural affection) values as opposed to the inhumanity of utilitarian political economy.[36]

The nineteenth century pantheon of creative artists and writers seems particularly sibling-rich: Wolfgang Amadeus and Maria Anna Mozart; Friedrich and Christophine Schiller; Johann Wolfgang and Cornelia von Goethe; François and Lucile Chateaubriand; William and Dorothy Wordsworth; George Byron and Augusta Leigh; Charlotte, Emily, Ann, and Branwell Brontë; Friedrich and Elisabeth Nietzsche; Felix and Fanny Mendelssohn; William, Henry, and Alice James; Thomas and Carla Mann; Virginia Woolf and Vanessa Bell (Stephens), to name but a few.

Undoubtedly the intensity of sibling relationships at this time cannot be denied, but why this should be so is complicated. New sources of wealth divorced from land were enabling the emergence of family enterprises centred on near kin and focused on the survival of individual household "establishments".[37] It has been argued that these developments encouraged a gradual shift in kinship from widespread alliances of lineages to a heightened emphasis on narrower family ties, middle and upper class women were seen more as the sexual property of fathers and brothers, as "avatars of themselves rather than co-carriers of family blood".[38]

Not surprisingly, this intensity focused on the issue of incest. As Ruth Perry has suggested, although it is impossible to know whether the "actual incidence of incest increased in the eighteenth century, or whether it was simply its social and cultural meaning that changed, incest loomed larger than ever before as an issue and a problem."[39] The key to understanding nineteenth century attitudes to sibling incest lies in more general conceptions of sexuality. As with all bodily functions, by the end of the eighteenth century, the open expression of sexual desires was becoming more shameful. In part this was due to Enlightenment ideas about rationality, but also to emotional refinement as an enhancement of sexual expression. It was a period of intense "talk" about sexual desire, its many forms, objects, and outcomes.[40] The gradual development of a sterner sexual code owed even more to the stalwarts of the religious Evangelical movement. Those who had been converted and their followers feared all forms of licence, particularly uncontrolled sex. For example, the Vice Society (1802) spearheaded the attack that, in Byron's telling phrase, created the shift "from cunt to cant".[41]

These debates over sexuality cannot be separated from the radical political atmosphere in the wake of the French Revolution. The symbolic dethronement of fathers in the form of kings stressed instead the model of sibling relationships. *Fraternity* might flourish, but *equality* between men and women in terms of sexual practice was both threatening and short-lived.[42] The poet Wordsworth, with his sojourn in France in his early twenties, and others of his radical youthful circle in their youth had drunk deeply of this refreshing atmosphere. By the turn of the nineteenth century, originators and followers of the romantic movement also repudiated Enlightenment sensuality as gross and materialistic. The idealization of love, and particularly of women, had become central to the Romantic quest for a more transcendental form of human relationships.

We cannot be sure how widely beliefs about purity and the asexual woman spread. But there is no doubt that it was accompanied by increasing emphasis on the *maternal* aspects of women's physical and emotional life. In this schema, sexuality and sexual behaviour, at least for women, became increasingly domesticated. Sex and reproduction were more firmly than ever seen as one fixed solely in the maternal role. Masculinity and male sexual behaviour, while affected by these changes, remained more varied. For both men and women, but particularly the latter, sexual intercourse as leading to conception was the dominant fact, even when transmuted in various forms of fantasy, ranging from pornography for men and the Gothic novel for literate women. For the generations of the late eighteenth and early nineteenth century, sexual desire was not the problem; it was penetration and pregnancy.

A belief also framing understanding of sexuality was that in a marriage the couple became literally "one flesh". This had long been proclaimed by the church and subsequently accepted by the medical fraternity as well as the public at large. According to Christian teaching, the mingling of sperm and women's "fluids", which she was believed to release on orgasm, was the mechanism that produced one body. The husband and wife thus became related as "blood" kin. Both these factors—the inevitable association of sex with reproduction and the belief in one flesh through intercourse—are important in understanding the way *incest* was regarded.

Given these beliefs it is understandable that, within Church doctrine, incest was defined by the kinship relationships that were allowed or disallowed for marriage by the church. However, from the Medieval period onwards there had been a steady narrowing of these forbidden categories.[43] By 1662, the Church of England had published in *The Book of Common Prayer* a table of prohibited degrees for marriage partners that was also displayed in every parish church. In-laws within similar relations as blood kin were also prohibited from marriage; e.g., one-half the forbidden categories were not genetically related at all. On the other hand, by this time, even first cousins *were* allowed to marry.[44] Within nineteenth century culture, it was *marriage* that defined the permitted categories of sexual activity.[45]

The confusion and ambiguity over sibling incest is exemplified by attitudes to the relationship of William and Dorothy Wordsworth, exemplars of the Romantic brother and sister. Interest in the nature of the Wordsworths' relationship, already raised in literary studies of the 1930s, was revived in a long-running discussion in the *Times Literary Supplement* in 1974. The writer of the opening letter takes exception to the suggestion of an incestuous relationship between the Wordsworths, an accusation that, she claims, has been "authoritatively refuted" by the author of the then most recent biography of William. Yet, even while refuting these imputations, the letter writer goes on to admit that: "the feelings for each other of many nineteenth century siblings were warmer, stronger and more lasting than anything felt today. They constituted a relationship for which the word 'incest' is totally inappropriate but for which some special word is nevertheless needed."[46]

By November, the American scholar, Reiman, who had commented from the beginning, was maintaining that it was really of little interest whether the sibling relationship resulted in physical intercourse—the hunt for the historical "did they or didn't they". Rather, he maintained that, as in the case of the Wordsworths: "Our real subject is emotional attachment between brothers and sisters so strong as to parallel or exceed in romantic intensity attachments to other members of the opposite sex. A man may not sleep with his sister (or mother) and yet never be able to feel an equally strong emotional bond to another woman".[47] This is exemplified by the ultimate Romantic hero, Lord Byron, who wrote to his half sister, Augusta Leigh, with whom he was passionately involved: "I have never ceased nor can cease to feel that perfect and boundless attachment which binds me to you—which renders me utterly incapable of *real* love for any other human being—for what could they be to me after you?"[48]

It is only recently that the connections between sibling incest and the culture of romanticism has been investigated. Previously, many commentators found it an inexplicable obsession. For example, in 1925 a study of the Romantic poet, Shelley, pondered:[49]

> One of the most peculiar traits in Shelley's psychology was his interest in the theme of incest between a brother and sister. To most of his readers this preoccupation with such a subject appears repulsive and inexplicable, for there is nothing attractive or even interesting in incest *per se*. Nevertheless, for some obscure reason, the subject fascinated Shelley.

Twentieth century discussions have also focused on the pathological psychology of brother–sister involvement. When these relationships went beyond the "normal", they were often regarded as a result of parental failure—a sign of a dysfunctional family. There is no doubt that many of the well-known very close brother–sister relations in the period under discussion were in families where one or both parents had died, leaving orphaned children, some of them still quite young, or a parent or parents were absent or ill. But in an era of high mortality such situations must have been common. The absence of a parent (or parents) is not enough to explain the intense and intimate nature of brother–sister interaction at the time or the heightened cultural attention it attracted.

Given these problems of definition, for historical analysis, it might be more useful to consider the anthropologist David Schneider's approach, where he maintains that the *meaning of incest* for a particular culture can be regarded as a "symbol of desecration", a symbol of "ungrammatical love".[50] For example, the particular power of sibling incest for nineteenth-century people is hinted at in its prime place in pornographic fantasy. Here the search for resemblance to the self is not held back, but is a social limit to be passed, directly and physically.[51]

Under what circumstances would these limits be transcended? As we have seen, much of the current debate about sibling incest centres on whether it is the experience of growing up together that, in some as yet unknown way, dampens erotic attraction (in short, "familiarity does not breed") or whether, on the contrary, the attraction is so strong that the prohibition needs to be extremely powerful.[52] After an early childhood spent together, Dorothy and William Wordsworth had experienced *both* separation and closeness. When they were reunited in their early twenties, to William, Dorothy was his "Beloved Woman", his touchstone and a link with the emotional, softer–feminine side of his nature. "Blessed Dorothy who had given him 'humble cares and delicate fears' as well as 'love and thought, and joy'".[53]

The form and intensity of his love for Dorothy has been interpreted in the series of poems written in the late 1790s, when they had been living together for several years; a period that included some of their most extended walking tours as well as a trip through Germany when they had been isolated by both lack of funds and knowledge of the language. A fragment written at the time eulogizes:[54]

> The dear companion of my lonely walk
> My hope, my joy, my sister and my friend
> Or something dearer still, if reason knows
> A dearer thought, or in the heart of love
> There be a dearer name

One commentator maintains that by this period, William had realized that his love for Dorothy was growing out of control. He used these poems as both a displacement of feeling and an imaginative exploration of alternatives for the outcome of his passion.[55] Another believed that in this type of "double singleness", the poet felt that he and his sister "were *interchangeable*. In writing about her he was writing about himself and vice versa" (original italics).[56]

Stephen Gill, in his biography of William, states how the strong love of Dorothy and William had a crucial domestic element, since they spent virtually all their time together. In the house they follow a conventional division of labour, but did many communal tasks such as gardening in common. A typical entry in Dorothy's journal records: "I went with William and walked backwards and forwards in the orchard til dinner time—he read me his poem. I broiled Beefsteaks. After dinner we made a pillow of my shoulder, I read to him and my Beloved slept." Dorothy called William "my darling" quite unselfconsciously. She records how she soothed him by touching or sat close to him in silent communion, an atmosphere "created by an acknowledged and expressed love".[57] Other journal entries seem to confirm this view: "I petted him on the carpet . . . After dinner we made a pillow of my shoulder and my Beloved slept". In another entry they "lay together deep in Silence and Love".[58] When William was away from the cottage she records that she "slept in William's bed and slept badly for my thoughts were full of William", but she also occasionally slept in his bed when he was there.[59] However we might interpret this behaviour, it should be remembered that people often shared beds at this time, not only out of necessity for the less well off but also for warmth and companionship.

William and Dorothy's domestic solitude, which they shared for half a dozen years, came to an end in 1802 when, at the age of thirty-two, he decided to marry. He had gradually become attracted to one of Dorothy's closest friends, Mary Hutchinson, who had already spent long periods visiting the Wordsworth cottage. Dorothy was extremely fond of Mary, but she also was understandably apprehensive about how life in the cottage would change after the marriage. In a striking passage she wrote to Mary at the time: "my dear Sister be quiet and happy . . . do not make loving us your business, but let your love of us make up the spirit of all the business you have . . ." the use of "us" here is noticeable. Mary appears to have acquiesced, for when Mary took William as a husband she also became Dorothy's "chosen companion in life", despite the fact that her own sister, Sara, was already in the nature of a "second self".[60]

Julia Barker, a more recent biographer of Wordsworth, who seems to have taken a dislike to Dorothy throughout, sees her becoming more and more possessive of William the more imminent the marriage became. She claims that Dorothy writes as "if she, not Mary, were his lover". When he was away for a few days, her journal records, Barker reports, with some distaste, that "the night before the wedding, William brought the ring to Dorothy for safe-keeping and she slept with it on her forefinger all night. Early next morning, he came upstairs to collect it and say goodbye". In what Barker describes as "an oddly repellent gesture", which was clearly meant to be an endorsement of his continuing love for his sister, William slipped the ring back on her finger and blessed her "fervently".[61]

By 1975 the debate over "Victorian brothers and sisters" in the *Times Literary Supplement* had come to an end. But interest in the topic never quite disappeared. F. W. Bateson, who put forward the incest idea most strongly, had to back-pedal in his second edition because of outrage this caused. T. S. Eliot, among others, were "seriously distressed by the notion".[62] Nevertheless, Stephen Gill, in 1969, felt that William and Dorothy's relationship "was also, unquestionably, profoundly sexual".[63]

By 1998, Kathleen Jones felt "that Dorothy was in love with William is indisputable. His feelings for her were also very great, but he, perhaps more than Dorothy, was aware of the nature of his involvement and the dangers of their situation". Because William had had an affair when he was in Paris in his early twenties, which resulted in an illegitimate child, and then later married Mary Hutchinson, Jones speculates that while there may have been physical lovemaking between the brother and sister, it stopped short of physical intercourse. [64]

At present, the denial of incest spearheaded earlier by Mary Moorman and followed by Julia Barker, seems to be uppermost. She cites previously unknown letters between William and Mary, after eight years of marriage (and five children).[65]

their passion shines out with all the ardour of a pair of teenage lovers. What is more, this rare expression of their love is convincing proof that, however deeply William cared for his sister, his love for her was altogether of a different kind. Had these letters been available to earlier biographers, it would have been difficult for them even to have posited the case for an incestuous relationship between brother and sister.

In a 2004 popular book on friendship, the brother–sister relationship is foregrounded as the prototype of *non-sexual* love, specifically using the Wordsworths as an example. Here, the sexualizing of the sibling relationship in contemporary fiction and film is deplored.[66] It would seem we are left with the conclusion that "the nature of their passion for each other is a nettle left ungrasped".[67]

The depths of emotional attachment among nineteenth-century siblings—including erotic overtones—is brought out in that feature of English Victorian culture so puzzling to twentieth-century commentators, the intense debates over legislation that had outlawed marriage with a deceased wife's sister early in the nineteenth century. Because, on marriage, the kin of each spouse became as their own blood relatives, the marriage of a man to his deceased wife's sister was considered incestuous but was first prohibited by law rather than just Church doctrine in 1835. State intervention in such a moral and personal issue was unusual (incest *per se* was not made a criminal act in England until 1908). For over seventy-five years until the law was revoked, debates in and out of Parliament, in novels and a stream of articles (even mentioned in a celebrated Gilbert and Sullivan song), centred on the dangers of sister-in-law liaisons.[68]

Much of the tension arose because of the practical exigencies caused by a wife's death in childbirth and the attraction of remarriage to the most likely caretaker of the bereft young children, especially among the less affluent. Nevertheless, the preoccupation with the "Deceased Wife's Sister" may indicate some "displacement" of anxieties about relationships not with the wife's sister but with the husband's own sister(s).[69] In this context it should be noted that the remarriage of a widow to her brother-in-law was usually absent from the discussion.

* * * * *

Our incredulity about how seriously this issue was taken shows that at least some of the intensity around kinship relationships in general and siblings in particular has faded. Individuals are supposed to be judged on their own merits; not to do so hints at negative charges of *nepotism*. Then, too, the accelerating decline in the birth rate in all classes has meant that for generations born after the First World War, the number, if not the importance, of siblings has declined sharply. In the last half century, with the two-child family as the norm, there is no longer an intermediate generation of elder siblings while the extensive network of uncles, aunts, and cousins has melted away. To a certain extent the "composite" families of step- and half-kin have replaced these familial categories created by divorce and remarriage, but the meanings attached to these relationships are not yet clear.

Although family and kin networks still operate in occupational choice and recruitment, and despite the survival of small family businesses and farms in most Western countries (in varying proportions), it is evident that at the beginning of the twenty-first century sibling relationships are no longer central to the organization of economic life. Economic organization has, in turn, been shaped by the falling birth rate, which has drastically stripped the numbers of siblings in each family. These changes have undoubtedly narrowed the experience of living with kin, but they are not enough to explain the curious absence of interest in and recognition of sibling ties manifest in twentieth-century culture.

The reasons for this neglect in academic and intellectual circles are complicated. In addition to the structural and demographic changes already cited, the dominance of psychological, particularly psychoanalytic, interpretations of the family have tended consistently to draw attention to the vertical ties of parent and child. Yet, despite the overwhelming amount of material on this issue, a sociologically and culturally informed theory of childhood remains sketchy. And, despite the efforts of historians of childhood, it is still unclear what relations were held to constitute "the child" or when childhood in its contemporary sense was first instituted.[70]

The dominance of psychic models in this field has meant that when sibling interaction is actually noted, it often figures as displacement for a deeper Oedipal pattern; brothers and sisters are regarded as pale reflections of the central parental drama. One unfortunate result of this view has been to downplay the importance of brother–sister incest and violence.[71] The authors of one of the few full-scale American studies of siblings remark that none of the classical theories of personality and psychological development portrayed brothers and sisters, aunts and uncles, as important in socialization, although in the past decade there has been an upsurge of interest, as witnessed by this volume.[72]

It is true that recent interest in inequalities within the family has drawn attention to birth order among siblings, especially over the issue of primogeniture and the allocation of resources. Nevertheless, what emerged from a large historical conference and subsequent publications on this topic was that what the contributions "collectively demonstrate is the complexity of inter-sib relations".[73]

Nor did the move from using snapshot images of the family to a "life-course" approach necessarily alter the focus. Generational studies have concentrated on vertical transmission and again neglected horizontal ties.[74] Even where the numbers of children in the family are recognized as important, the comparison has been *between* families of different sizes rather than an examination of relationships *within* the family.

Only a handful of "urban anthropologists", with their sensitivity to kinship systems, has recognized the continued saliency of brothers and sisters in mid- and late twentieth-century life.[75] In particular, the disruption brought about by emigration and geographical mobility away from parents, other kin, and local community leads to special dependence and cooperation among siblings lasting into adulthood; for example, shared housing and other resources. As, in one American study, the brothers and brothers-in-law joined one another in small shops or worked in the same factory, the sisters shared housework and motherly duties so that, if there were more than one baby crying, whichever lactating mother happened to be around would pick up and breast-feed the child. But when the immigrants had settled into the new culture and the generation born in the new country grew to adulthood, sibling relationships, like those between neighbours, lost their primary place.[76]

It should not be surprising that within the other social sciences there persists a similar lack of attention to peer-generation relationships. Economic thought focuses either on the single individual or takes the household (family) as the unit. When "household" constitutes the main economic "actor", its internal relationships are ignored, not only those of husband and wives (as feminists have pointed out), but also those of siblings, other kin, lodgers, and servants.[77]

Political theory, too, stems from a tradition which names the senior male as representing the household, a construction ultimately derived from Western and Middle Eastern traditional religious thought. It is this model of the family that has been used as the basis for the state, with wives, children, younger siblings, and servants representing categories of "non-person". In the nineteenth century, as a concept of contract replaced particularistic notions of kin within political thought, the underlying ideas about kinship and gender remained integral to that construction.[78] Unfortunately, the centrality of kinship in the formation of political theories has not often been recognized. Thus, despite massive attention to history of the family by historians such as Peter Laslett and Lawrence Stone, there has been little effort to link specific family relationships to the formation of the state.[79] David Schneider, as previously stated, an anthropologist, does suggest that societies built around democratic values would tend to stress egalitarian ties and here siblings would provide a prototype. Referring to American society, he claimed that "horizontal solidarity with collateral kin can be thought of as an integral part of a social system that requires a high level of coordination and mutual dependency but which at the same time, values a high level of autonomy, freedom of choice and egalitarianism".[80]

But the connections between such democratic expectations and actual kinship remain obscure. It is true that notions of brotherhood and sisterhood have been used to invoke ideas of inclusion and identity in national or racial terms. A well-known example is found in the early nineteenth-century anti-slavery campaign that coined the slogan: "Am I not a man and a brother? Am I not a woman and a sister?"[81] The idea of brother and sister as used here, however, implies a childish immaturity and expectations of subordination to the "parent" culture.

There is also evidence that siblings have provided the model for utopian communities in many times and places, which is not surprising since, despite the growth of both contract theory and bureaucratic organization, kinship remains even now in many ways a primary model of all social relations.[82] Enclosed monastic communities (of either sex), confraternities, fraternal organizations such as the Freemasons, millennarian sects, as well as trade unions and socialist parties, have all used fictive sibling and friendship structures with their naming practices (Brother, Sister, Comrade) to signify a levelling of social position. For example, in a study of a mixed-sex utopian community, Lyndal Roper calls attention to the title "marital sister" *(eeewester)* used for wife, and she believes that the model of brother–sister relations was meant to emphasize equality, kinship, and similarity, rather than difference, and thus spiritualize the marriage relationship.[83]

However, if fraternal organizations are examined carefully, there is almost always a tension towards reverting to parental models, or at least leadership with a "Big Brother", while mixed-sex communities invariably stress masculine authority. Even Brotherhood exhibits the tension with power relations, tending to slip into the emergence of a father figure; the existence of all-male groups which aimed at internal equality, were part of a wider culture based on senior masculine privilege.[84] Although in studies of these various organizations and communities the sibling metaphor is noted, it has tended to be taken for granted; siblings are part of the air we breathe, while it is parental, particularly patriarchal, hierarchy that gets explanatory attention.

Nevertheless, less formal evidence based on childhood memories, written autobiography and oral histories, shows that the lives of ordinary people as much as those of the famous resonate with vivid portraits of actual brothers and sisters—cherished, detested, admired, reviled. Much of our literary and cultural heritage harks back to such individuals, who had strong, complicated, and sometimes difficult relationships with siblings. Our own childhood imagination continues to be filled with many brother–sister scripts in the staple of fairy tales that have such an abiding hold on Western imagination, even if in a "Disneyfied" form.[85]

How long will this continue? In the last analysis it is the experience of sharing a life with other people within an identity labelled "family" that turns an abstract kinship model into a concrete relationship. For young children in our own time, it seems to be the *person* who is more important than the category, and even with older children it is the relevance of the relationship that influences children's knowledge of kinship terms.[86] The unusually low mortality rates in contemporary societies have inevitably changed the meaning of sibling relationships. The experience of being "chosen" to replace a dead sibling, especially for the parents, is now very rare but was once widespread (hence the custom of sometimes giving the new same-sex sibling an identical name to the dead child). The powerful psychic and emotional effects of being such a replacement or surviving child are now much less often an enduring childhood experience.[87]

Because parents now have a greater possibility of surviving until their children are self-sufficient, there is little necessity felt to use siblings as guardians of their nieces and nephews—in fact, many modern parents prefer to name friends—although informal contacts and mutual exchange between adult siblings are clearly present in many cases. Especially in old age, many siblings appear to re-establish closer relationships. A large grey area between personal preference and duty colours relations between the middle-aged dyads and triads of the small-family era. However, there usually remain two issues where these ties are forced to come to the fore: the care of elderly parents and the division of property and resources, particularly after the death of parents, and even sometimes before. Little attention has been paid to either of these issues in professional social work or family counselling literature, although modern novels often take the death of the parents and the gathering of the grown-up brothers and sisters as a focus for dramatic construction.

The reasons for "not seeing" the importance of sibling relationships are manifold—economic and demographic change, legal constructions, political and psychological theories, social practices, psychic processes of denial and projection. Historically, there has undoubtedly been a reduction in the saliency of this relationship along with changes in its form, shifts that may be further complicated by the growing numbers of single-parent, one-child families. Yet both the idea and reality of brothers and sisters, uncles and aunts, nieces, nephews, and cousins, still have remarkable purchase in making sense of contemporary life. In an American report on sibling rivalry, few adult siblings had severed their ties completely and one-third of those interviewed used words like "competitive" and "hurtful" to describe their relationship—negative but still emotionally charged evaluations.[88]

We continue to take for granted siblings as a constant and universal presence dictated by our common humanity. At the same time, as Martine Segalen has asked, "If relationships with the kinship group are such an abiding phenomenon, why has their existence been so often hidden and, indeed, denied over the last twenty years or so?"[89] Such a paradox may tell us something about the gap between everyday existence and the categories used by academics and intellectuals. In stretching horizontal bonds away from the nuclear triad, siblings are capable of building a web of intimate and trusting relationships and could be a model for nascent civil society. Their dearth, for example in those areas of China where the one-child family policy has been successful, has made for highly competitive and self-centred individualism. Where there are very few or no siblings, the symbolism of siblingship may loom larger, part of our yearning for a historical Golden Age. Perhaps it is only when siblings are no longer part of everyday experience that we can begin to talk and write about them.[90] At present, most people's experience is growing up with only one or possibly two siblings. While this gives much less choice than the long families of the past, it may, in fact, intensify such relationships, at least in childhood. As the doyen of nineteenth century bourgeois cultural history, Peter Gay, has said: "At their most wanton, romantic lovers, seeking to blend into a single being, found their identity by losing it".[91] Siblings were, and still are, closest at hand in the making and unmaking of that identity. Even now, to many people Jane Austen's dictum still holds true that "fraternal love, sometimes almost everything, is at others worse than nothing".[94]

Nevertheless, modern cultures must come to terms with a much reduced kinship pool. In such an era, with a substantial minority of one-child, lone-parent families, what might take the place of siblings, aunts, uncles, nephews, nieces, and cousins? In psychic terms, egalitarian friendship can also evoke the search for intimacy. One of the few serious studies of friendship concludes that friends can overcome the isolation of individuals, "by subtraction, as it were when two become one, or by doubling, when each of the friends acquires a second self". As siblings once did, friends promise wholeness, but wholeness is also friendship's problem; the delicate balance in wanting to be ourselves and wanting to be close to other people as well.[93] But the striking difference is that while friends—to an extent—are chosen, siblings remain a "given". It is just possible that trust among friends may hold one key to genuinely democratic structures and values, embedded in a kind of intimacy unknown to our historical past.[94]

Notes

1. In particular the importance of the sister relationship has been recognized in feminist literature: Adrienne Rich, *"Sibling Mysteries"*, *The Dream of a Common Language* (New York: W. W. Norton, 1978); see also Brigid McConville, *Sisters: Love and Conflict within the Lifelong Bond* (London: Pan, 1985); Toni McNaron, *The Sister Bond: A Feminist View of a Timeless Connection* (London: Pergamon Press, 1985); Drusilla Modjeska (Ed.), *Sisters* (London: HarperCollins, 1993); Patricia Foster, *Sister to Sister: What Women Write About the Unbreakable Bond* (New York: Anchor Books, 1995).

2. Rayna Rapp, "Toward a nuclear freeze? The gender politics of Euro–American kinship analysis", in Jane Collier and Sylvia Yanagisako (Eds.), *Gender and Kinship: Essays Toward a Unified Analysis* (Stanford: Stanford University Press, 1987); Marilyn Strathern, *After Nature: English Kinship in the Late Twentieth Century* (Cambridge: Cambridge University Press, 1992).

3. Jane Collier and Sylvia Yanagisako, *Gender and Kinship: Essays Towards a Unified Analyasis* (Stanford: Stanford University Press, 1987, p. 7).

4. Susan Staves, *Married Women's Separate Spheres: Property in England, 1660–1833* (Cambridge, MA: Harvard University Press, 1990); "the law dealt with family issues as 'partly value but partly love and affection'", Halsbury's *Laws* of *England* (London: Butterworth, 4th edn, 1977, vol. 18, p. 137).

5. Naomi Tadmor, *Family and Friends in Eighteenth-Century England: Household, Kinship and Patronage*, (Cambridge: Cambridge University Press, 2001).

6. The ambiguity this creates is well brought out in legal wrangles over the ruling that if a tenant died without issue having a half-brother, the latter could not inherit as he was only related by half-blood, a rule finally abolished in 1833. J. H. Baker, *An Introduction to English Legal History* (London: Butterworth, 1979, p. 228).

7. Esther Goody, "Separation and divorce among the Gonja", in M. Fortes (Ed.), *Marriage in Tribal Societies* (Cambridge: Cambridge

University Press, 1972). See also Martine Segalen, *Historical Anthropology of the Family* (Cambridge: Cambridge University Press, 1988).

8. Ruth Perry, "Brotherly love and brotherly hatred in the fiction of Frances Burney", unpublished paper delivered to the Modern Languages Association, December 1990; Elaine Jordan "Literary doubles. Brothers and sisters", unpublished notes—by kind permission of the authors.

9. George Eliot, "'Brother and sister', in 'The Spanish Gypsy'", *Collected Works* (London, 1901, p. 587).

10. Alfred Tennyson, *The Lover's Tale* (C. Kegan Paul, London, 1879, p. 20).

11. G. Einstein and M. Moss, "Some thoughts on sibling relationships", *Social Casework*, November 1967, p. 553; M. Straus, R. Gelles, & S. Steinmetz, *Behind Closed Doors: Violence in the American Family* (New York: Anchor Books, 1980).

12. Francine Klagsbrun, *Mixed Feelings: Love, Hate, Rivalry and Reconciliation Among Brothers and Sisters* (New York: Bantam Books, 1992).

13. See Leonore Davidoff and Catherine Hall, *Family Fortunes: Men and Women of the English Middle Class 1780–1850* (London: Routledge, 2002).

14. William R. Beer, *Strangers in the House: The World of Stepsiblings and Half Siblings* (New Brunswick, NJ: Transaction Publishers, 1989).

15. Extreme identification seems to occur when other support systems for children break down. Even opposite-sex siblings sometimes identify strongly, as, for example in the case of Charles Lamb, who became the carer of his sister Mary after she had murdered their mother. In his caring role, Charles felt as if he had thus avoided the "impertinence" of manhood. Jane Aaron, " 'Double singleness': Gender role mergence in the auto-biographical writings of Charles and Mary Lamb", in Susan Gloag Bell and Marilyn Yalom (Eds.), *Revealing Lives: Autobiography, Biography and Gender* (Albany, NY: SUNY Press, 1990).

16. Envy of brothers' opportunities is found in memoirs spanning centuries and class groups. For example: *Memoirs of the Life of the Late Mrs. Catherine Capp*, edited by her daughter, Mary (London: Longman, 1822); Hannah Mitchell, *The Hard Way Up: The Autobiography of a Suffragette and Rebel* (London: Virago, 1977). In religious households the realization that they, unlike their brothers, could never become preachers seems to have been particularly painful. *Autobiography of Elizabeth M. Sewell*, edited by Eleanor Sewell (Longman's, Green, 1908); Katherine Sklar, *Catherine Beecher: A Study in Domesticity* (New Haven: Yale University Press, 1973).

17. Leonore Davidoff, "The legacy of the nineteenth-century bourgeois family and the wool merchant's son", *Transactions of the Royal Historical Society*, *14*, 2004; Margaret Homans, "Eliot, Wordsworth and the scenes of the sister's instruction", *Critical Inquiry*, *8*(2): 39 (winter 1981).
18. Harriet Martineau, *Autobiography* (London, 1877, 3 vols, vol. 1, p. 99).
19. Ruth Perry, *Novel Relations: The Transformation of Kinship in English Literature and Culture 1748–1818* (Cambridge: Cambridge University Press, 2004, p.156); Mary Ryan, *Cradle of the Middle Class: The Family in Oneida County New York, 17901–1865* (Cambridge: Cambridge University Press, 1981).
20. This truism of everyday life has a long history, as in the biblical story of Jacob, the wicked, and Esau, the righteous; brothers completely different in character and destiny. "How could it be that these two, who were for one another day and night, could have come from the same womb?" Lawrence Kushner, *Honey from the Rock: Visions of Jewish Mystical Renewal* (Woodstock, VT: Jewish Lights Publishing, 1977, p. 38).
21. Bert N. Adams, *Kinship in an Urban Setting* (Markham, Chicago, 1968, p. 117); for the concept of "reference group", see Robert K. Merton, "Continuities in the theory of reference groups and social structure", in *Social Theory and Social Structure* (Glencoe, ILL: Free Press, 1975).
22. Robert Brain, "Friends as twins", *Friends and Lovers* (London: Paladin, 1977); Penelope Farmer, *Two or The Book of Twins and Doubles* (London: Virago, 1996).
23. For example, Viola and Sebastian in Shakespeare's *Twelfth Night*, but there are many other examples; e.g., Sarah Grand's *The Heavenly Twins* (1893); Valerie Sanders, *Brother–Sister Culture in Nineteenth Century Literature From Austen to Woolf* (Houndsmill: Palgrave, 2002).
24. In particular, the widely used Germanic/Scandinavian legend of Sieglund and Sieglunde, the brother–sister pair who were parents of the hero, Siegfried (basis for the Wagnerian Ring Cycle) which also became the basis for the powerful short story, "Blood of the Walsings" by Thomas Mann; Luciano Santiago, *The Children of Oedipus: Brother–Sister Incest in Psychiatry, Literature, History and Methodology* (Roslyn Heights, NY: Libra, 1973).
25. Ann Shearer, "Sisters and brothers—brothers and sisters: intimate relations and the question of 'incest'", paper delivered at the European University Institute, September 2000, by permission of the author; Kathryn B. Maguire, "The incest taboo in *Wuthering Heights*: A modern appraisal", *American Imago: A Psychoanalytic Journal for Culture, Science and the Arts*, *45*(2): 218 (summer 1988).

26. See W. M. Shields, *Philopathy, Inbreeding and the Evolution of Sex* (Albany, NY: State University of New York Press, 1983); Alan H. Bittles, "The role and significance of consanguinity as a demographic variable", *Population and Development Review, 20*(7) (1994).

27. See the extensive debates including evolutionary and sociobiological positions in Nancy W. Thornhill, "An evolutionary analysis of rules regulating human inbreeding and marriage" (with commentaries), *Behavioural and Brain Sciences, 14* (1991).

28. Gregory C. Leavitt, "Sociobiological explanations of incest avoidance: A critical review of evidential claims", *American Anthropologist, 92*(4) (December 1990).

29. Carroll M. Pastner, "The Westermarck hypotheses and first cousin marriage: the cultural modification of negative sexual imprinting", *Journal of Anthropological Research, 42* (1986).

30. Jaroslav Cerny, "Consanguineous marriages in Pharonic Egypt", *Journal of Egyptian Archaeology, 40* (1954); but see an alternative view in Keith Hopkins, "Brother–sister marriage in Roman Egypt", *Comparative Studies in Society and History, 22* (1980).

31. Martin Ottenheimer, "Lewis Henry Morgan and the prohibition of cousin marriage in the United States", *Journal of Family History, 15*(3) (1990).

32. David Schneider, "The meaning of incest", *Journal of the Polynesian Society, 85*: 150 (1976).

33. James B. Twitchell, *Forbidden Partners: The Incest Taboo in Modern Culture* (New York: Columbia University Press, 1987, p. 243).

34. Peter Jagger, *Gladstone: The Making of a Christian Politician: The Personal, Religious Lfle and Development of William Ewart Gladstone* (Harwarden, Clwyd: Pickwick Publications, 1991); Leonore Davidoff, "Kinship as a 'categorical concept': a case study of the Gladstone Siblings", paper prepared for the Festschift for John Gillis, 2004.

35. Robin Fox, "The virgin and the godfather: Kinship law versus state law in Greek tragedy and after", in *Reproduction and Succession: Studies in Anthropology, Law and Society* (New Brunswick, NJ: Transaction, 1983). George Steiner, *Antigone: The Antigone Myth in Western Literature, Art and Thought* (Oxford: Oxford University Press, 1984).

36. Daniel Daneau, "The brother–sister relationship in *Hard Times*", *The Dickensian, 40* (1964); see also Michael Slater, *Dickens and Women* (Stanford: Stanford University Press, 1983).

37. Davidoff and Hall, *Family Fortunes*, Part II.

38. Perry, *Novel Relations*, p. 371; David Sabean has been the prime promoter of the idea of this shift, see *Kinship in Neckerhausen, 1700– 1870* (Cambridge: Cambridge University Press, 1998).

39. Perry, R., *Novel Relations*, p. 180
40. Tim Hitchcock, *English Sexualities 1700–1800*, (Houndsmill: Macmillan, 1997).
41. Roy Porter, "Mixed feelings: the Enlightenment and sexuality in 18th century Britain", in P. G. Bouce, *Sexualities in 18th Century Britain* (Manchester: Manchester University Press, 1982, p. 8).
42. "Between 1792 and the middle of 1794, radical iconography instantiated a new family romance of fraternity: brothers and sisters appear frequently in this iconographic outpouring, mothers rarely and fathers almost never" Lynn Hunt, *The Family Romance of the French Revolution* (London: Routledge, 1992, p. 53).
43. Jack Goody, *The European Family: An Historico-Anthropological Study* (Oxford: Blackwell, 2000).
44. Sybil Wolfram, *In-laws and Out-laws: Kinship and Marriage in England* (London: Croom Helm, 1987, pp .25–27).
45. Significantly, in the latest twentieth century *Oxford English Dictionary*, incest is defined as "the crime of sexual intercourse or cohabitation between persons related within the degrees within which marriage is prohibited by law".
46. Althea Hayter, "Victorian brothers and sisters", *Times Literary Supplement*, 9 August, 1974, p. 859.
47. D. H. Reiman, *Times Literary Supplement*, 1 November, 1974, p. 1231.
48. Quoted in Errol Durbach, "The *Geschwieter-Kamplex*: Romantic attitudes to brother–sister incest in Ibsen, Byron and Emily Bronte", *Mosaic*, 12(4): 65 (1979).
49. Edward Carpenter and George Barnfield, *The Psychology of the Poet Shelley* (London: Allen and Unwin, 1925, p. 91).
50. David Schneider, *op cit.*, p. 166.
51. James B. Twitchell, *Forbidden Partners*, p. 176.
52. In the nineteenth century this was defined as the "Westermarck effect", as opposed to Freud's conception in "Totem and taboo". In the late twentieth century the Westermarckian position has been resurrected by sociobiologists.
53. "William Wordsworth", *Chambers Encyclopedia*.
54. Fragment written in 1800, published in Mary Moorman, *William Wordsworth: A Biography* (Oxford: Clarendon Press, 1957–65, p. 282).
55. Reiman, *Times Literary Supplement*, 1 November, 1974.
56. F. W. Bateson, *Wordsworth: A Reinterpretation* (London: Longmans, 1963, p. 153).
57. Stephen Gill, *William Wordsworth, A Life* (Oxford: Clarendon Press, 1969, p. 203).

58. Quoted in M. LeFebure, *Times Literary Supplement*, 8 November, 1974, p. 1261.

59. Kathleen Jones, *A Passionate Sisterhood: The Sisters, Wives and Daughters of the Lake Poets* (London: Virago, 1998, p. 117).

60. *Ibid.*, p. 130.

61. Julia Barker, *Wordsworth* (London: Viking, 2000, p.293). Note that John Wordsworth, Dorothy and William's brother, who had been in love with Mary, was also hurt by the marriage although he never referred to this openly.

62. Kathleen Jones, *op. cit.*, p. 119.

63. Stephen Gill, *op. cit.*, p. 203.

64. Kathleen Jones, *op. cit.*, p. 118.

65. Julia Barker, *op. cit.*, pp. 493–494.

66. Lisa Gee, *Friends: Why Men and Women Are From The Same Planet*, (London: Bloomsbury, 2004, pp. 12–17).

67. Kathleen Jones, *op. cit.*, p.119.

68. C. F. Behrman, "The annual blister: a sidelight on Victorian social and parliamentary history", *Victorian Studies*, XI(4) (1968); N. Anderson, "The 'Marriage with a Deceased Wife's Sister Bill' controversy: incest anxiety and the defence of family purity in Victorian Britain", *Journal of British Studies*, 21(2) (1982).

69. Harriet Martineau's one novel, *Deerbrook* (1839), centres on a doctor who realizes he is in love with his resident sister-in-law; Charles Dickens had a close attachment to his wife's younger sister, which he, after her death, transferred to a yet younger sister; both sisters lived for long periods in his household; Slater, *Dickens and Women*.

70. Diana Gittins, *The Child in Question* (Houndsmill: MacMillan, 1998).

71. For this view of sibling incest, see G. W. Berry, "Incest: Some clinical variations on a classical theme", *Journal of the American Academy of Psychoanalysis*, 3(20) (April 1975); Vera and Allen Frances "The incest taboo and family structure", *Family Process*, 15(2) (June 1976), and a feminist challenge in Ellen Cole, "Sibling incest: The myth of benign sibling incest", *Women and Therapy*, 1(3) (fall 1982).

72. For an early statement see Michael Lamb and Brian Sutton-Smith, *Sibling Relationships: Their Nature and Significance Across the Lifespan* (London: Lawrence Erlbaum, 1982, p. 4); Klagsbrun, *Mixed Feelings*; Prophecy Coles, *The Importance of Sibling Relationships in Psychoanalysis* (London: Karnac, 2003); Juliet Mitchell, *Mad Men and Medusas: Reclaiming Hysteria and the Effects of Sibling Relations on the Human Condition* (London: Penguin, 2000); Juliet Mitchell, *Siblings: Sex and*

Violence (Cambridge: Polity Press, 2003); Robert Sanders, *Sibling Relationships: Theory and Issues for Practice* (London: Palgrave, 2004).

73. Richard Wall and Lloyd Bonfield, "Dimensions of inequalities among siblings", introductory essay to a special issue of that title, *Continuity and Change*, 7(3): 269 (December 1992). For a one-dimensional approach to siblings historically see Frank Sulloway, *Born to Rebel: Birth Order, Family Dynamics and Creative Lives* (New York: Pantheon, 1996).

74. For a recent study that counteracts this approach through the idea of lifetime attachment, see Victor G. Cicirelli, *Sibling Relationships Across the Life Span*, (New York: Plenum Press, 1995).

75. Bert Adams, *Kinship in an Urban Setting*; Raymond Firth, Jane Hubert, and Anthony Forge, *Families and their Relatives: Kinship in a Middle-Class Sector of London* (London: Routledge & Kegan Paul, 1969); Yanagisako, *Transforming the Past*.

76. Judith E. Smith, *Family Connections: A History of Italian and Jewish Immigrant Lives in Providence, Rhode Island 1900–1910* (Albany, NY: State University of New York Press, 1985, p. 102); Yanaisako, *Transforming the Past*.

77. Michele A. Pujol, *Feminism and Anti-Feminism in Early Economic Thought* (Cheltenham: Edward Elgar, 1992).

78. Leonore Davidoff, "Regarding some 'Old Husband's Tales': public and private in feminist history", in *Worlds Between: Historical Perspectives on Gender and Class* (Cambridge: Polity Press, 1995).

79. Robert Wheaton, "Observations on the development of kinship history 1942–1985", *Journal of Family History*, 12 (1987).

80. Elaine Cumming and David Schneider, "Sibling solidarity: A property of American kinship", *American Anthropologist*, 63: 505 (1961).

81. Catherine Hall, "Competing masculinities: Thomas Carlyle, John Stuart Mill and the case of Governor Eyre", in *White, Male and Middle Class: Explorations in Feminism and History* (Cambridge: Polity Press, 1992, p. 270).

82. Kinship relationships, for example in terms of "big brother–little brother" are also implicit in modern corporate bodies. Michael Roper, *Masculinity and the British Organization since 1945* (Oxford: Oxford University Press, 1993).

83. Lyndal Roper, "Sexual Utopianism in the German Reformation", *Journal of Ecclesiastical History*, 42(3): 404 (July 1991).

84. Mary Ann Clawson, "Fraternalism and the patriarchal family", *Feminist Studies*, (Summer 1980), and her *Constructing Brotherhood: Class, Gender and Fraternalism* (Princeton, NJ: Princeton University Press, 1989).

85. Lily E. Clerkx, "Family relationship in fairy tales: a historical socio-logical approach", *The Netherlands Journal of Sociology*, 23(2) (October 1987). It might be argued that children identify with the brothers and sisters as segmented parts of themselves *vis-à-vis* an orphaned state, wicked stepmothers, etc. Significantly, Marina Warner's magisterial study of fairy tales does not specifically discuss siblings: *From the Beast to the Blonds: On Fairy Tales and Their Tellers* (London: Vintage, 1994).

86. Nancy Benson and Jeremy Anglin, "The child's knowledge of English kin terms", *First Language*, 7(19/1) (1987).

87. For a striking account *of* this phenomenon see Andrew Birkin, *J. M. Barrie and the Lost Boys* (London: Constable, 1979).

88. Janet Mersky Leder "Adult sibling rivalry", *Psychology Today*, (January/February 1993).

89. Segalen, *Historical Anthropology of the Family*, p. 103.

90. John Gillis, personal communication.

91. Peter Gay, *The Naked Heart,* volume IV, *The Bourgeois Experience: Victoria to Freud* (London: Harper Collins, 1996, p. 101).

92. Jane Austen, *Mansfield Park* (Oxford: Oxford University Press) p. 212.

93. Graham Little, *Friendship: Being Ourselves With Others* (Melbourne: The Text Publishing Company, 1991, pp. 15, 250, 255); Ray Pahl, *On Friendship* (Cambridge: Polity Press, 2000).

94. When totalitarian regimes begin to invade personal relations, a retreat inwards to the closest bonds may, at least for a short time, hold at bay the political invasion of trust between people. Thomas Mann's story of a post-First World War brother and sister whose semi-incestuous games cut them off from the destruction of their bourgeois security by the effects of massive inflation ("The Blood of the Walsings") was eerily played out in real life by his son, Klaus, and daughter, Erika, during the rise of Nazism. See Klaus Mann's novella and play *Siblings and the Children's Store*, translated with an introduction by T. Alexander and P. Eyre (London and New York: Marion Boyars, 1992).

CHAPTER TWO

Ishmael and Isaac:
an enduring conflict

Estelle Roith

"Mankind never lives entirely in the present. The past, the tradition of the race and of the people, lives on in the ideologies of the super-ego, and yields only slowly to the influences of the present . . ."

(Sigmund Freud, "New introductory lectures on psychoanalysis, 1933a, p. 67)

"Very deep is the well of the past. Should we not call it bottomless?"

(Thomas Mann, *Joseph and his Brothers*, 1933, p. 3)

"Take now thy son, thine only son Isaac, whom thou lovest, and get thou into the land of Moriah; and offer him there for a burnt offering" (Genesis 22: 2).[1] The words of Genesis, echoing down the millennia, herald the supreme trial of Abraham's faith. Often described as the defining moment for Judaism, the words stand at the crossroads of all three monotheistic faiths. In this paper, whose theme is the story of two half-brothers, Ishmael and

Isaac, the sons of Abraham, I am going to look at the event known to Judaism and Christianity as the "Binding of Isaac" (in Hebrew, the Akedah), and to Islam as the "sacrifice of Ishmael", the founding myth of the saga of monotheism whose heirs today are so deeply troubled.

Myths dramatize all kinds of significant watersheds in the early history of civilized development. It is generally agreed that what we see dramatized in the Akedah is a major stage in the psycho-social transition of early civilized development from human to animal sacrifice and, crucially, from polytheism to monotheism. Robert Graves and Raphael Patai define myths as: "dramatic stories . . . either authorizing the continuance of ancient institutions, customs, rites and beliefs . . . or approving their alteration (1966, p. 11).

Anthropologist Carol Delaney, writing specifically on the Akedah, emphasizes that the story has been "a structuring force . . . on human psychology and the dynamics of history" (2000: p. 184). Like other "origin myths", it represents not truth or reality but ways in which people can "situate and interpret their lives . . . identity and orientation in [the] world . . . Jews, Christians, and Muslims have been able to say: 'We are the children of Abraham'" (*ibid.*, p. 20).

Richard V. Kaufman (1983) uses the Akedah story as an example of the "early stage in the development of morality" both between parent and child and in the formation of early Western civilization. From a "presuperego myth", with the breakthrough in Abraham of infanticidal impulses, magical reversals, retaliations, and bloodshed, the development is to the acquisition of superego functioning, to parental protection and restraint and the transformation of idolatry into "ethical monotheism" (*ibid.*, p. 248). Kaufman believes that the story depicts the mythic birth of civilization out of barbarism through the "emergence of the morally bound parent" and, importantly, through the child's discovery of the parental conscience (*ibid.*, p. 250). Other psychoanalytic commentators have seen the story in terms of a reversal of classical Freudian Oedipal theory. In this reading, the destructive fantasies of fathers for sons are emphasized with the ambivalent wish on the part of Abraham to murder his son and its resolution in Isaac's redemption (Ross, 1982; Stein, 1977).

I am not going to venture far into the vast body of philosophical and theological debate about Abraham's near-sacrifice of his son on Mount Moriah. Nor will I address the question of the different biblical authors and editors and their re-workings of the ancient texts. I intend to draw on the texts themselves as they have come down to us over the millennia. Here, I would just note that from the earliest Jewish commentaries and legends onwards, for both the Church Fathers and philosophers such as Kant, Kierkegaard, and Martin Buber, the focal point in the Akedah has devolved on issues surrounding the morality of Abraham's faith and of his unquestioning obedience to God's command.

My main focus in this paper is a different one. My aim is to examine the nature and implications of the sibling relationship underlying the myth of the Akedah. I am aware that a theologian or historian would do more justice to some of *my* themes. I am also aware that, at times, I shall seem to treat the characters concerned as real people rather than as figures in a religious myth that happened to grip the popular imagination. My justification for this is that whether or not they ever lived, these characters *have* remained real in the popular imagination. The story of Abraham, "central to the nervous system of Judaism and Christianity" (Goldin in Spiegel, 1993, p. xxi), is, in a different version, also central to Islam and the events in those stories are celebrated in teaching and prayer, ritual and custom, by millions of followers and worshippers around the world. Here, I am going to look at the connections between the Biblical and the Koranic versions of the myth. I will try to show that long before the factors usually cited as the causes of the conflicts between Islam and the West, Jews and Arabs (the first Muslims) were struggling with a deep-seated cause of dissension whose roots, shrouded in the mists of ancient history, have remained buried in the biblical story of the two sons of Abraham. I believe that the relationship of Judaism and Christianity on the one hand, itself fraught with tension for so long, to Islam on the other, has been haunted by the omission of this complex connection between Ishmael and Isaac.

The fact is that in the Old Testament a gap yawns from the very start between Abraham's relationship with his elder son, Ishmael, and that with his younger son, Isaac. It is a gap of affection, privilege, inheritance, and, ultimately, of the identity of the chosen and favoured child of God.

Genesis 16 tells us that Hagar, the mother of Ishmael, was maidservant or slave to Abraham's wife Sarah; in the Arab—and later

Muslim—tradition Hagar was Abraham's second wife. Sarah was barren and, in the couple's declining years, "sent in" Abraham to Hagar, as was the custom, in the hope that she would conceive and produce the heir necessary to fulfil God's prophecy to him that he would father a great people. Surrogate mothering evidently being no less complex than it is today, Hagar, when pregnant, grew tactlessly smug about her new role. The jealous Sarah (complaining angrily to Abraham that she was: "despised in her eyes" Genesis 16: 5), treated Hagar so harshly that the maidservant fled into the wilderness, a flight that foreshadowed her later exile. There, she was found by "an angel of the Lord" and instructed to return to Sarah. She was pregnant with a son, she was told, who would also father multitudes. Hagar returned and gave birth to Ishmael (the name means "Heard by God", testimony perhaps to the fact that he was heard by no one else. (Barchilon, 1985)).

Once again, God appeared to Abraham and renewed his promise of "descendents as the stars of heaven and as the sand upon the seashore". Puzzled, Abraham asked that Ishmael, at that time his only child, be made heir to the promised covenant: "O that, Ishmael might live before thee" (Genesis 17: 18), but is told sharply by God that this will not do. "Sarah thy wife shall bear thee a son indeed; and thou shalt call his name Isaac; and I will establish my covenant with him" (Genesis 17: 19). Some years after this (the exact chronology is uncertain but it is suggested in the text that Ishmael is in his teens), Sarah conceived miraculously and gave birth to Isaac, thus fulfilling God's second prophecy. Again, Sarah prevailed upon Abraham to cast Hagar out, this time, when the young Ishmael was caught "mocking" Isaac at the feast celebrating the young child's weaning. (Hertz, 1929, like many rabbinic authorities, interprets the term to mean "an act of impurity", i.e., sexual abuse (p. 176, n.9).)

With the next mention of Isaac comes what Kierkegaard (1985) describes as the great "paradox", which seems to cancel out not merely God's covenant with Abraham but the entire divine plan. God makes his shock announcement: "Take now thy son, thine only son, Isaac, whom thee lovest, and get thee into the land of Moriah; and offer him there for a burnt offering" (Genesis 22: 2). The Old Testament account is quite specific. It is Isaac, Sarah's son, whom God is demanding, the loved and favoured son, surprisingly, called his "only" one. Yet Isaac is, of course, Abraham's second son. Ishmael, therefore, when cast out into the wilderness together with his mother, has been rejected not only by his father, family, and tribe, but also by God. He was also left by his mother when the water provided by Abraham ran out as they wandered in the desert. Distressed, Hagar went "an arrow's distance" away to avoid watching Ishmael, who, perhaps in a metaphor for helplessness is mysteriously represented here as a small child, die of thirst (Genesis 21: 16). It is important to note here that Ishmael is not excluded from the divine "promise", for he too, Hagar is told once again by an angel, will have progeny too numerous to count (Genesis 16: 10). Yet, the destiny prophesied for him is very different to that of his half-brother. This first-born son of Abraham, venerated by Islam as its founding prophet, is to be a rebel and an outcast: "a wild man; his hand will be against every man, and every man's hand against him" (Genesis 16: 12).

How has Islam dealt with this bleak account of its beginnings, which casts its founding father in the role of the rejected and dispossessed other? After all, the Hebrew text of Genesis, as I have said, is the source of all successive interpretations of the sacrifice story and was, including for early Moslem scholars, the definitive account; the *Torah* remains for Islam "the Book of God" and Abraham, Isaac, and Jacob, as well as Ishmael, are still, today, revered as prophets.

One way Islam has chosen to deal with the issue has been to dispute the authenticity of the biblical account. Long before the advent of Islam, writes Kanan Makiya (2002), the close affinity between Arabs and Jews was noted by Christian scholars. Both peoples drew extensively on the Hebrew scriptures and commentaries, with Jews interpreting them to the Prophet's followers in Arabic (*ibid.*, p. 281). But in the early centuries of the Muslim era (which began in 622 AD), the belief that both the Old and New Testaments had been falsified by Jews and Christians, respectively, gained ground. The "People of the Book" are frequently admonished in the Koran for denying God's revelations and refusing to bear "the burden of the Torah . . . like a donkey laden with books" (Surah 62: 5). Thus the burgeoning religion of Islam began to diverge from the bleak biblical account of its origins, while later Muslim scholars supported the Koranic view about the "Book of

God". Crucially, most—although not all—scholars agreed that the child who was to be sacrificed, unnamed in the Koran, was "Ismail". The renowned tenth-century Muslim scholar, Al-Tabari, observed that "The earliest sages of our Prophet's nation disagree" about which of Abraham's two sons were offered up for sacrifice (Noujaim, 1995, p. 161). Ishmael, it is argued, was quite literally Abraham's "only" son at the crucial time, since Isaac's birth, as described in the same section of the Koran, occurs later (Surah 37: 105). Moreover, the argument continues, God's prophecy that the chosen one will beget a "great multitude" and rule over Canaan, clearly came to pass for the Arabs, Ishmael's people, whereas Jews, exiled since the destruction of the second Temple in 70 AD, returned to the area only relatively recently (Sloan, 2002).

Muslim versions of the story differ in other ways. God does not directly command the sacrifice. Abraham dreams that he is sacrificing his "son"—who remains unnamed throughout this episode—then says: "Tell me what you think". "Father, do as you are bidden" comes the reply (Surah 37: 91). Abraham's decision then to sacrifice him is made not merely in response to Ishmael's own interpretation of his vision and willingness to submit to it, but to the boy's own instruction to his father to do so. There is an important difference here between the Old Testament and the Koranic versions. In the first, Isaac is given neither choice nor information about his fate. Indeed, his anxious question as to where was the animal intended for the sacrifice, is deflected by his father: "God will provide himself a lamb", Isaac is told (Genesis 22: 8). The Koranic "son", on the other hand, plays an active role in the drama. He knowingly accepts, indeed calls on his father to accept, his sacrifice and although he too is redeemed, it is from Abraham's own vision, which, admittedly, is deemed by Muslims to represent God's command. Most important, however, is the Muslim belief that the revelation by God to Muhammad, later inscribed in the Koran, represents the only accurate statement of the divine plan. Disclosed for the first time in full to the Prophet, it has been seen, in part, as the completion and fulfilment of the Jewish development.

Nevertheless, Abraham's willingness to obey in this account, as in its counterpart in the Old Testament, is taken as the ultimate test of his faith. Indeed, the interpretation that the unnamed son is Ishmael has carried enough weight to persuade Muslims throughout the world to commemorate the event annually with the festival of Id al-Adha. Interestingly enough, in a description of Ishmael, strikingly at odds with that of the Bible as an "outcast" and "man of violence", the Koranic version describes him as "a gentle son" as if to resemble the biblical image of Isaac (Surah 37: 105, p. 315). Isaac was later to be described by the Rabbis as the "first of the great kind ones" of the Bible, "the tame dove", of the daily Hebrew morning prayer (Wellisch, 1954, p. 68).

The Akedah has also played a major role in Christianity. The Church Fathers found close analogies between the binding of Isaac and Jesus—the "lamb of God"—at Golgotha. The earliest example of this is seen in the second century AD, when the emphasis of both Judaism and Christianity began to shift from Abraham, as the perfect example of faith, to Isaac. Thus, in the Epistle of Barnabas, Isaac's near-sacrifice is seen as prefiguring the Crucifixion. Irenaeus exhorts Christians that in "their faith they too must be on the alert to bear the cross just as Isaac bore the wood for the burnt-offering . . .". The image, found in midrashic–talmudic sources, of the "one bearing his own cross" was one of which the Church Fathers were "especially fond" (Spiegel, 1993, p. 84). Origen, writing early in the third century, links the Lamb of God, of John 1: 29, with the ram of Genesis 22, substituted for Isaac at his redemption (Doukhan, 1995, p. 111). This link is made more explicit still by St Augustine in his City of God, where he finds that the thicket in which Abraham found the ram recalled Jesus's crown of thorns. Both Jesus and Isaac, Augustine also notes, carried the wood for their own ordeals on Mount Moriah (in Wellisch, 1954, p. 72). St Paul concluded that those who believe in Christ were, like Isaac, "children of the promise . . . born after the Spirit", by contrast to those who, like Ishmael, were born "after the flesh" (Galicians 4: 23–29). (Paradoxically, Jews, since they remained "enslaved" by Jewish law, were identified by Paul with Ishmael as children of Hagar.) But the connection drawn between Isaac and Jesus is most direct in the opening words of the New Testament itself, where Jesus's lineage is traced directly to Abraham: "The book of the generation of Jesus Christ, the son of David, the son of Abraham" (Matthew 1: 1).

It might be objected that this topic is an obscure one, belonging in the scholarly preserve of historians and theologians. However, a glance at internet sites devoted to Islamic as well as Jewish and

Christian affairs reveals that the issue is very much alive today. Arguments entitled: "Isaac vs. Ishmael: the heart of the conflict"; "Ishak or Ismail: the Muslim dilemma"; and "The sacrifice of Abraham—the Koran or the Bible?" are being waged across the Web. Accusations of scriptural distortion are being hurled, inconsistencies and contradictions in the Bible—never difficult to find—invoked, and "proofs" of ancient editorial bias constantly "discovered". While the West, until recently, has remained largely oblivious to the crucial role of the sacrifice within Islam, as well as its claim to the sacrificial son, the sacrifice itself has constituted an article of faith—indeed, it is the central article of faith—for Muslims. As the Koran puts it, the submission of Abraham was "the bitter test" for which was bestowed on him "the praise of later generations" (Surah 37: 105), while Id al-Adha—the festival celebrating the "sacrifice"—is the holiest of festivals marking the culmination of the Hajj.

Edward Said (2001) has spoken of the "many-sided contest" waged over the centuries by the three monotheistic faiths, followers of "the most jealous of all gods". The original protagonists in this contest for the place of the favoured child of God, as we have seen, were Abraham's two sons, the half-brothers, Ishmael and Isaac. As remote in time and place from us as they are, interactions between parents and children, and siblings with each other, nevertheless embody features that are universal phenomena in families everywhere as well as in the internal world of object relationships. I would like, therefore, to take a brief look at some studies that describe features of sibling relationships to see how, in one way or another, they influence and have different meanings for each other.

Prophecy Coles (2003) has proposed that, following Freud, psychoanalytic orthodoxy has neglected, in both theory and practice, the importance of sibling relationships and the long-standing dynamic issues involved. She links this neglect to the centrality given by Freud, and subsequently by psychoanalysis in general, to the Oedipus complex and relationships with parents (ibid., pp. 21–22). Coles cites Juliet Mitchell's argument, that there has been "a massive repression of the significance of all the love and hate of sibling relationship and their heirs in marital affinity and friendships" (ibid., p. 3).

Freud's famous dictum that the first-born son as "his mother's undisputed darling" "retains . . . the triumphant feeling, the confidence in success, which not seldom brings actual success along with it", went on to become a psychoanalytic tenet (Freud, 1917b, p. 156). Although—or perhaps because—Freud, his mother's eldest son (his father had two older sons from a previous marriage), did remain "his mother's undisputed darling", he was acutely aware of his displacement from the "throne" of the only child following the birth of his brother, Julius. He acknowledged suffering a lasting sense of guilt when the baby died a few months later. He then found it deeply problematic when his first sister, Anna, was born. Freud seems to testify to this when, with what seems like an autobiographical note, he wrote: "A child who has been put into second place by the birth of a brother or sister, and who is now for the first time almost isolated from his mother, does not easily forgive her this loss of place; feelings . . . arise in him and are often the basis of a permanent estrangement" (Freud, 1916–17, p. 34). As Coles writes, "An eldest child may feel robbed of his unique position in the family when the next sibling is born" (Coles, 2003, p. 84). Juliet Mitchell, writing on the displacement of the eldest child says, "The sibling is par excellence someone who threatens the subject's uniqueness" (Mitchell, 2003, p. 10) Mitchell continues, "The older child is not just displaced, but for a time is without a place" (p. 47).

While Freud acknowledged his mother's faith and pride in him as the source of his self-confidence, his own earliest identification was with Joseph, the Biblical interpreter of dreams. It is interesting to note that, contrary to his dictum, this was an identification with the favourite, younger son of a loving father, whose fortunes were determined by his brother's envy and hatred of him, and whose mother died giving birth to his only sibling, Benjamin. Joseph, thus, grew up motherless. Freud's peculiar hostility towards old women (Wortis, 1940, quoted in Roith, 1987), juxtaposed with his well-known theoretical idealization of the mother–son relationship (Freud, 1933a, p. 133), point rather to a deeply problematic relationship with his mother.

In fact, Freud's view that the first-born son is usually the preferred child is challenged by a great deal of contrary evidence. The Bible is a particular case in point. Starting with Abel, Abraham himself, Isaac, Jacob, Joseph, Joseph's son, Ephraim, Moses, as well as

Kings David and Solomon and others, it is younger brothers, we are shown, who are usually preferred by God and by their parents and, where possible, have been chosen to carry on the line of descent.

The findings that parents and children will influence and have different meanings for each other, that different parental identifications and projections are made with each one and different conscious and unconscious attitudes are recreated and enacted, is supported by Rosemary Balsam (1988). She emphasizes the important observation that parental attitudes will, in turn, influence how each child perceives the other. Parental preferment of one child over another can compound the hostility and envy of siblings for each other (Balsam, 1988, pp. 66–67).

No story could better reveal this tension than the Genesis account of the biblical twins, Jacob and Esau. Meissner's (1994) analysis of the warring brothers reveals the elements of sibling rivalry and "envy that reach back to their childhood days and carry with them their unabated burden of resentments and recriminations" (ibid., p. 461). This particular story, however, illustrates not merely a state of rivalry that began before birth, but shows also how, in each choosing one of the pair of twins to favour and promote over the other, the parents clearly failed to provide their sons with an essential developmental framework in which relations between the two could prosper. The story of Jacob and Esau demonstrates, more than anything else, the narcissistic investment for each parent in keeping their respective favoured twin apart from his sibling and identified symbiotically with themselves, rather than available to develop an adequate sense of a separate, non-threatened self with each other. It is no coincidence that it was Isaac, himself the unwitting infant participant in a drama of parental favouritism, betrayal, and abandonment, who was the father of these envious and covetous brothers.

However, the case of Ishmael and Isaac is different in important respects to that of Esau and Jacob. Whereas even an older child might experience some degree of difference in the quality of his mother's attention during pregnancy and the birth of the sibling, Ishmael and Isaac were, like Joseph and his brothers, the sons of different mothers who were themselves separated from each other by their roles, their social and legal status in the family and community and, crucially, by their relationships to Abraham, father of their respective sons. Yet, in spite of Hagar's dependant status, Ishmael must himself have been greeted as the longed-for and long-awaited son of the aged Abraham. For he was far from being the product of a casual encounter by Abraham with one of many concubines. The Bible is at pains to show us that the tie between Abraham and Sarah was such that Hagar was "taken" by him only at Sarah's own behest in the couple's old age. Abraham, before the birth of Isaac, had pleaded with God for Ishmael to be made heir to the covenant with its precious endowments of the blessing and the land. Thus, this surrogate son of Sarah might well have expected acceptance and protection from both her and his father. On the other hand, Ishmael might already have experienced a change in his father's perception of him and his place in the family after the birth of Isaac. That Abraham loved him is made clear in the text, as we shall see shortly. But the focus of his affections had clearly shifted. Perhaps the now-adolescent Ishmael was perceived by him as threatening, rather than gratifying the sense of narcissistic completeness he had gained at the long-awaited birth of this first son. Perhaps, as Mortimer Ostow succinctly observes: "Isaac is preferred to his brother Ishmael because Sarah is preferred to Hagar" (Ostow, 1989, p. 489). Whatever the reason, Abraham's hopes were now transferred to the "true-born" son, ordained by God to inherit the precious covenant, the son miraculously born to his wife Sarah.

Chosen by God over his elder brother, made heir to the precious covenant, Isaac was the "cuckoo in the nest" in which Ishmael was once the only, long-awaited son (Vivienne Lewin, personal communication). Significantly, the young Isaac was not only the child of a loving parental couple, he also enjoyed the "blissful union of His Majesty the Baby" with the full "parental retinue" (Meissner, 1994, p. 461), which, with Hagar's lowly status and her history of strife with Sarah, was never available to Ishmael. Small wonder, then, that Ishmael was found "mocking" the young Isaac, his newly-arrived successor, heir to the unbounded love of both Abraham and Sarah, at the child's great feast of weaning. The feast, which celebrated the "true-born" son's separation from the enticing feminine world ruled over by his mother and his graduation to the masculine realm of his father, also relegated Ishmael to the role of the "other", the "son of the bondswoman". Whatever the meaning ascribed to the term, "mocking", Genesis leaves us in no doubt that

Ishmael was perpetrating some kind of mischief and persecuting his toddler rival in some way.

Abraham expelled Hagar and Ishmael in obedience to Sarah's wish and God's command, although his grief at the loss of his eldest son is such that God was moved to console him: "Let it not be grievous in thy sight because of the lad" and promises to create from "the son of the bondswoman" a nation for Abraham's sake (Genesis 21: 12–13).

Missing from the story of the two sons of Abraham, apart from the "mocking" behaviour I have described, is any evidence of the brothers' feelings for each other or, indeed, of any presence in each other's minds. However, in a terse and obscure passage, Genesis conveys a startling piece of information. It relates that Abraham died and "his sons Isaac and Ishmael buried him in the cave of Machpelah" with Sarah (Genesis 25: 8–10).

Ishmael's return to help bury his father must represent a considerable psychic achievement on his part, since he was likely to have been nursing feelings of sibling rivalry, envy, and narcissistic injury, both consciously and unconsciously. In returning to help Isaac bury Abraham, Ishmael was clearly able to find the capacity for sorrow and grief and the ability to mourn, as well as to cooperate with Isaac. In this moving episode, we can imagine in this Ishmael something of the lonely, exiled son who longs to re-experience his father's lost love. He might also have wished to find again an affection he once felt—along with the jealousy—for the baby brother, who did not, after all, choose their present situation. In Isaac, on the other hand, we might also see the wish to share with his brother a loss common to them both and, with it, a bond in their mutual descent from Abraham.

Sarah herself holds a unique place among women in the Bible. The first of the biblical matriarchs, she was destined to be seen as the "great mother of Israel", revered by Muslims as well as by the Church. Sarah is the only woman in the Bible to be addressed directly by God, rather than through an angel (Wellisch, 1954, p. 68), and one of the few women to be depicted as an individual in her own right. Coveted by kings for her great beauty, her gift of prophecy was, according to the rabbis, greater than that of Abraham. She was also, as we have seen, hot-tempered, jealous, and, once Isaac was born, fiercely protective of his rights of inheritance.

Her burial place in Hebron on the West Bank remains a place of pilgrimage for all three faiths.

I believe that Sarah's role in the story is, more often than not, underestimated. For example, Delaney (2000), in a feminist reading of the Akedah story, criticizes biblical commentators for their focus on God and Abraham, to whom the child appears to belong in a more specific way than he does to the mother. She proposes that the voices of both Sarah and Hagar have been silenced; they have been excluded not merely from the sacrifice event but from the whole story (*ibid.*, pp. 22–23). It is true that the next time Sarah is mentioned in Genesis it is with the announcement of her death and burial. Indeed, a rabbinic legend relates that she died of grief on being told the truth (Spiegel, 1993, p. 31, n. 13). Yet, we might speculate about her role in the story as a whole. Although it is clear that Sarah was unaware of the planned sacrifice of Isaac, we do know that she had a decisive influence on other major family decisions, such as the expulsion of Hagar with the young Ishmael.

Parental failure of children, of one kind or another, is common to both versions of this myth. We have seen how Sarah's destructive impulse against Ishmael was given full rein but also how Hagar, helpless as she was to protect her son from expulsion, then left him alone, unable to watch him die of thirst. In the best-known Muslim accounts of this episode, mother and child are, once again, left to fend for themselves in the wilderness, although Abraham has initially accompanied them to Mecca. In this account too, the child Ishmael is left alone by Hagar who leaves him to go on a frantic search for water, a search that is commemorated in every Hajj when the pilgrim runs seven times, as Hagar did, between two rocky hillocks in Mecca. The child, meanwhile, is guided by the angel Gabriel to discover the Zamzam spring, thereby saving them both. (Guillaume, 1955, p. 45). Like Sarah in Judaism, Hagar holds a unique place in Islam. Muslims are expected to identify with her faith in God and in Abraham (Fakhry Davids, personal communication). Yet, in both the biblical and the Muslim accounts, Ishmael is deprived both of water—the element most basic to survival—and of the nurturing he needs (Melanie Hart, personal communication). Thus, he is obliged to resort to a narcissistic or prematurely self-reliant provision; that is, he must depend on divine rather than on parental intervention. Although the miracle is forthcoming and death is averted, Ishmael, like Isaac, has had to survive a near-death experience.

In a certain sense, Islam, like Judaism, is reluctant to recognize the human failures of the mothers in the stories. It seems that, like Sarah, Hagar can only be idealized. It is as if the real mother—emotionally absent or destructive—must be defended against, as well as, simultaneously, defended and preserved from attack herself. We seem to glimpse here the vestige of an earlier mother, the mother of a pre-monotheistic age, or of infancy, transposed into a submissive relationship with a punitive God-the-father. The splitting involved in this precarious psychic exercise suggests anxieties about survival that might well have been projected away on to a punishing, omnipotent father-God.

I began this chapter with the story of the Akedah, the Biblical account of the "binding of Isaac", and went on to show the different version of the event given by the Koran. However, the question that presents itself throughout the controversy between the Biblical and the Koranic accounts, and between Judaism and Islam, remains unanswered. Why should both sides wish to compete for what seems like the dubious honour of having their founding father offered up for slaughter by a so-called loving father, in unquestioning obedience to a demanding deity? If we compare Abraham's impulse to kill Isaac (or Ishmael), both much wanted sons, to Laius's wish to kill Oedipus, a much *un*wanted child, whose only crime was to be born at all, we can see that Abraham must have been moved by a quite different impulse. So, before going any further, I would like to look at the meanings invested in the idea of sacrifice. For nowhere is the "many sided contest" between Ishmael and Isaac, waged within the pages of the sacred texts, more apparent than in the claim made by the followers of each to be the son chosen by God for the sacrifice (Said, 2001).

Andresen's (1984) study of the "sacrifice complex" shows that the act of sacrifice has been a "fundamental element of religious practices on every continent and in every time . . ." (p. 529). There are different bases for sacrifice across different cultures and Andresen summarizes the "nodal fantasies" constituting the three main divisions, each involving different motives and objectives. Here, I am going to take only the briefest look at the issue of child sacrifice and at some of the elements involved in the story of the Akedah.

While the Israelite sacrifice of animals came to a halt with the destruction by the Roman Titus of the second Temple in Jerusalem in 70 AD, the topic of child sacrifice—whether it occurred at all and if it was still practised when Abraham and Sarah arrived in Canaan— remains endlessly controversial. Many Jewish scholars reject the "Christian" notion that the message of the Akedah was to substitute animal for child sacrifice. By that time, it is claimed, it had long been abandoned (Berman, 1997). However, the frequent prophetic warnings against the practice throughout the Bible, commencing in about the eighth century BC, suggest that it remained a problem.

Graves and Patai (1966) are in no doubt that the sacrifice of first-born sons was common in the Palestine of antiquity and, in support of this literal reading, cite the verse in Exodus 22: 29. "the firstborn of thy sons shalt thou give unto me" (p. 175).

For theologian, Jon Levenson (1993), the distance on this point between ancient Israel and its Canaanite cousins was not so great as the "heated prophetic critique" suggests. However, around the sixth century it became acceptable in both cultures to sacrifice an animal as a substitute for a child (*ibid.*, p. 36).

Raphael Patai (1977) writes that when Abraham and Sarah arrived in Canaan around the seventeenth century BC, their Israelite religion already had as its credal basis the monotheistic belief in Yahweh, with circumcision as an established rite. The Yahwist struggle between Israelite monotheism and Canaanite polytheism was to involve, at times, paying due homage to Canaanite and Phoenician gods and their sacred rites, including the sacrifice of the first-born son (*ibid.*, p. 50).

Wellisch (1954) believes that the story of the Akedah mirrors a universal psychic truth about parental ambivalence towards the child. He proposes that primordial infanticide was probably practised before primordial patricide by all races and nations across the ancient world (*ibid.*, pp. 9–10). Euripides' play, "Iphigenia at Aulis", in which Iphegenia is rescued by the Goddess Artemis from sacrifice by her father, Agamemnon, is invoked by Wellisch as a parallel story to the Akedah. Wellisch argues that the "Akedah Motif . . . is the Biblical extension of the Oedipus Complex", since it too depicts the experience by a child of a father's infanticidal impulse but, in addition, points to its resolution by means of paternal love and restraint (*ibid.*, pp. 113–115).

Contrary to these views, Freud's emphasis on the destructive wishes sons harbour towards their fathers has, itself, become one of the organizing myths of Western culture. From 1897, when he abandoned his seduction theory, proposing instead the Oedipus complex and its vicissitudes as the essential psychic paradigm, Freud did not waver on this emphasis. He largely ignored the role of Laius in Sophocles' drama, and the destructive fantasies of parents towards their children. (Ross, 1982). Thus, in Freud's "myth of origins", "Totem and taboo" (1912–1913), the prototypical crime is not infanticide but parricide, with the sacrifice by the sons of the primal father. The rebellious sons, denied a share of the women of the horde, murder and then devour the primal father. Their subsequent feelings of guilt, love, and remorse, and the renunciations they then imposed upon themselves constitute the beginnings of culture, religion, and civilization. "Primitive men actually *did*" what the neurotic only wishes to do. As Freud wrote; "in the beginning was the deed" (*ibid.*, p. 161). In "Moses and monotheism", his study of the origins of Judaism and of religious belief, written in 1939, Freud again concluded that the repressed memory for that first parricide, with its phylogenetically acquired sense of guilt, became "inherited property" that in each generation "called only for awakening" (1939a, pp. 132–133). Kept alive by the prophets, these traces of an earlier primal reality found expression in the religion of Moses and his father-God (*ibid.*, p. 52).

Freud virtually ignored the biblical Abraham, dismissing claims to regard him as the source of monotheism and of the religious rite of circumcision, both of which he attributed instead to the Egyptian Pharaoh, Ikhnaton. Nevertheless, he did detect in a "prophetic dream" that he dreamt during the First World War a murderous wish of his own. He writes that he saw "very clearly the death of my sons," [all of whom were then on military service] "Martin first of all" (in Gay, 1988, p. 354). Freud did, in fact, acknowledge the filicidal wish involved. He thought he discovered the "concealed impulse" in himself when he interpreted years later: "*the envy which is felt for the young by those who have grown old . . .*" (Freud, 1900a, p. 560, in Ross, 1982, p. 173, italics added). However, such insights were not integrated by him into his developmental theory which "remained essentially a psychology of sons and their filial conflicts" (*ibid.*). Interestingly, given the biblical preference for younger sons I have described above, we might note that it was the death of Martin, his eldest son, that Freud saw "first of all".

Stein (1977), writing from the vantage point of both psycho-analysis and anthropology, maintains that the idea of sacrifice remains, unconsciously, "deeply enshrined" in Judaism. Like several other writers, he cites as evidence of this the special conditions that still apply in Judaism to the first-born son of each wife. Based on the verse in Exodus 22: 28 quoted above, when the first-born son (of each wife) is thirty-one days old, the observant Jewish father must redeem him from a "Kohen" (priest) in a ritual known as the "redemption of the first-born". A rabbinic reason sometimes given for this ritual is that the firstborn son, as in the time of the Temple, had to be redeemed from consecration to the priesthood (Jacobs, 1995, p. 168). However, it also serves as a reminder of God's slaying of the Egyptian first-born (Exodus 4: 21–23). Whatever reason is chosen, the survival of the ritual denotes that the impulse to sacrifice the eldest boy remained potent long after the literal practice was rejected.

In his celebrated book on the Akedah, Shalom Spiegel (1993) dis-cusses an important strand of rabbinic opinion, widely influential in the Middle Ages, which, with many rabbinic embellishments and variations, suggests that Abraham did, in fact, slaughter Isaac on Mount Moriah. This is said to be the explanation for the puzzling description in Genesis 22: 19 of Abraham's return from Mount Moriah, in which he appears to be accompanied only by his two servants. No mention is made of Isaac (Spiegel, 1993, pp. 30–33). Again, the degree of anxiety reflected in the urgency with which the angel of God halts the sacrifice is striking. The command: "Lay not thine hand upon the lad", is immediately followed—unusually for the Bible—by a repeated one, "neither do thou any thing unto him: (Genesis 22: 12).The second command suggests that Abraham's urge to kill Isaac is so strong that, in his struggle to resist it, he toys with the idea of inflicting a lesser injury—a wound or scratch— before the cautionary voice warns him against harming him at all. But Isaac's absence here from the text—indeed, the two are not mentioned together again until Abraham's burial—might also be showing us that he is now lost to his father, driven away by his real-ization of his father's intention. Kierkegaard says, that for Abraham, it was better, after all, that Isaac should think his father a "monster" than that he should lose faith in God (Kierkegaard, 1985, pp. 45–46).

After arguing for the ubiquity of parental ambivalence for the child, Wellisch then makes the point that the fate of many mythical and biblical figures can be seen to show the exact opposite (Wellisch, 1954, p. 23). For example, the stories of Moses, Oedipus, Isaac, and Ishmael, all of whom were redeemed after near-death experiences, reveal, Wellisch suggests, the unconscious wish of parents *not* to kill their children. Exposure on a mountainside, in the desert, or in a woven basket, or the change of mind by a fickle god, each leaves open the possibility of "accidental rescue". The subject of many myths and legends, the survival of such children, regarded by the ancient world as miraculous, often initiated a "new epoch in the moral development of man" (*ibid.*). Internally, we might say, the aged Abraham seems to represent here a new capacity in himself— and in culture—to tolerate and nurture, rather than envy and kill, the child who is to succeed him and who therefore heralds his father's death.

An essential feature of the rescue myth is its link with the theme of redemption. Although the son in each story is different, his near-sacrifice and resurrection constitutes the fundamental metaphor of death and rebirth for all three monotheisms. In the Jewish story, Isaac, after his near-death experience, becomes symbolically reborn, and hence the product of divine rather than human birth. He is "now the bearer of the divine seed and blessing in the place of Abraham" (Kunin, 1995, p. 41). Thus redeemed, Isaac redeems the sins of others, a role in which he is portrayed most fully in Genesis, later in early rabbinical texts (Doukhan, 1995, pp. 166–167).

> for because thou hast done this thing, and hast not withheld thy son, thine only *son*: That in blessing I will bless thee, and in multiplying I will multiply thy seed as the stars of the heaven, and as the sand which is upon the sea shore; . . . And in thy seed shall all the nations be blessed; because thou hast obeyed my voice [Genesis 22: 16–18]

This redemptive feature of the story of the sacrifice of Isaac is also part of the Christian theology that I described earlier. It is because Abraham offered up his "only begotten son", and because this son showed his love for his father by his perfect obedience, that the story of the Akedah became for the early Church an analogy for the sacrifice of Jesus (Wellisch, 1954, pp. 58–59).

In Islam, the annual re-enactment by Muslims on Id al-Adha, the Feast of Abraham, has the sacrifice of an animal at the core of its ritual. Its most important commemoration takes place in the Hajj in Mecca. Muslim jurisprudence holds that on the Day of Judgement, the animals' remains are offered up to be counted as good deeds (Yunis, 1995, p. 154). Like "Ibrahim", the worshipper will also feel that he submits himself to God's will. He will be carried across the "Sirat", the bridge leading to Paradise (Berman, 1997).

I have tried in this paper to show the essential differences between the stories of the two sons of Abraham and their theological and symbolic roles. But what of the fates of the two brothers themselves, of Ishmael and Isaac and their lives? Although I have already said something about Isaac and his sons, Jacob and Esau, his place in this story warrants a more detailed examination. Thomas Mann discusses Isaac's blindness in a way that reveals his own early interest in psychoanalytic ideas. In his biblical saga, *Joseph and his Brothers* (1978), Mann writes, "Is it possible for a man to become blind . . . because he does not like to see . . . because he feels better in a darkness where certain things can happen which *must happen?*" (p. 130, my italics). In this interpretation, Mann has intuited some quality in Isaac that many of the legends and commentaries have noted. In terms coined by John Steiner, we might say that it was only by "knowing and not knowing", by "turning a blind eye" (Steiner, 1987), that Isaac, at Rebecca's instigation, could collude with the substitution of his younger son for the elder. Moreover, Isaac had already been obliged to turn a blind eye to certain events in his life, first, to his unwitting role in the casting out of his own older brother, who, with his fertile concubine mother, was clearly experienced enviously by Sarah as a narcissistic threat, then to the sight of his father, knife in hand, acting in unquestioning obedience to his jealous, possessive God.

Although Oedipus's self-blinding continues to be much debated, I see it here in the most general terms as expressing a moral blindness in which, struggling between insight and resistance, Oedipus attempts, albeit ambivalently, to lay bare the truth. Isaac's blindness is different. For him, it reflects a need to split off his awareness of a catastrophic psychic situation in which his own place as the loved and "only" son, is experienced as dangerously insecure. Isaac's blindness, it seems to me, reflects what Melanie Hart aptly describes as a "static internal state" (personal communication). He is the subject of a cruel God. It would not be surprising, therefore, if Isaac has sought in his blindness a "psychic retreat" in which to take refuge from both inner and outer reality (Steiner, 1993). He seems to have found such a retreat in that "darkness" described by Thomas Mann in which he "might be betrayed" and in which, he might, in turn, betray his own elder son, Esau (Mann, 1978, p. 131).

If, as Freud wrote, "The super-ego fulfils the same function . . . that was fulfilled . . . by the father and later by Providence or Destiny" (1923b, p. 58), then Isaac's super-ego was punitive indeed. Louis Jacobs (1995) observes that the Talmud asks why Isaac submitted to "what virtually amounted to an act of suicide" (p. 19). But, as Britton writes in his explication of Freud's phrase above, "If the ego feels hated by the super-ego it abandons its hold on life" (2003). The "gentle" Isaac, with his "tame dove" quality, so prized by Rabbis and theologians, becomes, in the Jewish tradition, "the one in the middle", whose activities are more "constricted" than either those of his brooding, tormented father or his squabbling sons (Jacobs, 1995, p. 271). Exceptionally obedient, Isaac waxed "very great", i.e., he became rich, but he is the least visible, least well-defined of the patriarchs. Zornberg (1995), discussing Isaac's blindness, writes that "death haunts his imagination" all his life. "'Look, now, I am old, and I don't know the day of my death. . . .'" (p. 156), he pleads, some sixty years before he is actually to die. Most of the stories about Isaac are concerned with his anguish at his mother's death, or with his wife Rebecca and their sons.

The fate of Ishmael is more uncertain. Less detail is available because the focus of the Koran, unlike the Torah, is on teaching and guidance rather than history (Zaki Badawi, personal communication). However, it does show us that Ishmael, rather than being cast out by Abraham and Sarah after the near-sacrifice, leaves with him to build the Ka'bah in Mecca (Surah 2: 121–131). Abraham then returns to Sarah and Isaac while Hagar sent to her people in Egypt for a wife for Ishmael (Genesis 21: 21). From the Old Testament we learn that Ishmael had twelve sons, the princes of the Arab people founded in accordance with the promise made by God to "make him a great nation" (Genesis 17: 120). Abraham, in some rabbinic commentaries, visits him later in Mecca, but is given Sarah's permission to do so only on condition that he does not alight from his camel during his stay (Graves & Patai, 1966, p. 157).

Although we know so little about him, it is interesting to note the precise moment in the Bible narrative at which the descendants of Ishmael, the Ishmaelites, crop up. It was to a group of their merchant tribesmen, Genesis tells us, that the Midianites sold Sarah's great-grandson, Joseph, after rescuing him from the pit to which his jealous brothers consigned him. Joseph, of course, was taken to Egypt, the homeland of Hagar, where he was sold as a slave (Genesis 37: 28). Levenson (1993) points to the irony involved in this sequence of events in which the Israelites—through Joseph—came to know the bitter experience of slavery in a strange land (p. 96).

The psychological revolution that began with Abraham and his monotheistic vision can be seen as the first move towards an early stage of psychic unity. With many stops and starts, it initiated a process that led to a cultural shift from human to animal sacrifice and, from there, to the development of the impulse to protect and nurture the infant and child. However, we neglect to notice in what, I maintain, is our idealization of Abraham's achievement, his all-too human propensity to separate and segregate good from bad, while using others, in this case, his eldest son, Ishmael and his mother, as repositories for what appear to be unwanted and unrecognized parts of himself. We see that in the internal world of Abraham, as well as that of Sarah, psychic equilibrium and a sense of value and goodness were maintained by means of this process of splitting and projective identification, a process which has its source in the infantile tendency to salvage the sense of a good maternal object from a less satisfying experience.

"Ethical monotheism", therefore, carried with it much that was "pre-ethical". The Abraham who could plead with God for the errant people of Sodom—"Shall not the Judge of all the earth do right?" (Genesis 18: 25)—was more sanguine about the fate of those that he himself cast out. In the story of the Akedah, Ishmael and Isaac represent, psychologically, the loved and hated parts of their parents and the splits between them. They are the "good" and "bad" sons. As such, they remained separate and divided and this separation and division, as much as anything else, is an essential part of the legacy bequeathed to us by Abraham.

In the earliest accounts of the origins of both Judaism and Islam, there lies deeply embedded a set of paradoxical messages. First, it is the loved and favoured child who becomes the sacrificial victim but it is this son who is chosen to inherit the sacred promise and father its people. Second, it is a faithful, loving God who issues the command, not as punishment, but as a measure of true devotion. However, descent from Abraham is not sufficient in itself to ensure the central role in the divine plan. Both sons were descendants, yet only one was offered up in sacrifice, and it is in the near-sacrifice that the redemptive role is invested. The contest between the faiths to be the heirs of the sacrificial son is waged for this redemptive role. Thus, the importance of the sacrifice story to the descendants of Abraham is that the blessing of God depends on—and is a consequence of—the obedient submission by the son to the fearsome directive by his father to make of him a burnt offering.

The two stories of the Akedah, taken together, reveal how Judaism and Islam have each claimed that their founding father was the best-loved son of Abraham, the son chosen by God for the burnt offering. This claim has formed the basis for the supposed right to an exclusive identification with righteousness and power, a right seen as justified by virtue of sacred descent. In these two accounts of the half-brothers, Ishmael and Isaac, we recognize the universal story of the struggle for the place of the preferred child, the true heir to the parents' "promises" of love and favour. We recognize here a story of sibling rivalry writ large.

Note

1. All Biblical references, except where authors' own versions are quoted, are taken from *The Holy Bible. King James Version* listed below.

References

Andresen, J. J. (1984). The motif of sacrifice and the sacrifice complex. *Contemporary Psychoanalysis*, 20: 526–529.

Badawi, Z. (2004). Principal, Muslim College Ealing, West London

Balsam, R. H. (1988). On being good: The internalized sibling with examples from late adolescent analyses. *Psychoanalytic Inquiry*, 8: 66–87.

Barchilon, J. (1985). Meeting of the New York Psychoanalytic Society. *Psychoanalytic Quarterly, 54*: 143–145.

Berman, L. A. (1997). *The Akedah. The Binding of Isaac.* Northvale, NJ; Jason Aaronson.

Britton, R. (2003). The use of theological terms in psychoanalytic practice. Lecture to the London Centre for Psychotherapy.

Coles, P. (2003). *The Importance of Sibling Relationships in Psychoanalysis.* London: Karnac.

Delaney, C. (2000). *Abraham on Trial: The Social Legacy of Biblical Myth.* Princeton: Princeton University Press.

Doukhan, J. (1995). The Akedah at the "crossroad": its significance in the Jewish–Christian–Muslim dialogue. In: F. Manns (Ed.), *The Sacrifice of Isaac in the Three Monotheistic Religions* (pp. 165–176). Jerusalem: Franciscan Printing Press.

Freud, S. (1900a). The interpretation of dreams. *S.E.,* 4–5. London: Hogarth.

Freud, S. (1912–1913). Totem and taboo. *S.E., 13.* London: Hogarth.

Freud, S. (1916–1917). Introductory lectures on psycho-analysis. *S.E., 15–16.* London: Hogarth.

Freud, S. (1917b). A childhood recollection from Dichtung und Wahrheit. *S.E., 17.* London: Hogarth.

Freud, S. (1923b). The ego and the id. *S.E., 19.* London: Hogarth.

Freud, S. (1933a). New introductory lectures on psycho-analysis. *S.E., 22.* London: Hogarth.

Freud, S. (1939a). Moses and monotheism. *S.E., 23.* London: Hogarth.

Gay, P. (1988). *Freud: A Life for Our Time.* London: J. M. Dent.

Graves, R., & Patai, R. (1966). *Hebrew Myths. The Book of Genesis.* New York: McGraw-Hill.

Guillaume, A. (Trans. & Ed.) (1955). *The Life of Muhammad: A Translation of Ishaq's Sirat Rasul Allah.* Oxford: Oxford University Press.

Hertz, J. H. (Ed.) (1929). *The Pentateuch and Haftorahs: Genesis.* London: Oxford University Press.

Jacobs, L. (1995). *The Jewish Religion. A Companion.* Oxford: Oxford University Press.

Kaufman, R. V. (1983). Oedipal object relations and morality. *Annual Psychoanalytic Review, 11:* 245–256.

Kierkegaard, S. (1985). *Fear and Trembling.* Translated with an introduction by Alastair Hannay. London: Penguin Classics.

Kunin, S. D. (1995). The death of Isaac: structuralist analysis of Genesis 22. In: F. Manns (Ed.), *The Sacrifice of Isaac in the Three Monotheistic Religions* (pp. 35–38). Jerusalem: Franciscan Printing Press.

Levenson, J. D. (1993). *The Death and Resurrection of the Beloved Son. The Transformation of Child Sacrifice in Judaism and Christianity*. New Haven: Yale University Press.

Makiya, K. (2002). *The Rock. A Tale of Seventh-Century Jerusalem*. London: Constable.

Mann, T. (1978). *Joseph and his Brothers*. Harmondsworth: Penguin.

Meissner, W. W. (1994). Psychoanalysis and ethics: beyond the pleasure principle. *Contemporary Psychoanalysis*, 30: 453–472.

Mitchell, J. (2003). *Siblings: Sex and Violence*. Cambridge: Polity.

Noujaim, H. (1995). Response to Dr Amer Yunis, "The sacrifice of Isaac". In: F. Manns (Ed.), *The Sacrifice of Isaac in the Three Mono-theistic Religions* (pp. 35–38). Jerusalem: Franciscan Printing Press.

Ostow, M. (1989). Sigmund and Jakob Freud and the Phillipson Bible (with an analysis of the birthday inscription). *International Review of Psycho-Analysis*, 16: 483–492.

Patai, R. (1977). *The Jewish Mind*. New York: Jason Aronson.

Roith, E. (1987). *The Riddle of Freud. Jewish Influences on His Theory of Female Sexuality*. London and New York: Routledge.

Ross, J. M. (1982). Oedipus revisited—Laius and the "Laius Complex". *Psychoanalytical Study of the Child*, 37: 169–200.

Said, E. (2001). *Al-Ahram Weekly Online*, Issue no. 555, 11–17 October.

Sloan, I. (2002). Proof that the Bible is wrong and that Ishmael and not Isaac was to be sacrificed by Abraham. http://shamema.best.vwh.net/isaac.htm[27/04/02].

Spiegel, S. (1993). The last trial. On the legends and lore of the command to Abraham to offer Isaac as a sacrifice. *The Akedah*. Translated with an Introduction by Judah Goldin. New Preface by Judah Goldin. Woodstock, VT: Jewish Lights Publishing.

Stein, H. F. (1977). The binding of the son. Psychoanalytic reflections on the symbiosis of anti-Semitism and anti-Gentilism. *Psychoanalytic Quarterly*, 46: 650–683.

Steiner, J. (1987). The interplay between pathological organizations and the paranoid–schizoid and depressive positions. *International Journal of Psycho-Analysis*, 68: 69–80.

Steiner, J. (1993). *Psychic Retreats*. London: Routledge.

The Holy Bible. King James Version. (1957). London: Collins.

The Koran (1999). Translated with notes by N. J. Dawood. London: Penguin Classics.

Wellisch, E. (1954). *Isaac and Oedipus. A Study in Biblical Psychology of the Sacrifice of Isaac. The Akedah*. London: Routledge & Kegan Paul.

Yunis, A. (1995). The sacrifice of Abraham in Islam. In: F. Manns (Ed.), *The Sacrifice of Isaac in the Three Monotheistic Religions* (pp. 147–158). Jerusalem: Franciscan Printing Press.

Zornberg, A. G. (1995). *Genesis. The Beginning of Desire*. Philadelphia: The Jewish Publication Society.

CHAPTER THREE

Orestes and democracy

R. D. Hinshelwood and Gary Winship

D emocracy is a political notion, and is often used simplisti-
cally in political debate. But what are its emotional and
psychological roots in the individual? And do they support
the simplicity of the political ideal? The story of Electra and Orestes
as told by Aeschylus is a fascinating study in sibling relations.
Aeschylus used the family dynamics in the House of Agamemnon
as a basis for political observations about democracy in Ancient
Greece. Locating the political concept of democracy within the
family is an idea that is no less resonant today with the resurgence
of neo-conservative appeals to family values. From a psychoanalytic viewpoint, the notion of democracy is problematic, and we
trace the development of democratic ideals as an internal psychic
process that is influenced by, and in turn influences, familial, social,
and political dynamics.

Democracy was often dramatized in the works of the Greek
playwrights, where matters of civil concern such as war and
government were compressed into family dramas, such as that
played out in the *Oresteia* by Aeschylus. The relations between
mother and father (Agamemnon and Clytemnestra) and the sibling dynamics between Orestes and Electra were mirrored with

dramatic effect in the ebb and flow between traditional authority and experiments in democracy in the ancient world. Aeschylus was highly critical of these political experiments, as were other ancient scholars and playwrights. Those debates contrast with the modern espousal of democracy as unthinkingly good.

We need, like the ancients, to problematize "democracy". It may be worth retracing our cultural footsteps to remake the link between political democracy and attitudes towards the family and siblings. Or rather, attitudes towards democracy and towards siblings may show a telling correspondence, and psychoanalysis could have a useful say in understanding the passionate levels of unconscious rivalry or solidarity that characterize both areas of life—politics and the family. The sibling bond is usually cast in familiar terms in relation to rivalry, murder, and guilt. A psychoanalytic theory of a "bond of devotion" might be added.

In line with Freud, we point to the sibling relation as a feature of the internal psychic world. It develops in the family, influenced by parental authority. There the intergenerational boundary typified by the psychoanalytic "incest taboo" in a vertical direction (between parent and child), exists together with a horizontal frame for sibling "equality". Freudian psychoanalysis has always prioritized the vertical relations between self and parents, because that has been the abiding feature of the analyst–analysand relationship. That vertical relationship became enshrined within the Oedipus complex. But has the special setting of psychoanalytic work distorted the discoveries that have been made and reported?

The relative neglect of explanatory theories of sibling relations in psychoanalysis may also have been to do with the historical epoch in which psychoanalysis arose a hundred years ago, where emphasis on authority structures based on familial frames of references were dominant in society and in the clinical encounter. Should more attention be paid to the horizontal relations of sibling to sibling? It may be a consequence of the setting that "Siblings are the great omission in psychoanalytic observation and theory" (Mitchell, 2000, p. 23, see also Mitchell, 2003). Coles (2003) goes further, to speculate that early sibling relations have been positively repressed as "we fear the power of sibling relationships. Are they more passionate than parental relationships?" (Coles, 2003, p. 2).

To come to this point, psychoanalysis has traversed a long social journey. In the early days professional expertise was given high authority and status, and resulted in a wide differential of power and status between analyst and patient. Transferences in a psycho-analytic treatment naturally orbited around hierarchical relations. Today, professional expertise is being removed from professional life; authority is increasingly invested in the evidence of science rather than the experience of persons (see Hacking, 1999). This new location for authority could set psychoanalysis free to explore egal-itarian, lateral childhood relations. They could intrude more visibly into the transference–countertransference setting, beside or instead of the vertical ones of parental authority. In other words, a parental transference towards the analyst as father or mother could some-times give way to a transference in which the analyst is brother or sister. In fact, some analysts do now advocate an equal relation-ship between two struggling subjectivities jointly creating their analytic process (intersubjectivists such as Ogden, 1994; Stolorow, Brandschaft, & Atwood, 1987).[1]

There is increasing evidence that siblings recognize each other from early developmental stages—perhaps even as early as the adult care-givers;

> Infant/child observation research tells us that the child's sensory perceptions of siblings can occur almost as early and with as much frequency as those of the maternal object. While the mother is usually the first love object and the immediate source for identifica-tion and early learning, the existence of actual siblings as well as internal sibling representations within the mother's psyche exert a sizeable effect upon the child's ego development. [Agger, 1988, p. 3]

These observations raise the question whether a sibling can be a primary object in the psychoanalytic sense.[2] These and other authors suggest it is timely to contemplate a paradigm shift in psychoanalysis where the centrality of the Oedipus myth is balanced by sibling relations. It would be timely, therefore, to consider the Orestes–Electra myth neglected in the long history of psychoanalysis for these reasons.[3] Before looking in detail at it, we will briefly consider the psychoanalytic omission from a historical perspective.

Psychoanalysis and hierarchy

When Freud made his forays into social science, he was not oblivious to horizontal sibling-like relations. His views were made most explicit in "Totem and taboo" (Freud, 1912–1913). Freud designated the band of brothers as the primal horde who were envisaged as overthrowing the father and internalizing him in cannibalistic rites. Thereafter, said Freud, the horde formed a unifying bond based on an agreement not to usurp the position of the father with another singular leader. Thus, the brotherhood replaced the malignant authority of the patriarch with a democratic pact. In this model, democracy emerged under the common conditions of patricidal guilt. It is a formulation that suggests an early Freudian starting point for a psychoanalytic theory of democracy—an "emotional democracy", we might say. In 1921, in "Group psychology and the analysis of the ego", Freud developed a further hypothesis about the bond between members of a group, arguing that it was devotion to a leader rather than aggression and guilt towards him that brought the group together. Freud surmised that a part of a group member's personality could be replaced by submission to the leader. This part was what he had previously called the "ego-ideal" (Freud, 1914c). Freud gave the example of the church to illustrate how devotion is heaped upon Christ as a leader-ideal.

The creation of a collective vertical allegiance, at the same time leads to a second bond, according to Freud. This is a horizontal one, the relations between all the members of a group (in this case the Christian church); they have a solidarity with each other precisely because they have a common vertical bond. The horizontal relation is one of equality, deriving from a common characteristic. The individuals are all alike in having Christ as their ego-ideal. Freud likened this dynamic to that which exists within the family in relation to the father. The horizontal dynamic emerges as siblings give allegiance to their shared parents. Vertical relations have no single quality, they may be suffused by patricidal feelings or by a devotional allegiance.[4] The character of the vertical relations has an important bearing on the sibling relations. Thus, sibling rivalry can be said to occur only through the shared relationship with the parents and it is not possible to consider the sibling relationship in isolation from the parental one.[5]

Horizontal[6] sibling dynamics have held various alternative statuses in psychoanalytic theory: (i) as being substitutes for relations with primary parental objects; (ii) as primary object relations in their own right; or (iii) relations with a special reference to the relations with the primary parental objects. The latter alternative, the interaction of vertical and horizontal relations, is in line with Freud's account in 1921. Further characteristics of sibling relations concern a mixture of impulses that include rivalry and aggression, but also love and eroticism. When considering sibling relations, we often conceive of them in negative terms; particularly as "sibling rivalry" (such, for instance, as the daughters of King Lear); or, as Mitscherlich commented, a move "from Oedipal rivalry to sibling envy" (Mitscherlich, 1963, p. 268). However, this tendency leads to a psychoanalytic neglect of the positive aspect of sibling relations; those ordinary bonds of horizontal solidarity. Hard-pressed parents know well the power of cooperativeness between their children. In fact, as Coles pointed out: "Many of the foundation myths of ancient civilisations have involved sibling incest" (Coles, 2003, p. 60). In this case the sibling relationship is not concerned with the act of procreation but rather with the creation of a whole world order. It could hardly be a more creative union between siblings.

Orestes and Oedipus

The myth of Electra and Orestes makes a significant counterpart to Oedipus—though not in the simplistic rendering that gave rise to the term the "Electra Complex". While Oedipus is *the* story of an only child, Orestes and Electra is *the* psychoanalytic template for brother and sister. Orestes and Electra are bonded by their mutual devotion to a joint duty; the avenging of their father's (Agamemnon's) murder by their mother (Clytemnestra). In the second part of Aeschylus's trilogy of plays[7]—*The Libation Bearers*—Orestes is returning from war while Electra is waiting. Orestes' exile is over and he returns home to surprise his sister. He lays two locks of hair upon their father's grave. Electra enters with a procession bearing libations and Orestes hides behind the grave. Electra spots the locks of hair and recognizes them as identical to hers. She declares hesitantly that the hair must belong to Orestes. She sees some footsteps and places her own in them saying; "Two outlines, two prints, his own, and there a fellow traveller's. The heel, the curve of the arch, like twins" (lines 206–207). Electra follows Orestes footsteps, one by one, until she reaches the grave, whereupon Orestes then shows himself. Electra cries; "We meet—oh the pain of labour—this is madness" (lines 209–211). Electra has doubts about their destiny and the task of matricide that lies ahead of them. Orestes reassures her by seizing a piece of cloth that he is wearing and reminds Electra that she wove it for him when he was born. The cloth appears to be a symbol of their swaddling unity, the weaving of their conspiracy. In these dramatic exchanges Orestes volunteers to do the deed of matricide, sparing his sister the burden.[8] Electra and Orestes' pact becomes the moral of the story and not Electra's rivalry with her mother. This act of devotion to each other where the brother and sister conspire to overcome the malignancy of the matriarch (Clytemnestra) reaches a crescendo in the trial of Orestes, in the final act. Orestes is brought before a jury of his peers who preside over various character witnesses, one being Apollo himself. The jury cannot decide whether Orestes is guilty of murder or whether he acted righteously. The jury is split half-and-half and Athene intervenes in the end to pronounce Orestes innocent. The Furies[9] that have harassed Orestes since the act of matricide are outraged at Athene's decision. In order to quell their outrage Athene offers them a home.

There are two levels at which we can interpret the dynamics of the trial. On the one hand, there is a very intimate relation between the siblings and their negotiations (and we will say more about this presently) while there is also something politically emblematic about justice and democracy at a high social level. Aeschylus used the micro-politics of a family tragedy in the house of Agamemnon to highlight the macro-political dynamics of Greek life at the time. The play encapsulated Aeschylus's[10] own critique of democracy as he alluded to many of the outstanding features of Athenian politics at the time; war especially, given Greece's numerous overseas interests. The various oscillations between democracy, oligarchy, and monarchy in the trilogy showed Aeschylus deftly warning of the possible collapse of traditional authority under the thrust of democracy, as Farrar commented, "The trilogy reflects Aeschylus's concern that the thrust toward full democracy at the expense of traditional authority could result in anarchy" (Farrar, 1992, p. 21).

Aeschylus's drama concerned the ruin of rulers and the reliance on the wisdom of the populace, and concluded that anarchy results from the indecision and impasse of the jury in the trial represented in the Furies going berserk. Aeschylus suggested that traditional authority remained superior; the democratic assembly flunked its responsibility and brought inertia. The return of Athene signalled the necessary resort to a higher traditional authority. Aeschylus determined that such authority was needed to bring about order and to quell the anarchistic furies that democracy invites.

However, what might we conclude about the more intimate sibling dynamic in the play? This brother and sister are deeply engaged together in mutual outrage and they agree to the murder of the mother that Orestes carries out. The unifying bond in the play echoes Freud's original formulation (in "Totem and taboo") of a social extension of the Oedipus complex. After the overthrow of the patriarch, the brothers formed a unifying bond derived from the guilt of homicide. However, in the case of Orestes and Electra, the overthrow is of mother and the homicidal horde is the fraternity of brother–sister. These are variations in the myths that cannot be ignored, and cannot therefore be reduced to a simple female re-rendering of the Oedipus complex. The dynamic between Orestes and Electra becomes a surrogate, or micro-democratic, unity. It is a space smaller than the horde, but offers a more intimate window into the democratic exchange between siblings.

The unifying sibling bond that seeks justice in *The Oresteia* contrasts with the role of siblings in the Oedipal myth of the primal horde. In *Oedipus at Colonus*, the second part of Sophocles' trilogy (set after Oedipus has discovered the truth of his incest and blinded himself), we discover that the mutual relations between Oedipus's children was saturated with the conflict designated psychoanalytically as sibling rivalry. Ismene (Oedipus's daughter), brings news to Oedipus of his sons (her brothers) and she starts by saying that all is not well with them. However, before she can qualify her bad news Oedipus flies off into a diatribe, accusing the sons of having the ill manners of Egyptians and being disloyal to his name. Ismene tells Oedipus that the brothers have become rivals for the throne of Thebes and she interprets this ambition as like-father-like-son: "lust

of their sinful hearts has filled them with an evil spirit of emula-
tion" (*Oedipus at Colonus*, lines: 347–416). Having been ousted in the
contest by his younger brother,[11] Polynices comes to his father to
seek a blessing for his idea to muster an army with which to overthrow Eteocles. At first Oedipus refuses to see Polynices: "It is my
son, my worst enemy," moans Oedipus (line: 1172). When Oedipus
is persuaded by his daughter to see his son, Polynices tells his
father of his plan. Oedipus's response is chilling. Just when we
might expect Oedipus to try to put an end to the family bloodshed
by dissuading Polynices from following the dread but well-trodden
path of murder in his family, Oedipus disowns his son, curses
Polynices and his brother, predicting that blood will fall on both
their heads. Oedipus calls these curses his "weapons—that you
may learn the lesson of piety to parents" (lines: 1374–1375). In
completely ignoring what is happening between the brothers,
Oedipus can only see the conflict self-referentially, insisting that
they learn to respect him. As the play proceeds to the third part of
the trilogy, Oedipus's prophecy is fulfilled and we discover that the
sons have indeed engaged in fatal mutual mortal combat.

The death of the two sons in this way is a reconfiguration of the
original patricide. The deathly triangle in the first place of Oedipus,
Jocasta, and Laius is succeeded by the triangle of Oedipus, Polynices, and Eteocles. Arguably, the tragedy of the two sons' death
surpasses the original patricide. These transgenerational features in
the myth suggest that the trauma of one generation may exert
greater disturbance for future generations if unresolved. The
violence of the parents is transmuted into a greater internecine
sibling slaughter. This instalment of the Oedipus story does not
confirm the origin of civilization as Freud postulated it in the band-
ing together of the brothers out of guilt. The significance of sibling
relations is clearly a much richer tapestry of emotions and relationships.

Comparing Orestes and Oedipus also raises contrasting features
of social and sibling relations. While the story of Orestes might
suggest a construction of sibling union, the evolving story of
Oedipus is emblematic of its collapse into murderous strife. Freud
created an even more multivalent view of civilization, when he
moved beyond his theory of guilty patricide (Freud, 1912–1913), to
the theory of identification in "Group psychology and the analysis

of the ego (Freud, 1921c), where he described the bonding that comes from a common and devoted allegiance to the father-ideal. Later, in 1930, he returned to a modification of the primal horde idea in "Civilisation and its discontents", where he thought the social bond was aimed at controlling and repressing innate destructiveness. It seems necessary, therefore, to suggest that sibling relations can be classified as various, distinct, and emotionally intense forms of relatedness. We suggest the following bald delineation as a model for further discussion of the characteristics of sibling relations: (i) a love-devotional bond (Orestes and Electra), (ii) a bond of guilt (as in Freud's primal horde), and (iii) fratricidal hate–rivalry (Polynices and Eteocles).

Developmental democracy

Because of the initial hierarchical relations of a psychoanalytic treatment, Freud arrived at an understanding of the internal hierarchy of the superego. His line of thought always directed attention to the internal world of the person and the infant. He was impressed, even shocked, by the harshness of this cruel, domineering, "moral" superego. He was concerned to understand how children experience a harsher world than their actual childhood;

> . . .The severity of the super-ego which a child develops in no way corresponds to the severity of the treatment which he has himself met. . . . A child who has been very leniently brought up can acquire a very strict conscience. [Freud, 1930a, p. 130]

This is the harshness of a hierarchical internal world of experience, rather than the actual world of the real family. Melanie Klein showed that the younger the child the greater the experienced harshness. This suggests a very powerful internal demanding playing on the self. It would seem to be an internal paradigm that is antithetical to democracy, and suggests that the attainment of democratic attitudes in the external real world of others and the family is an emotionally daunting developmental task. In this respect, Winnicott's views of infantile omnipotence are in line with Freud's categorizing of the early relations of power and equality. The infant demands, and indeed Winnicott says must be given, an omnipotent place; then slowly needs it to be wrenched from his/her protesting grasp. The implication is that the world is seen at the beginning of life, refracted through intrapsychic expectations that are suffused with power and with a superior morality pursued with an energetic sadism.

Developmental democracy must gradually be won from this primary state. Inevitably, it must come about through the effectiveness of the parents' actual powerful influence in the long process of their gradual supremacy—for the fortunate child, this is a benign supremacy, but for some unfortunates it will be abusive. The development of parental "control" is a necessary achievement on both sides to ensure the safety of the infant and child. All being well, this process is a progressive grounding in what may become a democratic adult life. The process of ameliorating and modifying internal expectations must surely be influenced by the existence of siblings. Siblings must struggle with the multiple influences they represent for each other. The dynamics oscillate as the infant handles his own internal states and primitive urges in the context of his/her siblings struggles as well. How this arena develops inside each one will determine how the eventual attitudes towards democracy and authority will congeal. The following is an illustration of the to-and-fro of this process in infancy:

> A young boy of 2½ years had a three-month-old baby brother. When I visited the mother, she was breast-feeding the baby. I was sitting at the other end of the settee where she and the baby were, and chatting to the mother while she fed. The boy had been breast-fed until 12–15 months. After a while, the little boy came across from where his toy box was, and said with some force, looking at the baby at the breast, "That is my milk." He then climbed on his mother's lap too, put his head down to where the baby was feeding as if to suckle as well. Then he changed his mind and gave the baby a kiss on the cheek. He looked up and smiled into his mother's face. Then he said, "I going to give him a raspberry." And this time he bent his head down with his lips against the baby's cheek again and blew a very juicy raspberry. Mother was surprised and amused by this display, but took a phlegmatic view of how normal and understandable it was. The boy stood on the floor and then said he was going to give Mummy a raspberry too. Mother gently told him not to, and to go back and play with his toys, which he did, and we resumed our chat.

Shortly afterwards the boy turned to mother from the other side of the room and said, "Don't talk. Please, don't talk." He sounded quite stern in an adult long-suffering way, as if we were tiresome children he had to keep in order. A little later father came into the room and took the boy off into the garden.

This illustration conveys the struggle of the boy to deal with his own imperative to control his mother. Her attention was visibly and bodily turned to the baby, and mentally to the visitor. He felt very left out of the centre of attention, and was faced with the experience of exclusion, jealousy, and the decline of his position in the family. He was confronted with sharing his mother, and being merely a part of the group, rather than a privileged member of it. He was torn between taking away "his milk" for himself again, or giving a loving kiss to his brother, or then displaying simple aggression and contempt for the nursing pair. His father rescued him from this conflicted experience, but not before he had a good opportunity to work at it.

The exercise of authority in the family is a developmental learning curve for the infant, through infancy and childhood into adolescence. If we envisage democracy as an emergent family dynamic located specifically with the maturation of the child and/or siblings, we can than see how it maps on to similar processes in the social and cultural order.[12] The first step we take beyond these family struggles, is into the social culture of a playgroup or primary school. Playground democracy is an ethic of fairness, and little children attempt to control each other with claims such as, "That's not fair". As a result of the child's immature harsh conscience, this can be a very strict culture, and is the beginning of what Freud called "the ethical demands of the cultural super-ego" (Freud 1930a, p. 143). Children's playground culture seems to embody the belief that a quite outrageous inequality has to be controlled and mastered. That culture appears to be a contest of fairness versus bullying. This was observantly recorded by William Golding (1954) in the book *Lord of the Flies*. On the island, the stranded boys literally played out a contest between democratic fairness and bullying autocracy. The novel was written in the context of the Cold War, but it engages its readers through the verisimilitude of children's struggle between bullies or democrats. In *Lord of the Flies* strict democracy is symbolized by the use of the conch as the symbol of speech;

that is to say, only the holder of the conch is permitted to speak. Inevitably, this democratic device collapsed and cohesive, retributive gangs emerged. The conch might be thought of as a symbol of a sort of autistic democratic object, possession of which guarantees fairness of access to the means of influence.[13]

Both an individual move and a cultural one have to be made against these harsh ethical demands. Children struggle with the culture they set up amongst themselves. The tyrannous force in some has to be quelled by a superior force for equality, which is itself fought for with an almost tyrannous power itself. The goodness of the ethic of fairness is often mitigated by the destructive forcefulness by which children make their claims. Playground democracy based on fairness in power and possessions is the first move against the bullying systems inherent in the individual and in cultural forms.[14] Bullying is turned against bullies.

The family and social democracy

As Laing (1971) asserted "The family is not an introjected object, but an introjected set of relations" (p. 5). In terms of object-relations psychoanalysis, it could be said that what is primary is not the objects, but the relations. Henri Rey (1994) discussed the emergence of primary objects in the mind of the infant from the actions of other persons upon the infant, and upon each other, how they transform, mutate, and so on. Such primary action of objects deeply moulds the attitudes to democracy, and democratic object relations. And it surely includes the primary experience of relations with siblings.

In this chapter we are proposing a developmental sequence for the individual. It begins in infancy with the state of extreme helplessness that tyrannizes parents and family,[15] with an ensuing attempt to master that internal helplessness through games such as Freud's fort-da observations (Freud, 1920g).[16] The demand for objects, such as mother, to be within sight is slowly relinquished. That is to say, the infant begins to give up his tyrannical mastery of his family environment through a slow and painful process of mastering his own impulses. The relinquishment of this egoistic tyranny, though never entirely accomplished, is one that ultimately must be greatly assisted by the internalization of ethical systems from the family, then through the harsh ethic of fairness among "sibling" equals, and eventually through various levels of social and cultural engagement. If this is indeed the background to the development in adults of the democratic demand for equality and fair redistribution, we can see it has a complex history in each of us, composed of extremes of helplessness, tyranny, mastery, and ethical harshness. Where the infant's good experiences outweigh bad ones in reality, a thinking capacity (cognitive or emotional) develops, which acts as a template for social justice—a collection of good objects that out-vote the bad objects, we might say.

While we are presenting the view that democracy begins at home, it is clearly not an uncomplicated view. Both the multivalent emotional quality of sibling relations and their entanglement with vertical Oedipal issues problematize the origins of democracy. It is not a simple, ideal social form. The individual is embedded in a complex emotional turmoil by the demand for democracy. How might we compress the discourse of the family with the politics of social democracy?

Here we turn to the sociologist Anthony Giddens (1994). He envisaged a family model of democracy, arguing that the best model of democracy might resemble the best democratic family.[17] Giddens refers to this conception of democracy in terms of a *democracy of the emotions*. The idea of "emotional democracy" is an attempt to revitalize democracy amongst the citizenry, inserting democracy into everyday life; his aim being to bridge the hiatus between citizen and government.[18] Giddens envisaged the value of "dialogical democracy" and the supposed improved communication among the citizenry through heightened day to day family and social reflexivity.[19] A commitment rooted in emotional impulses and responses to democracy is one avenue for challenging the growing apathy and alienation from democratic society. It is notable that Giddens argues that those professions engaged in talking therapies might make a significant contribution to the development of dialogical democracy in the social sphere. However, Giddens does not say much more about a theoretical underpinning for emotional democracy in the family. This we have attempted to point towards as a developmental process arising from the struggles and passions of having siblings.

We can turn now to Winnicott's (1950) pithy paper, "Thoughts on the meaning of democracy". The notion of democracy arising in the Oedipal register suggested a process of upward identification among voting citizens where identification with political candidates was seen as the basis of decision-making in voting intention. At best, the democratic machinery necessarily must be slow, allowing time for the voter to become familiar with issues at hand, identifying with representatives and then arriving at a decision. Winnicott proposed a hierarchical model of democracy that accepted a sort of functional immaturity in as much as he reduced the political hierarchy to a series of infantilizing interrelations. Politicians are elected *loco parentis*, and in turn they are themselves "children" to the parental authority of the House of Lords, who were then accountable to the authority of the Crown, and finally the highest parent of all, God. While in one throw Winnicott oversimplified the complex mesh of voting, he did propose a relatively feasible backbone to the *emotional* dynamics of democracy. He placed a theory of "family transference" (i.e., child–parent relations) at the heart of the democratic process and inferred how ordinary family matters and the vertical emotional and identificatory relations influence the democratic process. We might be most familiar with this as the monarchistic model of democracy in the UK.[20]

Raymond Williams (1961), who, like Winnicott, viewed democracy as a "structure of feeling and upward identification" (p. 353), nevertheless regarded it as fuelling the longevity of conservative social stratification. Williams suggested that as long as "upward identification" remained largely unconscious, systems such as monarchy would be perpetuated without modification. This upward identification is apparent even beyond the confines of traditional monarchies. We can see more generally how a democratic polity can be enraptured by a family in power; for instance, in the USA the Kennedy and Bush families, the Gandhis in India, even the Hussein family in Iraq. It seems that power, democratic or otherwise, can be assigned to a family across generations, where power is maintained, and abused, within the narrow confines of a family. Having said this, the idea that the family is the mechanism of popular democracy can only give erratic support to Giddens's theory of the ideal "democratic family". Chomsky (1991), too, argued that the Bush dynasty in the USA has done a great deal to deter democracy.

If some natural social law recognizes the family as a nodal point for identification at a supra-state level, sibling relations are subversive, instilling radically negative impulses against this *status quo*. Held's (1996) remarks in the preface to his *Models of Democracy* are also worth noting. He acknowledged various people for helping him write his book and then he thanked his children whom he announced as having: "grasped the basic elements of democracy even if they do not treat all citizens as free and equal, notably their parents" (Held, 1996, p. xiv). One presumes Held's children are young, maybe pre-adolescent and that, as we do, he posits democracy developing along a learning curve; younger children do not realize their democratic responsibility at first, and parenting is not necessarily subject to democratic engagement. Held's reference to the absence of "parental freedom" echoed Winnicott's (1949) assumption that as a parent to young children one is liable to feel more like a slave than a citizen. "His majesty the baby" is a time-honoured irony. On the one hand it is plausible to argue for a democratic family, but equally, parenting can be said to resemble a model of benign dictatorship; democracy is entirely irrelevant when the toddler is straying too close to a busy road, for instance. The infant, too, can, and sometimes needs to, employ a tyranny of helplessness for its survival, while parental tyranny guarantees the infant's survival. Power and democracy become extraordinarily complex notions when considered developmentally, much more complex than Gidden's (1994) account; and those complexities must influence the vicissitudes of the way the ideal emerges in practice.

It might be feasible to talk about democracy between parents, which evolves in an emergent democratic dynamic towards a three-body psychology of parent–parent–child. The introduction of a third party (a parental couple and child) makes disagreement possible while permitting democratic rule: the child wants to have another ice cream on a hot day, father says "no" (for whatever reason) but mother disagrees. There is a parental impasse but the exercise of democratic majority with the child as stakeholder may hold sway. This three-party nuclear democratic model may well differ from a more extended family system model. There may be a significant difference in conceptualizing two-body democracy (lone parent–infant), three-body democracy (parental couple–infant, or later where siblings band together) and many-bodied democracy (extended family–infant, or siblings and parents). The child's sense of participation runs through various levels of preverbal negotiation to more sophisticated levels of intellectual debate. The experience of involvement and enfranchisement emerges through these family, and subsequent, reconfigurations, to emerge as the basis of personal maturation and as a foundational education in civil process.

Given the truth of the adage, "his majesty the baby", we could say that developing democratic attitudes is as much about the baby giving up omnipotent power, as discovering one's rights. We might well look towards the family system as the initial template for the child's experience and education in democracy, though experience and outcome of this process will diverge according to the kind of family one emerges from. Certain affects (good, bad, or otherwise) attaching to external figures depends on the kind of relationship; even if mother is the first container for the projective processes, proximal relations from *in utero* onwards, of siblings and other key figures, such as father, grandparents, and so on, also play a part. The conglomeration of externality, the network of relations called the family, forms an internal social web or "protomental group matrix" in the mind of the baby (Winship, 2001). Family configurations provide the initial foundation of experience, so the relations between family members are the basis for the infant's first experience of the entanglements of democracy. A familial "proto-democracy" (for want of another term) among siblings and their parents is all-important as the starting point for the capacity to measure experiences and comprehend the concept of justice.

Conclusions

If we take seriously the determining quality of the internal world of the individual, it must influence the attitudes to democracy and authority. That state of mind can have the characteristics of either an internal democracy, or an internal tyranny. Which it is depends in part on the amelioration of the super-ego as the dominant vertical relation within the person; and that amelioration probably depends strongly upon the struggle with the richly ambivalent feelings towards siblings.

If psychoanalysis has tended to ignore the determinant effects of sibling relations, the wider culture has not—as Coles (2003) demonstrated, the importance of siblings goes back to the ancient world and to legends in other cultures that were contemporary with the European story of Oedipus. The prototype of equal, horizontal sibling relations, derives in part from the impact of the newborn on older siblings, as well as parental expectations (helpful or otherwise) of how to deal with that struggle. Later the institution of, and working through, the playground culture at an age between three and five years, transforms the family foundations of the internal world. That continuous introduction to more egalitarian fairness is also the period when gender relations are laid down—during the genital phases of development. Features of both the eventual sexuality and the receptiveness to democratic process are slowly solidified in the personality. Gender relations, sexual preferences, political commitments, and personal and marital relations are traceable back to these oscillating moments of vertical and horizontal relations. Relations with primary objects, both siblings and parents, can involve the erotization of hierarchical and/or egalitarian relations. In general, it would seem that sibling relations are likely to have profound effects on the way adults eventually emerge to conduct themselves in social roles. However, we contend that sibling relations are not independent factors; they exert their influence in the context of the overarching parental relations.

Given the emergent quality of democracy, its nature is to struggle free from its larval form—the infantile dynamic between tyranny and fairness, reflected in the cultural echo of divine authority versus liberation. In this context of a history of emotions, it is very tempting to push apart the twin pillars of authority and democracy. However, we risk the roof tumbling in. Instead, we need to hang on to the intertwining of horizontal and vertical relations, which forms the family context for all our origins. It is oversimplifying to eradicate authority from democratic systems, just as authority without the "brothers" participation is also a perversion of human culture. The Magna Carta that enshrined the right of peers in relation to the divine monarch, and so the march to democracy, needs to problematize the extremely complex emotional and conceptual environment from which it springs. The ethic of democracy was spawned from sibling fairness as the escape from helplessness, tyranny, and ethical harshness, and we should never forget that we can always atavistically be drawn back to this pedigree.

Notes

1. These egalitarian analysts are close to the Ferenczi-Balint tradition (Haynal, 1988).
2. See also Volkan & Ast (1997), who review the very early possibility of infant fantasy about siblings.
3. Melanie Klein's paper on the *Oresteia* (1963) was unfinished and published posthumously. She followed the narrative in detail viewing it as an account of the unconscious depths of the primitive psyche in relation to the oscillations between the depressive position and paranoid–schizoid level. Our reconsideration of the myth here in relation to a model of sibling democracy does not in anyway contradict Klein's findings; it merely teases out different features.
4. In "Totem and taboo", the rituals consequent upon the death of the father–leader involve cannibalistic rituals exemplified by the Christian sacrament.
5. In fact, parentless siblings can be conceived, a babes-in-the-wood syndrome. Cocteau imagined such a sibling relationship as *les enfants terribles*, an idyllic unworldly ménage. They are hardly the norm, though, and would not significantly contribute to the development of democracy as the wide social phenomenon it is.
6. This is aside from the complicating factor of age, size, and gender, which may place siblings in a vertical relationship as well as a horizontal one. This factor is invariably neglected in the sibling literature and though beyond the scope of this paper at present would seem worth investigating.
7. Aeschylus wrote his trilogy circa 470 BC. Aeschylus is the source interpretation of the story of Orestes, rather than Euripides' slightly later rendering. Euripides picks up the drama where Aeschylus left off.
8. Though incidental to our main theme, Electra does not actually commit the murder of the mother. This is mostly overlooked in accounts of the Electra Complex. In some ways, it is a rudimentary misrepresentation of the myth to suggest that Electra's position is the female equivalent of Oedipus's. The two myths seem more divergent than convergent, and minimize the intensity of the sibling loyalty and conspiracy.

9. The Furies are gorgon-like creatures that Klein sees as symbolizing Orestes' madness. They appear as psychotic hallucinations that externalize Orestes inner state, thus Klein views them as symbolizing Orestes' collapse from the guilt of his act to a paranoid–schizoid level of functioning.

10. Aeschylus was part of a group of poets who developed a genre of tragic drama that became influential in reflecting and shaping public opinion. Aeschylus's *Oresteia* trilogy masterfully crafted the tensions and moral dilemmas at the heart of democracy. From 500 BC, debate in Greek society had protracted phases when it was constituted by adversarial philosophy and politics. The nature of oppositional rhetoric appears to have spurred radical advances in science, medicine, cosmology, and so forth. The Athenian Empire flourished with the construction of antithetical argument and alternative proposition as new possibilities for social, political, and intellectual constitution were advanced through various ages of the regime. Democracy, as it came in and out of focus across times of peace and war, was cast and recast as a marker for various epochs of greatness in arts, literature, learning, and logic. Voices critical of democracy, such as Plato's, emanated, but none was more subtle post-Solon (500 BC) and pre-Pericles (300 BC) than Aeschylus's rebuttal of democracy in the *Oresteia* (Farrar, 1992).

11. There is some debate as to whether Polynices and Eteocles are twins. Even so, twins often refer to themselves chronologically as younger and elder, even if it is only by a matter of minutes.

12. For instance, it is possible to map various points where democratic events are institutionalized; for example, in the jury system (Winship, 2000). It is feasible to wonder more generally about an inherent inclination for social justice in group processes (Winship, 1997).

13. One might be mindful of this in relation to the number of symbolic objects that are deployed in the UK: Parliament, for instance.

14. That such fear of a bullying ethic lives on into adult cultural forms is seen in the criticism, and sometimes practice, of political correctness, which reaches tyrannical intensity in its demands for equality.

15. It is necessary to clarify what one means exactly by "family"; are we talking about a nuclear family or an extended family, or a two-body parental couple (heterosexual)? Plural, new orders of family construction have emerged to stretch our core conception of family, including single parenting, divorced parents, step-parenting, homosexual couples as parents, and so on. Democracy in the lone parent family may be an entirely different event compared to the family with a parental couple.

16. The peek-a-boo game of infants in their second year. There are some common aspects in all forms, and perhaps the most consistent is the sibling solidarity. The effective evolution of sibling relations towards democracy may vary with different family forms. Is it the case that the nuclear family of the West is the best grounding for participation in a political democracy?

17. Engels (1884), too, in a different vein, thought that capitalist property rights began in the family, and its undemocratic form of rights of possession over each other is "taught" in this social location. The family he regarded as both spawning property rights and evolving from them. Clearly, the family is a complex and ambiguous ally of democracy.

18. Giddens addressed the "crisis of democracy" in the West. While being impressed with the way in which democracy emerges in countries where it has not previously existed, Giddens argued that the paradox of democracy is such that where democracy is embedded there is much greater apathy. He argues that the West needs to undergo a period of redemocratization. Crouch (2000) suggests that we have already entered a post-democracy epoch where social agency is defined by corporate interest and not by citizen stake. This may be somewhat precipitous, but Chomsky (1991) likewise has argued that democracy, especially in the USA, has been profoundly deterred in the modern era.

19. A version of Habermas's "situational logic" and "communicative action" (cf: Giddens, 1978).

20. The Royal Family in the UK has pugnaciously remained greatly esteemed in its formal coupling with democracy. We might say that "democracy" has served the monarchy well and the monarchy has served democracy well. Indeed, the egalitarian, constitutional changes instituted by Cromwell probably did more to secure the basis of the monarchy than it did to destabilize it (as was the original intention). In maintaining the traditional order in the UK, democratic monarchy has identified itself with popular support. This may be surprising, given that the Royal Family perpetuates and represents the massive cleavage in the UK that generates class and privilege. The relationship between commoner/subject and the ruling aristocracy are signified in many rituals of pomp and pageantry decorated with emblems of affluence unchanged for several hundred years. These grand shows impress the way in which democracy has secured and perpetuated the deep inequalities in the polity. This paradoxical situation is entirely

explicable in term of the psychoanalytic complexity of Oedipal relations enmeshed with sibling ones.

References

Aeschylus (1976). *On the Oresteia*. Harmondsworth. Penguin Classics.

Agger, E. M (1988). Psychoanalytic perspectives on sibling relationships. *Psychoanalytic Inquiry, 8*: 3–30.

Chomsky, N. (1991). *Deterring Democracy*. London: Vintage.

Coles, P. (2003). *The Importance of Sibling Relations in Psychoanalysis*. London: Karnac.

Crouch, C. (2000). *Coping with Post Democracy. Fabian Ideas*, 598. London: Fabian Society.

Engels, F. (1884). *The Origin of the Family, Private Property and the State*. London: Lawrence & Wishart, 1972.

Farrar, C. (1992). Ancient Greek political theory as a response to democracy. In: J. Dunn, (Ed.), *Democracy, The Unfinished Journey 508 bc to ad 1993*. Oxford: Oxford University Press.

Freud, S. (1912–1913). Totem and taboo. *S.E., 13*. London: Hogarth.

Freud, S. (1914c). On narcissism. *S.E., 14*. London: Hogarth.

Freud, S. (1920g). Beyond the pleasure principle. *S.E., 13*, London: Hogarth.

Freud, S. (1921c). Group psychology and the analysis of the ego. *S.E., 18*. London: Hogarth.

Freud, S. (1930a). Civilisation and its discontents. *S.E., 21*. London: Hogarth.

Giddens, A. (1978). Positivism and its critics. In: T. Bottomore & R. Nisbet (Eds.), *A History of Sociological Analysis* (pp. 237–286). London: Heinemann.

Giddens, A. (1994). *Beyond Left and Right*. Cambridge: Polity.

Golding, W. (1954). *Lord of the Flies*. London: Faber & Faber.

Hacking, I. (1999). *The Social Construction of What?* Cambridge, Mass: Harvard University Press.

Haynal, A. (1988). *The Technique at Issue*. London: Karnac.

Held, D. (1996). *Models of Democracy*. Cambridge: Polity.

Klein, M. (1963). On the *Oresteia*. In: *Collected Works. Vol II*. London: Virago, 1988.

Laing, R. D. (1971). *The Politics of the Family*. London: Tavistock.

Mitchell, J. (2000). *Mad Men and Medusas: Reclaiming Hysteria and the Effects of Sibling Relations on the Human Condition*. London: Penguin.

Mitchell, J. (2003). *Siblings: Sex and Violence*. Cambridge: Polity.

Mitscherlich, (1963). *Society without the Father*. London: Tavistock (1969).

Ogden, T. (1994). Subjects of Analysis. Northvale, NJ: Jason Aronson.

Rey, H. (1994). *Universals of Psychoanalysis in the Treatment of Psychotic and Borderline States*. London: Free Association Books.

Sophocles (1947). *The Theban Plays*. Harmondsworth: Penguin Classics.

Stolorow, R., Brandschaft, B., & Atwood, G. (1987). *Psychoanalytic Treatment*. Hillsdale, NJ: The Analytic Press.

Volkan, V., & Ast, G. (1997). *Siblings in the Unconscious and Psychopathology*. Madison, CT: International Universities Press,

Williams, R. (1961). *The Long Revolution*. London: Chatto & Windus [reprinted London: Penguin, 1966].

Winnicott, D. W. (1949). Hate in the countertransference. *International Journal of Psychoanalysis, 30*: 69–74.

Winnicott, D. W. (1950). Thoughts on the meaning of democracy. In: *Home Is Where We Start From*. Harmondsworth: Penguin, 1990.

Winship, G. (1997). Justice as an inherent characteristic of group dynamics. *Free Associations, 7*(1): 64–80.

Winship, G. (2000). Jury deliberation: an observation research study. *Group Analysis, 33*(4): 547–557.

Winship, G. (2001). Notes on the research technique of infant group observation. *Group Analysis, 34*: 245–258.

CHAPTER FOUR

The siblings of *Measure for Measure* and *Twelfth Night**

Margaret Rustin and Michael Rustin

S ince its origins in ancient Greece, classical theatre has created great symbolic spaces in which the dilemmas of primary family relationships can be explored. There are many parallels between the investigations by psychoanalysts of the unconscious dynamics of families, and those of the great dramatists, from Aeschylus onwards.[1] Freud, of course, named the Oedipus Complex from Sophocles' great drama, *Oedipus Rex*, and seemed to identify himself with its hero's search for unacceptable but nevertheless necessary truths. In our book *Mirror to Nature: Drama, Psychoanalysis and Society* (2002), we explored many parallels between the discoveries of psychoanalysis and the representations of classical western theatre. What is so striking is how central issues of parenthood and marriage are to so many of the greatest plays of this tradition, in whatever period one considers.[2] Primary family connections are usually the prism through which dramatists explore the experiences of living in particular human societies.

---

*This paper was first presented in the Tavistock Clinic's Open Lecture Series "Reflections on Siblings: Drama and Psychoanalysis", in May 2004.

In this chapter, we are giving particular attention to sibling relationships, as a dimension of familial ties that has been neglected
until recently (Coles, 2003; Mitchell, 2000, 2003) in the psychoanalytic literature, though less so in writing about child analysis and
child psychotherapy, where the presence and significance of
siblings could hardly be missed by clinicians (Houzel, 2001; Klein,
1945, 1955; Tustin, 1972). In particular we examine two plays by
Shakespeare, *Measure for Measure* and *Twelfth Night*, which offer
contrasting pictures of relationships between sibs, both as reflections of a familial and social context, and as particular sources of
value and meaning. In *Measure for Measure* the fragility and breakdown of the connection between Claudio and his sister Isabella is a
sensitive indicator (or measure, indeed) of a much broader moral
crisis in the society Shakespeare depicts. In *Twelfth Night*, the
memory of loved siblings, even while their actual or imagined loss
is being mourned, sustains Olivia, Viola, and Sebastian in situations
of great vulnerability, recalling to their minds their shared memories of parents who had cared for them while they lived. These
plays enable us to recognize the significance of siblings, and
parents, as "internal objects", sustaining or failing to sustain
psychic integrity as major life transitions in young adult life have
to be negotiated.

Measure for Measure

In Elizabethan and Jacobean society, monarchical and familial
authority were closely allied with one another, patriarchy being
upheld, with religious sanction, as the natural condition of state
and household. In *A Midsummer Night's Dream*, for example, the
sovereign is urged to enforce a father's rightful authority over his
daughter, on the basis that the failure of patriarchal authority
within the family represents a threat to social order more generally.

Measure for Measure begins with Duke Vincentio handing over
his royal authority to Angelo, while he unexpectedly "hastes
away". We soon learn that there has been a change, and that war
has been declared on vice in the city, which is rife. Mistress
Overdone, a bawd, asks, "But shall all our houses of resort in the
suburbs be pulled down?", and is told by her servant, "To the

ground, mistress." Rumour spreads that an example has been made
of a gentleman, Claudio, who has been arrested. "Within these three
days his head is to be chopped off." Claudio explains to his
dissolute friend Lucio the reason for his arrest. His restraint comes

CLAUDIO: From too much liberty, my Lucio. Liberty,
            As surfeit, is the father of much fast;
            So every scope by the immoderate use
            Turns to restraint.

                              [I, 2, 117–120]

The Duke reappears, and explains to a Friar the background to
his handing over power.

DUKE: We have strict statutes and most biting laws,
            The needful bits and curbs to headstrong jades,
            Which for these fourteen years we have let slip;
            Even like an o'er grown lion in a cave
            That goes not out to prey. Now, as fond fathers,
            Having bound up the threatening twigs of birch,
            Only to stick it in their children's sight
            For terror, not for use, in time the rod
            Becomes more mock'd than fear'd: So our decrees,
            Dead to infliction, to themselves are dead,
            And Liberty plucks justice by the nose,
            The baby beats the nurse, and quite athwart
            Goes all decorum.

                              [I, 3, 19–31]

He thus describes the situation as a failure of his fatherly authority over his people. He has chosen Angelo to restore order, because
it would seem like "tyranny" for the ruler who has allowed laws to
lapse to start enforcing them now with punishments. The Duke is
concerned for his reputation. He is going to observe the situation,
in the disguise of a friar. Angelo has been selected for his role for
his puritanical character:

DUKE: Lord Angelo is precise;
            Stands at a guard with Envy; scarce confesses
            That his blood flows; or that his appetite
            Is more to bread than stone. Hence we shall see
            If power change purpose, what our seemers be.

                              [I, 3, 50–54]

Thus, the scene has been set for this drama of civic morality, in which the proper "measure" of justice will be explored and debated. The evocation of a "permissive society", and Angelo's "war on fornication", as we might call it, have many contemporary echoes.

Isabella and Claudio are brother and sister, and have made different choices in relation to the lax moral climate of the city. Claudio has a mistress who is pregnant by him.

CLAUDIO: upon a true contract,
I got possession of Julietta's bed.
You know the lady; she is fast my wife,
Save that we do the denunciation lack
Of outward order.
It seems the problem was that Julietta's kinsfolk had not yet come round to accept the marriage and provide the needed dowry.
. . . But it chances
The stealth of our most mutual entertainment
With character too gross is writ on Juliet.

[I, 2, 134–144]

Although Claudio is formally guilty of the crime of Lechery ("Call it so," he says) he has made a modern, private accommodation to the permissive social situation, merely postponing his marriage, as he and others see it, until circumstances would allow it to take place. Isabella, on the other hand, has chosen the path of purity and sexual abstinence. She is a novice, and is about to make her holy vows to join "the votarists of Saint Clare". Isabella appears to be on Angelo's side of a moral spectrum that has flagrant debauchery at one pole and monastic self-denial at the other.

The relationship between brother (Claudio) and sister (Isabella) is put to the test by the imminent threat to Claudio's life. Claudio asks Lucio to go to ask Isabella (who is taking her vows on this very day).

CLAUDIO: Acquaint her with the dangers of my state;
Implore her, in my voice, that she make friends
To the strict deputy: bid herself assay him. For in her youth
There is a prone and speechless dialect
Such as move men; beside, she hath prosperous art

When she will play with reason and discourse,
And well she can persuade.

[I, 2, 169–176]

Lucio goes to the convent with Claudio's message to Isabella. He is an unsuitable messenger to such a place. "Why don't they marry," she says of her brother and Juliet, but learning of the threat to his life, she agrees to intercede for him.

Lucio, with the perceptiveness of an experienced go-between or pandar, sees possibilities of gaining Angelo's attention that the innocent and at first somewhat perfunctory Isabella does not. He urges her, in effect, to "sex up" her approach, observing that Angelo's desires are being stirred up by her presence.

LUCIO (*to Isabella*):   Giv't not o'er so.—To him again,
Entreat him,
Kneel down before him, hang upon his gown:
You are too cold. If you should need a pin
You could not with more tame a tongue desire it.
To him, I say.

ISABELLA: Must he needs die?

[II, 2, 43–47]

And later in the same conversation:

LUCIO: O to him, to him, wench! He will relent:
He's coming: I perceiv't.

[II, 2, 125–6]

Angelo finds himself aroused to love, or lust, by Isabella, to his own surprise and horror.

ANGELO: What dost thou, or what art thou, Angelo?
Dost thou desire her foully for those things
That make her good? O, let her brother live!
Thieves for their robbery have authority,
When judges steal themselves. What, do I love her,
That I desire to hear her speak again?
And feast upon her eyes? What is't I dream on?
O cunning enemy, that, to catch a saint,
With saints doth bait thy hook!

> Most dangerous is that temptation that doth goad us on
> To sin in loving virtue. Never could the strumpet
> With all her double vigour, art and nature,
> Once stir my temper: but this virtuous maid
> Subdues me quite. Ever till now
> When men were find, I smil'd, and wonder'd how.
> [II, 2, 172–187]

Once aroused, and conscious of his hypocrisy, he plunges on, first offering to exchange Isabella's virtue for Claudio's life, then ordering Claudio's death, for his own protection. His embrace of evil from an initial position of virtue is reminiscent of Macbeth's. He has been initially attracted by Isabella's moral purity, identifying with her as someone whose special quality he admires. However, he and Isabella cannot but be thinking of her brother's sexual life and its fertility, and this excites both of them. Isabella's ill-judged and "innocent" suggestion that she will "bribe him" tempts him as well as provoking his self-righteousness. The presence of power also arouses both. "I would to heaven I had your potency, And you were Isabel!", she says. He abandons all self-restraint when she threatens to expose him, bringing his fear, guilt and lust together as he threatens her brutally:

ANGELO: Redeem thy brother
           By yielding up thy body to my will
           Or else he must not only die the death,
           But thy unkindness shall his death draw out
           To ling'ring sufferance.
           [II, 4, 162–166]

Isabella's virtue is in some respects the mirror-image of Angelo's. She refuses Angelo's sexual proposition, but is put into a state of moral self-righteousness by it. Angelo discovers his own sexual desires, which have previously been masked and projected into others by his persecuting purity. Isabella, on the other hand, responds to the experience of Angelo's passion by redoubling her own sense of virtue.

Just before Isabella goes to see her brother, to give him the news of her unsuccessful appeal to Angelo, the Duke in his Friar's disguise has been to see Claudio, and has prepared him to accept his impending death. Claudio is subdued, appearing to have abandoned hope for his life.

When Isabella visits him, Claudio at first goes along with her view of the situation.

CLAUDIO: Now sister, what's the comfort?

ISABELLA: Why,
              As all comforts are: most good, most good indeed.
              Lord Angelo, having affairs to heaven,
              Intends you for his swift ambassador,
              Where you shall be an everlasting leiger,
              Therefore your best appointment make with speed;
              Tomorrow you set on.

CLAUDIO: Is there no remedy?

ISABELLA: None, but such remedy as, to save a head,
              To cleave a heart in twain.

CLAUDIO: But is there any?

ISABELLA: Yes, brother, you may live;
              There is a devilish mercy in the judge,
              If you'll implore it, that will free your life
              But fetter you till death.

CLAUDIO: Perpetual durance?

ISABELLA: Ay, just, perpetual durance . . .

                                        [III, 1, 53–68]

As long as their conversation proceeds in these religious terms, Claudio goes along with his sister's view. He accepts her challenge of virtue, when she says "Dar'st thou die?"

CLAUDIO: Why give you me this shame?
              Think you I can resolution fetch
              From flowery tenderness? If I must die,
              I will encounter darkness as a bride
              And hug it in mine arms.

ISABELLA: There spake my brother: There's my father's grave
              Did utter forth a voice. Yes, thou must die.
              Thou art too noble to conserve a life
              In base appliances.

                                        [III, 1, 80–88]

Thus, Isabella invites her brother to endorse her conception of what virtue, and the honour of their family, require. But Isabella has still to tell him of Angelo's specific wickedness. At length, having prepared the moral ground, she does so:

ISABELLA: O, 'tis the cunning livery of hell
             The damnedst body to invest and cover
             In precise guards. Does thou think, Claudio,
             If I would yield him my virginity,
             Thou mightst be freed?

She has been so carried away by her own fervour that she has no doubt but that Claudio will concur. Initially, he appears to accept what she says. But when she tells him

ISABELLA: O, were it but my life.
             I'd throw it down for your deliverance
             As frankly as a pin.

he merely says "Thanks, dear Isabel", while different thoughts enter his mind, and he compares the horrors of death to this "least deadly sin".

CLAUDIO: Sweet sister, let me live.
             What sin you do to save a brother's life,
             Nature dispenses with the deed so far
             That it becomes a virtue.

Claudio's life instincts seems to have been brought to life again both by his sister's passionate eloquence, and by the sexual ideas put into his mind by hearing of Angelo's proposition.

Isabella is outraged by his wish to place his life before her virtue.

ISABELLA: O, you beast!
             O faithless coward! O dishonest wretch!
             Wilt thou be made a man out of my vice?
             Is't not a kind of incest, to take life
             From thine own sister's shame?

She suggests that her mother must have deceived her father, since "such a warped slip of wilderness / Ne'er issued from his blood", and equates Claudio's sin with the general vice that pervades the city.

ISABELLA: O fie, fie, fie!
              Thy sin's not accidental, but a trade;
              Mercy to thee would prove itself a bawd;
              'Tis best thou diest quickly. [*Going*]

Claudio's final "O hear me, Isabella" are the last words that brother and sister exchange during the play. Isabella's attack on her mother's honour is also suggestive of underlying anxiety about the moral character of the sexual woman and the reasons for her choice of chastity.

The Duke has overheard their conversation (placing him in the role of voyeur, and disturbingly preparing the ground for his later proposal of marriage to Isabella), and finds a kind of solution to their problems. Angelo has earlier abandoned a mistress, Mariana, who nevertheless has remained faithful to him. The Duke proposes that Isabella pretend to agree to Angelo's demand to sleep with her, but that Mariana should go to Angelo's bed as her substitute. The ends are to justify the means. He then returns to take up his role as ruler, and arranges Angelo's exposure. Angelo's hypocrisy, duplicity, and cruelty is revealed, but he is forgiven on condition that he marries Mariana. Claudio can now wed Juliet, and they can be parents together to their child. Lucio, whose disrespect to the Duke is not to be forgiven, has to endure the shame of being compelled to marry the prostitute whom he has previously got with child. Duke Vincentio proposes marriage to Isabella. An apparent moral respectability is restored, in the sense that all sexual coupling between the play's characters is returned to the sphere of legally-sanctioned marriage. But in emotional terms it is a compromised outcome, since Lucio's marriage is going to be founded on shame and loathing, and Angelo's on his indifference to Mariana. The Duke's voyeuristic manipulation of the situation culminates in his own proposal of marriage to Isabella: in enacting Angelo's desire for her on his own behalf, he demonstrates to everyone where power lies.

Isabella's accusation that Claudio is willing a form of incest in proposing her submission to Angelo to save his life has led to the argument by Marc Shell (1988) that the problem of what is incest and what is not lies at the centre of the play. Isabella's "marriage to Christ", implied by the holy vows she is about to make, and the indiscriminate sexual licence of the city, are held by Shell to be the opposite but complementary poles of an inability to differentiate between those sexual liaisons that are permitted and those that are not. Although the issue of boundaries, their collapse, and the response to this, is central to our interpretation of the play, we doubt if the concept of incest is so central to understanding it. Isabella's repressed passions are aroused by the presence of sexuality all around her—in Angelo as well as in her brother's liaison with her cousin Juliet—and it is this that accounts for her extreme moral fervour. The impersonation of her by Mariana, and Mariana's sexual encounter with Angelo in her place, suggest a kind of vicarious or displaced sexual experience. All this is publicly paraded when it is arranged that she should denounce Angelo on the Duke's return to the city, only to find herself initially disbelieved and humiliated. Although Claudio asks Isabella to save his life by sacrificing her virginity with Angelo, this seems by contrast to be to for the purpose of saving his life, and is not an act of vicarious sexual enjoyment. Claudio seems quite contented with Juliet, and appears less obsessed by sex than anyone else in the play. *Measure for Measure*'s exploration of sibling relationships seems to be more about the fragility of such ties in a weakened social order, than with incestuous passions. (Such issues are memorably explored in Jacobean drama.) What is most striking about the relationship between Claudio and Isabella is the emotional distance between them, despite the emphasis that is given to their status as brother and sister.

We suggest that *Measure for Measure* explores a world whose social bonds are unusually weak. It seems a "modern" situation, with many parallels to our own, but it is an unusual state of affairs to see represented on Shakespeare's stage. In fact the play is conducted like a social experiment. It is masterminded by the Duke, who, like the similarly omnipotent Prospero, seems to be a surrogate for the dramatist, even though his character is a major symptom and source of the crisis.

Marriages are, in Shakespeare occasions, almost invariably celebrated and sanctioned by ceremony, and are not merely the outcomes of decisions by consenting individuals to sleep or live together as they wish. Sexual partnerships and marriages are formed and contracted within a regulated social order in which kinship ties are central, and ceremonies symbolize and sanctify this.

Numerous of the comedies (*The Merchant of Venice, As You Like It, Much Ado About Nothing, A Midsummer Night's Dream, The Merchant of Venice, The Tempest, Twelfth Night*) end with a nuptial ceremony, or the promise of one. In some plays, such a recognized marriage has been the anticipated conclusion to the action, and its deviation from this course forms the essence of its tragedy (*Romeo and Juliet, Troilus and Cressida, Hamlet*). Even *Measure for Measure* ends with nuptial settlements of a kind. It is their hollowness and arbitariness—marriages imposed by law rather than by the happy reconciliation of lovers' own desires with the expectations of those in parental authority over them—which signifies what a depleted social order the play represents.

This is a world almost without ceremony or the possibility of it, so depleted are the normative bonds which bind members of this society.[3] The ease with which Isabella is extracted from her convent by Lucio, whom conventionally one would hardly expect to be allowed to set foot in such a place, and the entertaining confusion and irregularity surrounding the long-postponed execution of Barnardine in prison, are other indications of this breakdown of ruleful social order. So is the encroaching presence of sexual disorder and prostitution in this society, represented in the figures of Lucio and Mistress Overdone. The imposition of a draconian moral reform of this society, by the enforcement of long-neglected laws, under Angelo's censorious regime, is shown as a response to this disorderly situation, but it does not provide an acceptable substitute for good government.

Shakespeare is characteristically open-minded in exploring the implications of this new kind of "individualized" society, as we would now call it. The absurdity of the prison arrangements, in which the prisoner can put off his own execution by perpetual drunkenness, is shown to have its own odd humanity, and the Duke later pardons Barnardine because he has been under sentence of death for so many years. There seems nothing particularly wrong about Claudio and Juliet's relationship with each other, as it is represented in the play, though Angelo's earlier desertion of Mariana, and Claudio's lack of sympathy for his sister's feelings when his own life is put at risk, suggests that "sexual freedom" may place women at risk, as has indeed been found to be one aspect of our own post-sixties era of sexual liberation. *Measure for Measure* concludes with a rather unconvincing reconciliation of the contradictions and tensions of a deregulated society, through the restoration of a chastened Duke to his position as ruler. But in it we do seem to be on the edge of the disordered and deeply cynical world represented in Jacobean drama, which explores more extreme states of perversity.

Psychic realities in Measure for Measure

Let us reflect a little further on the psychic structures that are explored in this play. It is the disappearance of the Duke, the established authority, who represents a reasonably benign superego whatever his actual feelings may have been, that provides the space in which "common justice" collapses. (This is not the admired "reflective space" of Bion-influenced psychoanalytic theory, but rather a black hole in which no supporting structures remain.) The Duke's absence allows for the simultaneous emergence of a primitive superego and what the primitive superego is supposed to defend against, namely, moral breakdown and corruption. In fact, both these conditions have been incubating prior to the Duke's departure, in the form of Angelo's puritanical self-righteousness and the laxity and disorder that is pervading the "Vienna" of the play. The Duke's withdrawal is represented as a response to this situation of incipient crisis. Angelo's behaviour demonstrates the connectedness of harsh repression and unbounded licence, a conjunction very familiar in our own times. He is unable to discharge the Duke's commission, which is to sustain a form of justice in which "terror" is mitigated by "love" (I, 1, 19). But, of course, it is the Duke's distaste for the task of reasserting decency that underlies his choice of "bloodless" Angelo to do his dirty work for him.

The sibling themes of Measure for Measure are much more widely represented in the play than simply in the relationships between Claudio and Isabella, though their parentless state makes them ideal figures to explore the consequences of lost intergenerational support. Their bitter quarrel, in which neither can accommodate the point of view of the other, is one context in which Shakespeare illuminates the nature of extreme splitting. Isabella, the putative nun, is choosing chastity and renunciation, "honour" at the expense of personal fulfilment. Claudio, her brother, has opted for a sexual life without the commitment that a public marriage contract implies. In this respect, "honour" has been set aside, not maintained. A similar contrast is suggested between the Duke and Angelo, brothers in their sharing of the role of authority. The Duke is easygoing, Angelo the puritanical one. The failure to integrate human desires and fallibility within any supporting structure that could reliably look after people's needs—and particularly the needs of women and children for male support—is characteristic of all four protagonists. Here is Lucio's description of Angelo when he reports Claudio's condemnation to Isabella.

LUCIO: . . . Lord Angelo, a man whose blood
          Is very snow-broth; one who never feels
          The wanton stings and motions of the sense;
          But doth rebate and blunt his natural edge
          With profits of the mind, study and fast.

                                          [I, iv, 57–61]

Shakespeare, as so often in the comedies, uses a comic plebeian character to bring out the underlying confusion about what is good that the play is exploring. Elbow, the thought-disordered constable, is bringing a pimp and a bawd before Angelo:

ELBOW: I do lean upon justice, sir, and do bring in here before your good
          honour two notorious benefactors.

ANGELO: Benefactors? Well, what benefactors are they? Are they not
          Malefactors?

ELBOW: If it please your honour, I know not well what they are. But precise
          villains they are, that I am sure of, and void of all profanation in the
          world, that good Christians ought to have.

                                          [II, I, 48–56]

This nonsense makes us laugh, but also makes a point about the absurdity of the rule of law in a corrupt and misgoverned city.

If we think of Shakespeare's theme in this play as the breakdown of moral balance, both internal and external, we might see the choice of siblings as central figures as representing a central insight into the nature of the human mind. Each of the main characters demonstrates incapacity for entertaining a complex point of view, for tolerating confusion, contradiction, or psychic pain. This refusal of thoughts that would give rise to psychic conflict can be seen as the consequence of a mind in which there is no room for siblings. Thoughts that belong alongside one another but that are disavowed or thrown out are like the hated siblings who threaten to disrupt the child's domination of the family space. If relationships with siblings can be tolerated, a child's world is enormously enriched. In so far as they are refused, the child's world shrinks, is narrowed by narcissism, and becomes distorted by hatred and rivalry. Similarly, Isabella's initial dismissal of her desire for a sexual life, Vincentio's abdication of his responsibility to reassert public standards, Claudio's abandonment of concern for his sister,[4] and Angelo's betrayal of Mariana for the sake of material greed, serve for each of them to create a falsely simplified situation in which life's struggles can be avoided, guilt does not have to be tolerated, and the point of view of anyone else can be ignored. This represents a complete collapse of complex potential identifications with others, without which no tolerable social world would be conceivable.[5]

As Isabella puts it in her first encounter with the merciless Angelo:

ISABELLA: I would to heaven I had your potency,
             And you were Isabel! Should it then be thus?
             No: I would tell what "twere to be a judge,
             And what a prisoner.

                                              [II, 2, 66–70]

She imagines simply changing places with Angelo, not that there might be some other way of being.

Siblings being able to maintain mutual interest, concern, and respect for each other thus are a metaphor for a state of mind in which thoughts are allowed to come alive in the mind and be given house-room, even if they challenge the comfort of the status quo.

Twelfth Night

Twelfth Night depicts relationships between siblings of a very different quality from those of *Measure for Measure*. In the latter, the total breakdown of relations between brother and sister is a symptom of a wider collapse of a moral order, but in *Twelfth Night* the affection of brothers and sisters for each other, and their capacity to hold their memories in their minds, enables individuals to survive experiences of loss and danger. Relations between siblings in this play are shown to provide a foundation for the formation of loving sexual relationships in the next generation.

In *Measure for Measure*, the absence of living parents for the brother and sister, Claudio and Isabella, who are two of the principal characters, goes largely without mention. It seems that these parents can't be properly remembered or mourned, while, nevertheless, their two children cannot escape their preoccupation with them.[6] There is just one encounter between Isabella and Claudio in which their parents are referred to. When Claudio initially agrees to embrace his own death for the sake of honour, Isabella says, 'There spake my brother: there my father's grave / Did utter forth a voice" (III, 1, 85–86), thus identifying him with his dead father. But moments later, when Claudio has second thoughts about dying to save his sister's virtue, she calls into question her mother's faithfulness. "Heaven shield my mother play'd my father fair: / For such a warp'd slip of wilderness / Ne'er issued from his blood" (III, 1, 142). At this point, Isabella is contemplating her own dishonour, which she now imagines her mother having anticipated in her own life. But in *Twelfth Night* the death of fathers, and the real or believed death of their brothers, is ever-present in the minds and lives of Olivia and Viola, and their deepest struggle is to mourn them while retaining their hold on life. Where Olivia and the twins in *Twelfth Night* have good internal parents available to them, Isabella's and Claudio's are attacked and damaged objects.

Olivia, at the beginning of *Twelfth Night*, is reported to be mourning the loss of her father and brother. She says she intends to remain in this state for seven years. She is resisting the courtship of Duke Orsino. Her passionate response to Viola when she calls on her on Orsino's behalf, disguised as his page Cesario, suggests that what she may be fending off in her rejection of Orsino is the idea of him as a substitute for her dead father as a figure of patriarchal authority. Inside this young woman committed to seven years of mourning, and coping with the premature responsibilities of being head of her household, there seems to be a girl struggling to get out who desires to live in her own generational moment. Feste provides a more help-ful kind of fatherly interest in her, since he can keep her in mind, and even help her when she asks, while making few demands for himself other than to retain his place in her household. The bond between the two of them is in part their shared enjoyment of their intelligence—Feste's wit in particular—but Feste also uses his wit to convey to her that he understands her feelings of grief, and can share them with her. In their first encounter, he "catechises" her:

CLOWN: Good madonna, give me leave to prove you a fool.

OLIVIA: Can you do it?

CLOWN: Dexteriously, good madonna.

OLIVIA: Make your proof.

CLOWN: I must catechise you for it, madonna. Good my mouse of virtue,
           answer me.

OLIVIA: Well sir, for want of other idleness, I'll bide your proof.

CLOWN: Good madonna, why mourn'st thou?

OLIVIA: Good fool, for my brother's death.

CLOWN: I think his soul is in hell, madonna.

OLIVIA: I know his soul is in heaven, fool.

CLOWN: The more fool, madonna, to mourn for your brother's soul, being in
           heaven. Take away this fool, gentlemen.

OLIVIA: What think you of this fool, Malvolio, doth he not mend?
                                                    [I, 5, 55–72]

Viola lost her father when she was thirteen, before the action of the play, and since then it seems that she and her twin brother Sebastian have been very close. When she is brought ashore after the shipwreck, her brother's fate is the first thing in her mind. She is given hope that he may have survived, and this sustains her throughout the play. Such is Shakespeare's sense that no one could survive such catastrophes and remain emotionally in one piece without a dependable source of support that he gives both Viola and Sebastian quasi foster-parents, or perhaps in Sebastian's case a foster-brother, in the role of two sea-captains. They remain in the background after the shipwreck, fully committed to their charges, and emerge when they are needed.

In *Twelfth Night* Shakespeare explores the bisexual aspects of identity, especially in the context of young people's choice of love objects as they grow into adulthood. Are men and women different by nature, or similar, is one question that the play asks. Orsino self-regardingly asserts the difference between male constancy and female waywardness, imagining that he is instructing his young page Cesario in the ways of the world, while Cesario has to struggle in her mind with the fact that she is actually a woman and is in love with Orsino. At the same time, Viola recognizes that Olivia has fallen in love with her, believing her to be a man. She knows that Olivia is mourning her father and brother as she is hers, and identifies with her as a sister-in-grief. She also knows, from her own undeclared and unrequited love for Orsino, what it is to be rejected, and is compassionate towards Olivia in her state of infatuation. In working out how to represent herself as a man, she calls on her deep feeling for her twin brother. If it is a man she has to become, then it is Sebastian she will be, or as near to it as is possible. In fact, she is not very like Sebastian in character—Shakespeare seems perhaps to believe that there are few men who are as inward, as passionate, or as reflective about feelings as are his most passionate and intelligent female characters, and in this play Orsino and Sebastian are not they. (Antonio, in his passionate attachment to Sebastian, comes nearer to these qualities.) The men are made to seem shallower than the women. Sebastian only has to appear and make the best of the good fortune prepared for him by his sister, and Orsino just to have his eyes opened to see that his true love has been at his side, unrecognized, for weeks, to find joy.

The perfection in the resolution of the play lies in the way in which nearly everyone can have everything that they want, not just because they can live happily ever afterwards with their chosen lover, but because brother and sister will have each other, too, and Orsino and Olivia will acquire a quasi-brother and quasi-sister (brother- and sister-in-law) when they marry these twins. A polymorphous but non-perverse state of bliss—perhaps a prolongation of the benign aspects of adolescence—is being celebrated at the end of this play.

Another of the important questions being explored in *Twelfth Night* is: what is love? Sir Andrew is wooing Olivia, but he has been put up to it by Sir Toby, to extract money from him, and he is a gull. Maria, Olivia's diminutive maid, is truly in love with Sir Toby. She, unusually and interestingly, is allowed to win him by her display of wit and cleverness, though she is aided in this by the familial circumstances, in which it is much to the advantage of Sir Toby to keep on the right side of his rich niece. But there is real affection between Sir Toby and Maria, and the implication is that he may be made less disagreeable by his marriage to Maria. There is love, too, in the straightforwardly avuncular feeling of Viola's protective sea-captain for her. He helps her transform herself into the disguise of a man, and meanwhile is the keeper of her women's clothes. Quite intimate tasks these, though performed without complication. Antonio's passion for Sebastian is intense, and therefore more complicated, but the play allows their reconciliation, despite Sebastian's wrongly-imputed betrayal of Antonio, and the play avoids any suggestion that Antonio might be jealous of Sebastian's acceptance of Olivia. It seems that possible same-sex complications are being glossed over here.

Then there is Malvolio, and his love for Olivia, whom he serves as her steward. This is shown to be ridiculously confused with his vanity, and his aspirations for status and power over the rest of the household, of whom he imagines himself as lord once ensconced as Olivia's husband. His delusional conviction of his imminent upward mobility are fed by Maria's plot, and they echo her own plans or hopes to escape the status of servant and marry a nobleman, even a drunken one such as Sir Toby. The torment of Malvolio probably touches on her own fears of cruel rejection and humiliation, which are pushed away by making Malvolio the victim of their mocking trickery. Malvolio's capacity for absurd self-deception is established when he is overheard talking to himself, before he is trapped by the letter left for him by Maria, which leads him to believe that Olivia is in love with him. He is cruelly treated, but he is himself self-impor-tant and vindictive. Feste reminds Olivia when he confesses his own involvement in the plot that Malvolio had tried to humiliate him, and have him dismissed from her house, when he saw his chance to do so. Those dependent on these noble households are shown to engage in mean struggles to maintain their place.

Finally there is Olivia. What a subtle portrait this is. Here is a young woman who finds herself as the head of a large household and estate. Her household is unruly, and difficult to control. She is fending off the attentions of Orsino, the head of the greater house nearby. But when Viola appears, as Cesario, she throws herself at him, with no one to restrain her. The duel that Sir Toby sets up between Sir Andrew and Viola/Cesario is a sign of the alarm of the household, and of her family, at the risk to the family estate that arises if she gives herself in marriage to a stranger, about whose origins and fortune nothing is known, and whom the audience knows to be the wrong sex anyway. Her impulsive marriage to Sebastian, when he appears, only shows how at risk she really was, with no parents or family to help her to plan and negotiate her future. Sebastian thinks he must have arrived in paradise to be suddenly receiving the loving attentions of this beautiful rich woman (an echo of Bottom and Titania in the enchanted wood in *A Midsummer Night's Dream*). The Trevor Nunn film *of Twelfth Night* shows Feste observing her through the tumultuous climax of the play, the containing mind that is needed even if he is not in a position to do more than be there and watch. But his eyes represent those of the audience, too, embodying within the play the experience of containment that is given by the theatre itself. Feste represents the creative presence of the playwright and the company, being given the epilogue to speak.

FESTE:　　　But that's all one, our play is done,
　　　　　　And we'll strive to please you every day.

[V, 5, 406–407]

What a beautiful utopian fantasy it is, to imagine that a woman could be in a position to choose like this, and be enabled in the end to do so safely and well! And how does this happen? Because of the impregnation of this play by the presence of benign internal objects, in the minds of Olivia, Viola, and Sebastian in particular, but reinforced by Maria, Feste, and the rescuing sea-captains, which ensures that no lasting harm can be done. What a contrast with the world of *Measure for Measure*, where the parental role of good government has lapsed, where individuals pursue their own desires with little feeling for others, and where ideological and religious passions (whether of Angelo or Isabella) are left to fill a moral and emotional vacuum. At the end of *Measure for Measure*, every-thing is at best patched up. *Twelfth Night*, however, leaves us with a sense of the true complexities of love, where all remains to be worked out in the marriages celebrated so impetuously, and when the mourning with which the play opened has not really had time to run its course. But the relief and joy at the conclusion of this play, as at the end of *A Winter's Tale*, comes from the fact that an impor-tant part of the burden of mourning has been lifted with the restora-tion to each other of twin brother and sister, Viola and Sebastian, and from the miraculous good fortune that the two of them are there to fulfil needs which no one individual could do.

Twinship in Twelfth Night

One of the ideas implicit in Shakespeare's depiction of the closeness of the sibling link between Viola and Sebastian—and of course it is the special link of twinship, which goes way beyond ordinary sibling experience in the degree to which the whole of infancy and childhood has been shared—is that it comes to represent, once parents are lost, the familial identity and sense of fundamental safety that family membership represents. Viola is looking for a husband, as she reveals very early on.

VIOLA:	Who governs here?
CAPTAIN:	A noble duke, in nature as in name.
VIOLA:	What is his name?
CAPTAIN:	Orsino.
VIOLA:	Orsino! I have heard my father name him. He was a bachelor then.

[I, 2, 24–29]

But this is in the context of her thoughts about the husband her father might have thought suitable for her. The loss of Sebastian in the shipwreck leaves her without a male protector (though the captain steps in as a temporary shield) and it is the image of Sebastian, linked with her thoughts about her father, which support her in her adventure in Illyria, they together providing a "strong mast" to hold her as well as Sebastian.

CAPTAIN: ... I saw your brother
            Most provident in peril, bind himself
            (Courage and hope both teaching him the practice)
            To a strong mast that liv'd upon the sea;
            When, like Arion on the dolphin's back,
            I saw him hold acquaintance with the waves
            As long as I could see.

                                        [I, 2, 11–17]

It is tempting to link the dolphin with the lost mother in the background of these orphans' lives. The imagery of the mast and the ~~ ....~~ male and female elements linked together in the mind.

The background of sibling intimacy and trust is fundamental in both Viola's and Sebastian's adaptations to their temporary separation. Sebastian can respond with natural warmth to Antonio's brotherly protectiveness and affection, even accepting as natural the personal risks that Antonio is prepared to take on his account. This is the assumption of the loved individual that he is worthy of love (a little complacent, like a child who has been protected by parental love from too many shocks in life) and expects to find it anew in fresh contexts. Viola, whose character is more fully delineated in the play, draws on her link with Sebastian and explores its potential in two directions, both in her sibling-like tenderness and identification with Olivia, and in her readiness for a heterosexual love relationship with Orsino. As Melanie Klein suggested (Klein, 1932) and as Prophecy Coles' (2003) work has recently brought to the fore, the love between brother and sister can be a creative preparation for adolescent and adult sexual life.[7] Viola can adopt without difficulty a male persona and dress, and quickly understands Orsino. We might think that these capacities would have been less available to a young woman who had never had years of intimacy with a twin brother. Children's play, including the possibility of dressing up and trying out each other's gendered identities, is a rich source for the rituals of courtship that the play enacts. There is no problem for Viola in joining the all-male court of Orsino, organized around hunting (chasing the hart/heart) and aristocratic revels—she knows very well what young men do and feel and can join in the word games with ease and elegance. In her male disguise, she can revel in exploring the split-off male aspects of herself previously contained in her twin brother, in all probability. It is extraordinary how much Shakespeare enables us to imagine about the earlier life together of these twins, while actually putting them on the stage together for only brief moments.

Viola's attraction to Olivia suggests that alongside the tomboyish potential is a longing for womanly intimacy. The relationship that develops between them presages the actual sisterly relationship, in the future, that the dénouement sets in motion. They are natural sisters, and perhaps Olivia's more established position as the head of a household makes her a mother-figure for Viola as she certainly is for most of her dependents. (One of the choices in staging this play must be whether to give more emphasis to Olivia's girlish aspects, or on the contrary to emphasize her womanly qualities.) When Viola as Cesario is wooing Olivia on Orsino's behalf, her own longing to find a place in Olivia's heart is also to be heard, which is why she makes such a successful messenger. No one has previously got a foot in the door!

VIOLA:	If I did love you in my master's flame,
	With such a suff'ring, such a deadly life,
	In your denial I would find no sense,
	I would not understand it.

| OLIVIA: | Why, what would you? |

VIOLA:	Make me a willow-cabin at your gate
	And call upon my soul within this house;
	Write loyal cantons of contemned love
	And sing them loud even in the dead of night;
	Halloo your name to the reverberate hills,
	And make the babbling gossip of the air
	Cry out "Olivia!' O, you should not rest
	Between the elements of air and earth,
	But you should pity me.

| OLIVIA: | You might do much. |
| | What is your parentage? |

[I. V, 268–279]

Of course, her own growing love for Orsino is part of this (Viola can't resist him, so how can Olivia?) but the idea of camping at

Olivia's gate suggests just how much an attachment to the Olivia household appeals to this homeless girl.

Olivia's enchantment with Viola/Cesario has a narcissistic core. She is, after all, truly more alone than Viola (who is sustained by hope that her twin brother has survived) and there is little evidence of much support for her bereaved condition in her household. On the contrary, with the partial exception of Maria and Feste, they are exploiting her most of the time. So she is left having to be mother, father, and brother to herself. Having to play the male role as head of the household makes Olivia particularly open to falling in love with the girl disguised-as-a-boy who is also grieving her losses, a version of the position in which she finds herself. The ease with which she then later transfers her affection to the look-alike Sebastian suggests how little the love is to do with the actual person inside Viola/Cesario or Sebastian—they are seized upon as comfort, to allay her loneliness. A real relationship to a person recognized in her own right remains in the future. But perhaps there is also the suggestion, here as elsewhere in Shakespeare, that romantic love always entails wild projections and fantasies. What this play does is to prepare the ground for this adventure better than often happens, through its dramatic device of identical opposite-sex twins, which allows might-bes and might-have-beens to be explored and played with.[8]

At the same time, Olivia, in her head-of-household role, demonstrates more mature capacities for understanding. Implicit in her sympathy for Malvolio at the end of the play is the recognition that while he has been humiliated and punished for being mistaken—for being carried away by his narcissistic delusions of grandeur—Olivia and others have had the good fortune not to be humbled by their mistakes, but have been blessed with the magical resolution of their hopeless desires. In similar vein, one can imagine how well Olivia will understand Sebastian's precipitate assent to marrying her—he is so alone, he is not yet reunited with his sister, he is the one surviving member of his family as she is of hers. They throw in their lot with each other on the basis of their intense mutual need, but in the enchanted world of this play, we are left feeling that we need not be too worried for them.

Here in *Twelfth Night* is Shakespeare's representation of the benign possibilities of siblinghood. The loss of parents that each generation has to face is mitigated by the enduring intimacy of the sibling link when its loving aspects are in the ascendant.

Notes

1. Bennett Simon (1988) and W. Fred Alford (1993) have set out similar arguments.
2. Here we considered plays by Euripides, Shakespeare, Webster, Ibsen, Chekhov, Wilde, Miller, Beckett, and Pinter. In all of them this focus is central.
3. Our attention to ceremony, and its role in reflecting and maintaining social bonds, draws on the sociological writing of Durkheim, and its anthropological development by Mary Douglas. For a recent discussion of the social significance of ritual that develops both these sources, see Perri 6 (2002).
4. It should be noted, however, that Claudio does ask Isabella to listen to his point of view. It is she that refuses even to think with him about their shared dilemma.
5. Our article, "The relational preconditions of socialism" (1985), argues that the capacity for sibling relationships, and the parental functions which are necessary to nurture these, is the key to broader forms of social altruism.
6. In the absence of parents, Isabella turns to an order ruled by a prioress, a holy mother, and the Duke tries to solve the problems that he has created for the siblings in his abandoned role as kingly father in the assumed role of holy father. Claudio's unsolemnised liaison with Juliet is another expression of his parentless state.
7. Klein (1932, especially chapter 7) says that early sexual relations between brother and sister are common. She argues that whether this is harmful or not to later development, which it need not be, depends on the extent of guilt and sadism in these early explorations.
8. Cross-dressing allows this playful exploration of identity in other comedies, such as in the play *As You Like It.*

References

Alford, C. Fred (1993). *The Psychoanalytic Theory of Greek Tragedy*. New Haven: Yale.

Coles, P. (2003). The *Importance of Sibling Relationships in Psychoanalysis*. London: Karnac.

Houzel, D. (2001). The "nest of babies" fantasy. *Journal of Child Psychotherapy*, 27(2): 263–290.

Klein, M. (1932). *The Psychoanalysis of Children*. London: Hogarth Press.

Klein, M. (1945). The Oedipus complex in the light of early anxieties. In: *Love, Guilt and Reparation and Other Works*. London: Hogarth, 1975.

Klein, M. (1955). On identification. In: *Envy and Gratitude and Other Works*. London: Hogarth, 1975.

Mitchell, J. (2000). *Mad Men and Medusas: Reclaiming Hysteria and the Effects of Sibling Relations on the Human Condition*. London: Penguin.

Mitchell, J. (2003). *Siblings: Sex and Violence*. Cambridge: Polity.

Perri 6 (2002). What is there to feel? A neo-Durkheimian theory of the emotions. *European Journal of Psychotherapy, Counselling and Health (Special Issue: Theories of the Emotions)*, 5(3): 263–290.

Rustin, M. E., & M. J. (1985). Relational preconditions of socialism. In: B. Richards (Ed.), *Capitalism and Infancy* (pp. 207–225). London: Free Association Books.

Rustin, M. E., & M. J. (2002). *Mirror to Nature: Drama, Psychoanalysis and Society*. London: Karnac.

Shell, M. (1988). *The End of Kinship*. London: Johns Hopkins University Press.

Simon, B. (1988). *Tragic Drama and the Family: Psychoanalytic Studies from Aeschylus to Beckett*. New Haven: Yale.

Tustin, F. (1972). *Autism and Childhood Psychosis*. London: Hogarth.

CHAPTER FIVE

The replacement child as writer

Harriet Thistlethwaite

"Do not return. If you can bear to, stay
dead with the dead. The dead have their own tasks.
But help me, if you can without distraction,
As what is farthest sometimes helps: in me."

(Rilke, from "Requiem for a friend")

W hen a sibling dies, the parents and any other child or children in the family will have a devastating loss to contend with, and will in all likelihood have problems with mourning. What happens to an infant who is born into a family where an older sibling has already died and not been mourned? All normal use of projective identification with the family around will bring the infant into contact with the inner dead one, and this is likely to become a source of considerable confusion and difficulty in healthy living. For a newborn infant the effect in relation to the grieving mother is particularly devastating.

The term "replacement child" has been coined to denote a child born after a short time: conceived within six months of the miscarriage or death of the previous infant (Rowe et al., 1978). The essential factor is that there has not been sufficient time for the dead child to be mourned, by the mother in particular, so that an unconscious confusion is likely to arise in her mind between the dead and the live child who follows. Moreover, she will be unlikely to be able to provide containment for her infant.

The prime consideration of this chapter is how the replacement child is affected by the loss, and will be looked at through the material of two writers in particular: most extensively the playwright Eugene O'Neill, and more briefly, the poet Rainer Maria Rilke. These were both—in the sense of coming between the mother and her mourning a dead child—replacement children,

There are some interesting and significant psychoanalytic articles already written about the replacement child in clinical work (Cain & Cain, 1964; Etchegoyen, 1997; Poznansky, 1972; Sabbadini, 1988). Sabbadini says,

> I cannot say whether such consequences are always pathological but I believe that any child conceived, born and brought up under these circumstances develops serious problems in the area of self-identity and experiences intense difficulties, particularly at the critical separation–identification stage and during adolescence. [1988, p. 531]

Through the two writers used, I will argue that there are very varying experiences of being a replacement child but some strong resonances towards the dead siblings will be seen to occur in their lives and writing. In addition will be shown something about the ways in which writing functioned, in truly sublimatory ways, towards successful ego transformation and integration.

There are a good number of artists in the canon who are known to have been replacement children. Of course, in the days when families produced and inevitably lost several children this is not surprising. Chateaubriand, Beethoven, Stendhal, Goethe, Gorky, Hesse, Dali, for instance, and the list goes on even before we reach those less renowned or still in our own era. Vincent Willem van Gogh, now well studied in psychoanalytic literature, is known to have been a replacement child, who—it is convincingly argued (Lubin, 1975; Meissner, 1992, 1993, 1994; Nagera, 1967)—despite his art, and his brother's enormous support, could not survive the devastating results of an exceptionally unfortunate coincidence at birth. He was born on the same birthday a year later to a mother who had not mourned her previous stillborn infant, also named Vincent Willem, and who soon went on to have several more children.

Drawing psychological conclusions from an artist's work is a tricky business. There has of late been a culture of complaint about the desecration of literary works through attempts to confuse the imaginary aesthetic with biography. It is, at worst, to confuse the symbol with the symbolized. For this reason the writers chosen are two who knew and stated that they consciously drew from their inner lives for material, and wrote letters and journal entries alongside their creative works that add to our understanding of the interplay of the inner world and its conscious or unconscious use. That both writers lived at a similar time in history, which encompassed the convulsions in Europe around the First World War, is of added interest, but it is not intended to draw much from that or other external themes here. The aim is to pull into focus the inner world of the child with a dead sibling, specifically that of the replacement child.

Mourning a child's death

Klein (1940) makes a connection between mourning and the infantile depressive position. She suggests that the loss of a good external object reactivates unconscious anxieties about damage and loss of the good internal object in childhood. Mourning then involves working through both an external and an internal loss, and for that reason is an extremely painful task. She considers that the capacity to mourn in later life and to recover is dependent on the resolution of the depressive position in childhood.

The role of mourning is vital to the ego because, in the earliest stage after a loss or death, the reality of the loss is denied and parts of the subject are split off and projected into the lost object as a way of trying to hold on to it. The ego is weakened as a consequence. Only through the slow process of true mourning can the subject take back those missing parts and thus restore strength to his or her own ego. On the mourning process, Freud (1917e) states, "Each single one of the memories and expectations in which the libido is bound to the object is brought up and hypercathected and detachment of the libido is accomplished in respect of it" (p. 245). This letting go of omnipotent control of the object means encountering the infantile feelings of conflict between aggressive and reparative wishes towards the object, and the experience carries intense feelings of guilt, desolation and pain.

For mourning to be successful the reality of the loss has to be accepted. This can only be achieved by a process of differentiating self from object by sorting out what belongs to whom. As a result of this emotional work, disowned parts of the self are gradually taken back into the ego. Failing successful mourning, projected parts are never taken back and remain embedded in the object into which they have been projected.

The replacement child

Etchegoyen (1997) has written about the replacement child syndrome, delving deeply into the difficulties for the mother of mourning a dead child. Also a study by Rowe et al. (1978) discovered that where a pregnancy followed too closely—within five months—after a perinatal loss there were significantly more signs of a morbid grief reaction, whereby the reality of the child's loss could not be accepted. A bereavement is difficult to mourn during a pregnancy, and at such a time the process will be inhibited or incompletely carried out.

Etchegoyen (*ibid.*) writes that the more intense the denial of the loss, the more likely the damaging effects on the replacement, the family, and the network. She refers to the literature on the profound effect on the family and its relationships. Lieberman and Black (1987) refer to dysfunctional family patterns of avoidance, idealization, and prolonged grief in reaction to loss. And Lewis (1983) refers to family feuds, depressive anniversary reactions, and, in some cases, provocation of a replacement pregnancy over the next generation.

If a mother is still grieving or depressed while tending a new infant, the infant's own fear of dying is not metabolized through containment by the mother. Indeed, it is reintrojected in what Bion (1962) describes as the form of "nameless dread". Later, grasp of the nature of the lost sibling will perhaps be used consciously to "patch" the gap but behind that lurks an involvement with death, taken in to primitive depths, which may have life-long effect. The impact of this on the infantile psyche, and the likelihood of a *loss of meaning* is explored in a slightly different way by Andre Green's paper on "The dead mother" (1986).

Sublimation, and working through by writing

In an interview with Meltzer about the experience of viewing a work of art, Adrian Stokes said:

> When a discernment of inner states, however horrific, however dispensible by means of sadistic projection, is stabilized in terms of aesthetic oppositions and balances and other aspects of form, some coordination, some bringing together will have occurred at the expense of denial; and this bringing together will have required at the fount, the shadow of a reconstructed whole-object and part-object whose presence can at least be glimpsed in the very existence of an aesthetic result. [Meltzer & Williams, 1988, p. 217]

The aim for the best of writers, as in the examples to be discussed here, will be by the act of creating work through internal conflicts and thus arriving successfully at the depressive position. For the audience or readers, the work of art ought then to enable them to experience the one or more identifications they are there drawn into, and through their own inner resonances to understand the deeper issues more completely.

Eugene O'Neill

When Eugene O'Neill was diagnosed with tuberculosis in his early twenties, Ella, his mother, who was a morphine addict, went into an agitated depression. A nurse was called in, who knew nothing of the addiction, and she described a nightmarish day she spent with the family:

> When she arrived, the three O'Neill men were having a shouting match around the dining table. Ella paced the floor upstairs and

moaned, "My son, my son," her long white hair wildly undone, her dark eyes enormous and unfocused. After a time she would collapse and rock back and forth, clutching her knees to her breast or wringing her hands, and grieving for her son. The nurse said that when Ella moaned for "My son, my son," she sometimes meant Eugene and sometimes meant the baby Edmund, who had died twenty-eight years before. [Black, 1999, p. 128]

To those familiar with O'Neill's late, overtly autobiographical play, *Long Day's Journey into Night* (1956), that scene will sound very familiar. The play's most poignant utterance comes when Jamie quotes, near the end, from Swinburne's *A Leave-taking*: "yea, though we sang as angels in her ear, she would not hear". We then realize that the real failure had been Ella's withdrawal from her two surviving sons into an addictive space.

Early years

Eugene's father, James O'Neill, the son of impoverished Irish immigrants, had become a famous actor who, in his youth, played many great parts, including Shakespearean roles, but he became especially renowned for his success as the Count of Monte Christo, and was typecast thereafter to a degree that he never successfully played any other role. His handsome successes enabled him, in 1876, to woo and marry the nineteen-year-old Ella Quinlan, of a somewhat wealthier Irish Catholic background. James's acting career swept Ella away from her bourgeois aspirations, on tour all over the USA. As a dependent girl, but perhaps also because James was known for his seductiveness to women (before marriage he'd had an illegitimate son by an actress, whom he had abandoned), she tended to travel with him. Lonely in hotel rooms in strange places, she became very close to her first child, Jamie, born in 1878. Then in 1883 a second boy was born, Edmund. At the age of two, however, while the parents were away on tour, Edmund died of measles.

Eugene O'Neill, born two and a half years later, in 1888, can reasonably be called a replacement child in the true sense of being conceived to fill the unmourned loss. Ella's difficulty in mentally processing the loss of her child must have been compounded after the death of her father when she herself was still a young girl of sixteen. Evidence from her school-fellows (Black, 1999) suggests she had not mourned her father much at the time.

After Edmund died, Ella had a number of self-induced abortions, so it seems clear she did not want another child, who might die, or whom she might fail. She probably did not have the ego strength to mourn Edmund, so the abortions may also have been her concrete way of expressing hostility towards him for leaving her, and against her husband for his role in her guilt. This fear of pregnancy would also have been in tune with the attitude of little Jamie, who now had his mother to himself more. She no doubt also felt torn about effectively leaving him again. The family story, put about afterwards by Jamie, was that it was James who thought it would be good for her to have another child.

When she finally succeeded in bringing to term the healthy baby, Eugene, accounts have it that she was prescribed morphine for the pain, as was common at the time, and from that day on became addicted. The abusive gestures were now turned against herself, and morphine gave her the resort of a retreat.

In any form of addiction the drug symbolizes the ideal object. "The addict appears to regress to a phase of infancy where the infant uses hallucinatory wish-fulfilment fantasies in dealing with his anxieties" (Rosenfeld, 1965, p. 130). This is very apparent in the last act of O'Neill's *Long Day's Journey* (1956). Indeed, its long day is spent journeying towards this night. Finally, after a heavy dose of the drug, Mary (Ella) loses all track of time, reliving her convent school past and relationship with Mother Elizabeth: ". . . so sweet and good. A saint on earth. I love her dearly. It may be sinful of me but I love her better than my own mother" (p. 109). It becomes clear that in her mind Mother Elizabeth was responsible for suggesting that, rather than becoming a nun as she wanted, Mary should spend some time socializing like the other teenage girls, which led to her falling for the pin-up hero, James Tyrone (O'Neill). We begin to see that James had stood in for her beloved lost father. But for her to be in the role of mothering babies was not successfully achieved: having another baby was unbearable to her.

It is recorded (Gelb & Gelb, 1964) that Ella's immediate reaction to the death of Edmund had been to blame the seven-year-old Jamie for giving him the illness, so little could the fragile woman bear her own guilt at having been away. In fact, it was her mother who was left to care for the boys, and her mother's existence is practically denied. This suggests that Jamie already may have begun to serve a function of taking up the projection of her unwanted parts. In some sense, then, her addictive solution after another child was born becomes clearer. For in the addict the drug also appears as a symbol of the split-off bad part of the self. She was probably trying to protect her children from her bad parts.

Moreover, Rosenfeld's (1965) discussion of drug addiction makes a direct link to the dead object.

> The essential factor of the relation of drug addiction to depression is the identification with an ill or dead object. The drug in such cases stands for such an object and the drugging implies a very concrete incorporation of this object. The pharmotoxic effect is used to reinforce the reality both of the introjection of the object and of the identification with it. [Rosenfeld, 1965, p. 131]

This, then, was the mother of Eugene's earliest experience. She was in all probability fairly impermeable due to the drug. Addiction is closely allied to manic depression and involves too a deep splitting between idealized and denigrated objects. The nature of the sudden reversals we witness and experience in Eugene's plays would have been the very stuff of his earliest psychic intake. Ella was not able to be the object of trusted dependence, to contain, or be consistent.

Also her boundaries would have been unreliable. This failure contributed to Jamie, her first-born's inability—ever—to separate from her and live adequately on his own. It might be said that the two brothers shared the burden of becoming projectively identified with a dead part of Ella, linked to, but not identical with, her addicted aspect; the latter O'Neill was to characterize as "the fog" (see below). Even from early childhood—before the addiction— Jamie seems to have been symbiotically bound up with his mother, and after discovering her injecting herself in his early teens he immediately became addicted to alcohol. She was too fragile for either of her children to be able to express any negativity towards her, or get her to face any reality, and, with a frequently absent father, in their childhood they were unable to find ways of coping with aggressive and disappointed feelings. Thus, they would have resorted to evacuative projective measures, whether involving other people, or, in adolescence, using alcohol itself as the substitute object relationship. These factors also contributed to the two brothers being quite problematically entangled with each other, as was to become clear years later.

When, in 1902, Ella attempted suicide owing to an inability to get morphine supplies, Eugene was finally told of her addiction by his brother, and also made to feel guilty that the morphine had taken hold from the date of his birth. The shock of traumatic discovery is a continuing theme throughout his plays. At the age of fourteen he had effectively been told by his jealous brother that he was the mother-murderer.

Nevertheless, Eugene for a time followed and admired Jamie's dissipated ways, and swallowed Jamie's alternative view of their terrible father as having caused all Ella's troubles by forcing her to sacrifice herself for his touring, and to have another child. Eugene's acceptance of this "grievance" against the father suggests he was defensively idealizing his brother. He continued to do so until the early 1920s.

However, at seventeen Eugene followed a pattern laid down by his father and got a girl pregnant. He married her in panic, and yet, with James's approval, ran off on a long sea voyage. This was a close echo to his father's abandonment of a woman and son years before his own marriage to Ella. After Eugene returned from sea, the guilt about the girl, abandoned child, and the failure of heavy drinking to bury it all, led to severe depression. He made a serious suicide attempt through an overdose of veronal in 1912. It was an episode O'Neill glossed over all his life, but he was only just saved by the timely arrival of a friend.

Meltzer (1973) writes,

> Terror is a paranoid anxiety whose essential quality, paralysis, leaves no avenue of action. The object of terror, being in unconscious phantasy *dead* objects, cannot even be fled from with success. But in psychic reality the vitality of an object, of which it may be robbed, can also be returned to it, as the soul to the body in theological terms. This can only be accomplished by the reparative capacity of the internal parents and their creative coitus. [Meltzer, 1973, p. 148]

The internalized Ella, carrying one or more unmourned dead objects in her inner world, certainly would have added to such a persecution in Eugene, and his guilt about her addictive deadening, as well as all his responsibility for other losses perpetrated through the years of debauchery.

Early plays

The whole terrible episode may have contributed to scaring Eugene unconsciously towards increasing his identification with, and sympathy for, his maturer father. This link was to open up an internal space that would allow some real creativity. His slowly working at becoming a playwright is multi-determined, though one skein relates to the actor James, and thus to the parental dynamic. The position of playwright symbolically combined omnipotence and reparation in family terms. And Eugene had good reason to feel some gratitude towards his father by now, since he had supported and tried to help his son throughout all the years of dissipation. Rather than in relations with women and children, with whom he would continue to fail, playwriting was to be Eugene's chosen means to work through pain and back into living. The early plays deal with the terrors and private torments of his adolescence and early adulthood in direct ways, characterized by a talent for rhythm in monologue and dialogue that indicates what a close witness he was of fraught family dynamics, even if the endings were still often abrupt denials of reality.

The unproduced *Shell Shock*, for instance. In addition to its First World War theme, the play suggests the shock of the discovery of something shameful, similar to Eugene's discovery of his mother's addiction. It is built around a long, melodramatic confession on the part of a guilt-ridden, shell-shocked hero, which culminates in a primal scream—the result of which is a sudden and complete exorcizing of his guilt.

In 1920, another O'Neill one-act play was performed, called *Exorcism*. In it, a character decides to end it all by taking an overdose of morphine. When found and saved by a character, Jimmy, he feels that the demons that had been driving him have been exorcized and he turns to the world with renewed interest. After a brief performance O'Neill cancelled it and destroyed all the copies of the script. He may have found it too revealing of himself, and, knowing his mother's sensitivity, too challenging to her and his father. But also he may have understood that its final optimism was too pat. After seeing *Hedda Gabler* while still in his teens, O'Neill became passionate about Ibsen, and he was also much impressed by Strindberg. He had no doubt of his intention to portray true reality and get away from his father's generation of high melodrama on the stage.

In his early twenties, Eugene began to settle as he increased writing. He slowed up on drinking, saw less of Jamie, and married Agnes Boulton, who was from an artistic family and with a literary education. They were to have two children, Shane and Oona.

Stephen Black's biography of O'Neill (1999) tells us that he had a taciturn character, and was hard to read. Though his friends learned to take for granted his poker face and his concealed alertness, his first wife, Agnes, never did.

> Eugene for his part, must have realised the effect his silences had on her, but he did not or could not become more open . . . Both were believers in the mystical rhythms of love. Unable to find ordinary conversation, they were helpless when the mystical tides inscrutably drew them together and then left them to drift amid tense silences and guesswork. Neither could find a basic trust in the constancy of their bond that might have eased the ebb and flow of intimacy. [Black, 1999, pp. 229–230]

Those silences and guesswork must have been a reflection of Eugene's earliest experiences of his mother. Agnes had abandoned to her parents care a child born in her own teenage years, and Eugene seems to have found in her a wife who took up his projected difficulties with his internal needy mother. In the early years of the marriage they seemed to need to cling closely to one another.

After 1920, when his father died, Eugene wrote a play, *Gold* (1920), about a couple's unending grief over the death of their daughter years before. The father is an anthropologist, Jayson, who roams the world in search of a modern Golden Fleece. His wife, Martha, accompanies him everywhere and sacrifices everything to his goal. Then Martha finds herself pregnant and is afraid to tell her husband because they'd agreed not to have any more children who might die. She dies in childbirth and Jayson gives his son to an aunt to raise while he sets off on his quest.

This theme illustrates O'Neill, in normally mourning his father, consciously and unconsciously reliving some of the themes of his own childhood. It indicates his identification with his father, in seeking immortality in his writing "quest". It has a characteristic wry wit too, using the golden fleece, since his father was known to be miserly. The play shows that Eugene can now stand in the position of observer; or that of failed mother, or failed father, but not in that of being a good parent to an alive child. At this same time Eugene and his wife were becoming estranged, and he was on the verge of abandoning his second son, Shane.

Segal (1991) writes of the significance of the symbolic penis as drawing a boundary line against a vast amount of projective identification with mother. For Eugene, in the overall balance James must have had some function of this kind. But it is arguable that he was never a truly internalized good father, if *Long Day's Journey* reflects the inner truth. Jamie was also perhaps a protective buffer against mother, and guilt about this was to plague Eugene after Jamie's death. There is no doubt that Eugene wrote his greatest plays from a predominantly depressive viewpoint. Being in an observing position—literally as audience—he could place his parents, and this also enabled him to see the tragically impossible scenarios in which the four of them were entrenched. However, when it came to the responsibility of providing fathering for his sons he failed twice over. Both O'Neill's sons committed suicide years later, Shane after a long period as a drug addict.

In 1922 his mother finally died, of a brain tumour. That very day Eugene was at some social event with his old companions the Provincetown Players when a friend accused him of vanity: "You can't pass a mirror without staring at yourself." To which Eugene replied, "I'm just looking to see if I'm alive." It well may be that the death of his mother pulled him back to an infantile existential anxiety, so deep was his identification with her. Mourning her was for him a terribly obsessive process that involved him in compulsively writing and rewriting her character over the next two decades.

Middle plays

In the middle period of his playwriting O'Neill seems to be

conflicted by an uncertainty as to whether his mother's addiction betrayed him or he had betrayed his mother through debauchery. Was it her or was it him? He begins to delve deeper into his guilt.

Ella died shortly before the idea of *Desire Under the Elms* (1925) came to Eugene. Much of the play is about forgiveness and reconciliation but it ends in denying the possibility of either. Ephraim (whom O'Neill always said was his most autobiographical self) concludes that a destiny of unbroken loneliness—the loneliness of God himself, he says—is the true "hardness" God requires of man. Here is an indicator of Eugene's superego, and it does not seem that this God is very concerned about family relationships. More than that, there seems to lurk a quite defeatist shadow in him.

In *All God's Chillun Got Wings* (1923), the character actually named Ella goes through sudden reversals from love to hate and back in a quite mad way, and is at the extreme of all the chaotic reversals of feeling in O'Neill's plays. Obviously Jekyll–Hyde in manner, this Ella is at such a pitch of aggression that she has to be hospitalized, yet her feelings of love and dependency exist alongside the violence expressed in her racist hatred towards her black husband, Jim. The racial tensions are used here to denote a version of Eugene's mother's worst denigration of James O'Neill's impoverished Irish family background. Plays such as these have led commentators to wonder at O'Neill's capacity to get himself through the "vortex years of his suffering from the mid-20s to mid-30s which make one genuinely marvel at his avoidance of suicide" (Manheim, 1982, p. 40).

During this period, his female characters enact the madness O'Neill feared as he tried to deal with his brother Jamie's death. Jamie had given up alcohol after his father died—when he'd finally got his mother to himself—but deliberately drank himself to death within a year of Ella's death. Eugene, meanwhile, was not able to mourn and sublimate his mother's death either, the way he had done with a creative spurt after the death of his father. Part of the difficulty was that after the death he had discovered the full extent of Jamie's drunken helplessness. It involved a macabre tale featuring a crate of whiskey and a whore, on a train bringing the body of Ella in the baggage car, across the continent to the funeral in New London that neither son attended. These events were to be mercilessly and painfully detailed in *A Moon for the Misbegotten* (1945).

Also revealed were Jamie's attempts to cheat Eugene of a substantial part of the property Ella left in her will. His old idealism about his brother was at once ended, and he had no patience with Jamie's suicidal drinking thereafter.

In some sense his elder brother was the hardest for him to understand, and it wasn't until the mid-1930s that he began to portray his "Jamie self". It is likely that he dreaded the guilt of his own part in Jamie too much. Greed was another theme that was to join those in his writings at that point. In effect, he was now having to mourn both his mother and his brother. But also Ella's death had clearly revealed the real chasm that lay between the brothers, a chasm symbolized in the lost son, Edmund, and the neediness and guilt that his death had opened up years before in Ella, James, and Jamie. And which Eugene had, so to speak, inherited at birth.

It was a psychic hole that O'Neill's writing had not yet succeeded in either "patching" (Green, 1986), which perhaps the early writing was an attempt to do, or working through the awful realities for him. Much work lay ahead: his most painfully self-analytical, and also most successful plays, *Mourning Becomes Elektra* (1929–1931), *The Iceman Cometh* (1988, written 1939), *Long Day's Journey into Night* (1988, written 1939–1941), and *A Moon for the Misbegotten* (1945) were still to come. "Jamie" characters feature powerfully in the final three, particularly—as truly tragic anti-hero—in the last.

A conversation Eugene had, walking in Central Park with his friend and editor Saxe Commins, after Jamie had wired that their mother was dead, was reported later by Commins. At the time O'Neill ran through his family's misfortunes, ending with his brother's, suggesting that "Jamie was the most unfortunate of them all, for he had scarcely anything to sustain him, nothing except his love for his mother" (Commins, 1986, ref. Black, 1999, pp. 279–80).

After bouts of heavy drinking, and the increasing failure of his marriage, Eugene sought psychotherapeutic help between the years 1922 and 1925. In 1925 he succeeded fairly well in quitting drinking, and smoking. He often talked to doctors about his alcoholism, and read Freud's "Beyond the pleasure principle" (1920g) and then "Group psychology and the analysis of the ego" (1921c), saying: "Playwrights are either keen analytical psychologists—or they aren't good playwrights. I'm trying to be one" (Black, 1999, p. 321).

Never really a Catholic, he also read and was most impressed by Nietzsche's *The Birth of Tragedy* (1927), and was teaching himself from the Greek dramas.

The Great God Brown (1925) is in part from O'Neill's reading about Dionysus and Pan—and denied sexuality (*Panik*). In it lies an elegy that must have stood for his mother as perhaps he imagines Jamie saw her, once he had her all to himself. The identification with her girl-doll self is vividly apparent.

> I remember a sweet, strange girl, with affectionate eyes as if God had locked her in a dark closet without any explanation. I was the sole doll our ogre, her husband, allowed her and she played mother and child with me for many years in that house until at last through two tears I watched her die with the shy pride of one who has lengthened her dress and put up her hair. And I felt like a forsaken toy and cried to be buried with her because her hands alone had caressed without clawing. She lived long and aged greatly in the two days before they closed her coffin. The last time I looked, her purity had forgotten me, she was stainless and imperishable, and I knew my sobs were ugly and meaningless to her virginity. [O'Neill, 1925, p. 85]

This somewhat mawkish style obscures the mother and the son, the two are so intertwined, whereas Jim Tyrone's elegy for his mother, written two decades later in *A Moon for the Misbegotten* (1943), allows the listener to know the truth of the speaker's pain of remorse at having felt a burden.

> Suffer? Christ, I ought to suffer! . . . When Mama died, I'd been on the wagon for nearly two years. . . . She had only me to attend to things for her and take care of her. She'd always hated my drinking. So I quit. It made me happy to do it. For her. Because she was all I had. [p. 80]

Jim continues, to describe her in death,

> I could hardly recognise her. She looked young and pretty like someone I remembered meeting long ago. Practically a stranger. Cold and indifferent. Not worried about me any more. Free at last. Free from worry. From pain. From me. I stood looking down at her, and something happened to me. I found I couldn't feel anything. I

knew I ought to be heartbroken but I couldn't feel anything. I seemed dead, too. [*ibid.*]

In *The Great God Brown* (1926), O'Neill employs the device of masks—Brown takes up Dion's mask and is possessed by it. This suggests his having taken up his brother's mask, and writing the play enabled Eugene to recover and examine some fragmented images of his brother and try out the hostility behind his idealization. When Dion dies, Brown remarks: "So that's the poor weakling you really were! No wonder you hid! And I've always been afraid of you—yes, I'll confess it now, in awe of you" (p. 99). In Brown Eugene also expresses his envy of his brother Jamie's adolescent talents and being his mother's preferred child. By killing off Dion he also experiments with losing the part of himself that deadens with drink.

Since his adolescence, when he had discovered his mother's addiction, Eugene had coped with knowledge of his crime by splitting himself between his Dion (brother murder) self and his Billy (mother murder) self. Also, perhaps Eugene had projected his incestuous desire for his mother into Jamie, and by the device of having Brown take up the other's (Dion's) mask of desire he gropes towards this knowledge. In many of his earlier plays he'd used promiscuity in women as another mask. Jamie's promiscuity had certainly always been one of his characteristic attacks on Ella's delicate nun–madonna pose.

In *Mourning Becomes Elektra*, written between 1929 and 1930, O'Neill created the first character who truly mourns: an alter-ego and sister of Orin (Orestes), Lavinia, who—like Eugene at that point—has finally to endure living among all her dead. At the opening night Eugene consciously felt depressed and lost at the play's leaving him. It was the first time he acknowledged that his plays were like children, not only causing depression after he'd written them, but further suffering and mourning once they went out on stage to the public.

In that play the sexy suitor, Brant, who turns out to be the son of disgraced Uncle David Mannon and a servant girl, is a reminder that Eugene, too, had a half-brother somewhere: "Little Alfie", the early son of his father James's affair. Also he may have been exploring the vague future of his own illegitimate son, Eugene junior, who was now a regular house visitor. There is, in all likelihood, some split-off identification in Orin, as a son whose oedipal tragedy was enacted. Orin is driven mad by realizing he was not enough to keep mother alive—Jamie's lifelong issue from first Edmund's then their father's death. He is made to express the deepest distaste at his mother's sexual being, the intolerable primal scene lurking for him down that avenue.

However, Eugene himself seems to have begun to introduce a realistic element previously missing in women characters, who had been either idealized pure sensitive souls, or denigrated common whores. The women in the play, both Christine and her daughter later, are allowed to be sexual women. The sexuality is symbolized on stage in the sultry red hair they both carry (O'Neil always noticed women's hair), and the revealing green silk dress that recurs throughout. It is explicitly linked to a South Sea island fantasy experience, associated partly with Brandt, where lust is still somehow *innocently* possible. (Was there an apologetic note to O'Neill's mother in that?) This reality may also have come about in connection with his new love, Carlotta Monterey, who became his third wife, and was far more a sophisticated woman of the world than Agnes. Yet, it was a feature of this play that O'Neill never really developed further.

His alterations to Aeschylus's *Orestaia* reflect some of the internal psychic realities that he had to explore. (O'Neill was always more Sophoclean in approach, though he most admired Aeschylus.) Thus, Orin becomes increasingly mad, and kills himself, as Jamie had effectively done with drink. The one left is Lavinia. In some ways she is reminiscent also of Antigone, daughter of Oedipus, wilfully sacrificing her marriage in order to finally take back guilt after her two brothers' deaths. In O'Neill's play, Lavinia acknowledges at last her real role in the mother-murder, and it does not let her go. In reality, Eugene now stood carrying terrible guilt and self-hatred at being so unable to take responsibility for his mother's burial and his brother's completely suicidal debauchery. He had become the sole family mourner.

Late plays

Long Day's Journey into Night

Michael Manheim (1982) writes about kinship motifs in O'Neill's plays and his method of creating a rhythm: "this contrapuntal rhythm of kinship is one in which the initial beat is made up of acid recrimination and lacerating hurt, while the following beat invariably counters the first with split-second forgiveness and total if inevitably short-lived reconciliation" (p. 9).

In the late plays there is still much more recrimination than reconciliation, but the bitterness is never unrelieved and the tenderness never illusory. There is far less of the deceit and secrecy that was in the earlier plays. Now O'Neill portrays a kind of stoicism in which the hero is the one who can survive an illusionless life.

In *Long Day's Journey into Night* (1956) as Manheim points out, "Where there is contact, no matter how painful (and it is usually terribly painful), there is life—and where there is withdrawal there is death.' The dialogue itself becomes not solely a dramatic device but a life-sustaining one (Manheim, 1982, p. 11).

Fog is used throughout this play as metaphor for addictive withdrawal and the enveloping barrier to seeing. It may be seen as a "psychic retreat" such as described by Steiner (1993), and also an indicator of some blocking that destroys meaning, which is infantile in origin. O'Neill often used it from his youthful sea plays on, beginning with a play named *Fog* in 1913–1914 (O'Neill, 1988).

In Act One of *Long Day's Journey* (1956) Mary says, "thank heavens the fog is gone". She wasn't able to sleep with the foghorn going all night. She likens it to Tyrone's snoring in perhaps the most affectionate of exchanges with her husband, which, inevitably in this play, still contains the element of personal attack.

By Act Three, in which the characters are least connected, the fog has rolled back in again, in early evening. "*A foghorn is heard at regular intervals, moaning like a mournful whale in labour.*" We know then that Mary has given up the fight against her narcotic. The scene notes indicate, "*There is at times an uncanny gay, free youthfulness in her manner, simply and without self-consciousness, the naïve, happy, chattering schoolgirl of her convent days*" (p. 56).

Mary tells Cathleen she really loves fog. "It hides you from the world and the world from you. You feel that everything has changed, and nothing is what it seemed to be. No one can find or touch you any more." . . .

Then . . . "It's that foghorn I hate. It won't let you alone. It keeps reminding you, and warning you, and calling you back" (p. 57).

After Edmund returns, having learnt he has consumption, and has finally lashed out at Mary as a "dope fiend", she says, "Why is it fog makes everything sound so sad and lost, I wonder?" (p. 72). Later, in talk with his father, Edmund says,

> ... The fog was where I wanted to be. Halfway down the path you can't see this house. You'd never know it was here. Or any of the other places down the avenue. I couldn't see but a few feet ahead. I didn't meet a soul. Everything looked and sounded unreal. Nothing was what it is. That's what I wanted—to be alone with myself in another world where truth is untrue and life can hide from itself. Out beyond the harbour, where the road runs along the beach, I even lost the feeling of being on land. The fog and the sea seemed part of each other. It was like walking on the bottom of the sea. As if I had drowned long ago. As if I was a ghost belonging to the fog, and the fog was the ghost of the sea. It felt damned peaceful to be nothing more than a ghost within a ghost. . . . Don't look at me as if I'd gone nutty. I'm talking sense. Who wants to see life as it is, if they can help it? It's the three Gorgons in one. You look in their faces and turn to stone. Or it's Pan. You see him and you die—that is, inside you—and have to go on living as a ghost. [pp. 78–79]

In Act Four, after his father has talked at length of his own fears, hopes, and dreams, Edmund in a long speech describes moments while being at sea of feeling free and at one with beauty. One time:

> Dreaming, not keeping lookout, feeling alone, and above, and apart, watching the dawn creep like a painted dream over the sky and sea which slept together. Then the moment of ecstatic freedom came. The peace, the end of the quest, the last harbour, the joy of belonging to a fulfilment beyond men's lousy, pitiful greedy fears and hopes and dreams! . . .

> It was a mistake my being born a man, I would have been much more successful as a sea-gull or a fish. As it is I will always be a stranger who never feels at home, who does not really want and is not really wanted, who can never belong, who must always be a little in love with death! [pp. 94–95]

In the final act the fog appears denser than ever. Everyone is heavily entrapped in their own form of escapism. The play, and the day it records, pulls the spectator to feeling the terrible cycle of guilt and blame in a close-knit family; each one's presence and weakness causing guilt to another; no one with a strong enough inner core to withstand the lure to fall back into what we might see as one of Rosenfeld's (1987) "mafia gang" traps.

In the last act, Jamie, returning home very drunk, calls his mother a "hophead", and Edmund punches him. Then Jamie says: "I'd begun to hope. If she'd beaten the game, I could too" (p. 100).

In reality, Ella, with the help of her strong belief in the Virgin Mary, had given up her addiction in 1914; Jamie never managed more than two years without his.

The theme of personal rejection is most frequent throughout O'Neill's plays, but as time goes on there is usually also some hope. In *Long Day's Journey into Night* it is felt through the family's helpless love for the mother, and Jamie's confession about his dark ambivalence towards his brother. It is a poignant reflection that the author represented himself as the dying "Edmund", as though with his current, truer Eugene role in life he may have felt he could hardly be allowed to go on surviving.

O'Neill as writer

Whenever he felt fused with an internal object, O'Neill habitually tried to explore that character dramatically. He was working out his own salvation and trying to control the inner tormenting family members. Quite early in his career he was ready to write a confessional play, and to write the demons out. But by the time of the late plays he was working those relationships through internally much more, and the strain was telling. In 1934 he suffered a psychotic breakdown brought on by writing *Days Without End* (1933; O'Neill, 1988). In that play, which he redrafted many times, he tried to confront directly and actually bear (instead of escaping through addiction or adultery) the suffering at how his mother had hurt him, his own responsibility in defensively identifying with her, and his retaliatory wishes. From then on his work became much more deeply affecting.

However, it was through his identification with his father that Eugene originally found his playwriting avenue for sublimation. He makes witty use of a pun, twice in the last Act of *Journey*, as father and son, drunk and utterly despondent, play cards, they exchange two lines:

"Whose play is it?"
"Yours, I guess,"

replies Edmund first. The second time they reverse, and the now realistic old actor, Tyrone, is the one to give way (pp. 87, 91).

O'Neill also tried hard at writing lyrical poetry at times in his life, but found he was no good as something inside sabotaged him. As Edmund, his personification in *Long Day's Journey*, he says to his father as they talk about poetry:

> I'm afraid I'm like the guy who is always panhandling for a smoke. He hasn't even got the makings [of a poet]. He's only got the habit. I couldn't touch what I tried to tell you just now. I just stammered. That's the best I'll ever do. I mean if I live. Well, it will be faithful realism at least. Stammering is the native eloquence of us fog people. [p. 95]

A severe hand tremor—a sad link and a reminder of Ella's give-away hands—that he'd begun to suffer ultimately stopped his writing altogether. Eugene O'Neill survived to the age of 65 but his last marriage was, by more than one account (Black, 1999), always fraught with volatility and cruel rows, and living was still bleak for him. There is more of an echo of his mother, who'd always felt homeless, in his wry complaint at the end, that he was not only born in a hotel room but was to die in one too.

Rainer Maria Rilke

Background

Rilke was born in Prague in 1875, premature by two months. Both his mother and father had wanted a girl to make up for the loss of a daughter, Ismene, who had died at birth the year before. Rene Maria he was named—both female names, the latter since he'd been born on the day of Holy Mary, and his mother was very strongly Catholic. She had married a military man whom she felt was beneath her, and was unrealistic about hardships. Strait-laced and bourgeois, she also indulged in a sentimental theatricality, idealizing her only son as a genius, and treating him as a girl. One day in childhood—according to the mother—Rilke came to her saying

"Ismene stays with her dear mother, Rene is a good-for-nothing, I have sent him away, girls are more affectionate aren't they?" (Graff, 1956, p. 13).

Rilke early on felt chafed under the artificiality of his mother's airs, and gradually began to realize what a shallowly destructive woman she was. In a poem of 1915 he compares himself to a building which was laboriously erected stone by stone and his mother, whom "Christ comes to wash every day", insists on tearing it down with selfish unconcern (*ibid.*, p. 13).

His father, whose pride had been shaken when he was reduced to having to take a post in the service of the railroad, was stiffly conventional and a realist: when his son was seven, he sent him to a military academy school and Rilke was suddenly bereft of all the unreal laudation he'd had at home. His parents were divorced two years later. Throughout his school life in Moravia Rilke was very unhappy, and now made additionally claustrophobic by the intense militaristic regime that left him without space to think or write. He was often ill in the infirmary. He wrote that "It was like being totally submerged for five whole years" (Prater, 1986, p. 8). All these various childhood experiences would result in the avoidance of impingements becoming a central factor in his psyche for the rest of his life.

He discovered Goethe, and began to write poetry in which lay a deep yearning for some ideal past that he'd missed:

> If there had been someone to show me animals or flowers, or taught me how to be happily alone with a book, what love, what blessing I would have had in my heart for him. Instead of which, I walked myself to a standstill ... and passed the time ... which I would later find never long enough. Theseus came into the world in an underground chamber, no matter, he came up like a shoot from a plant: but I grew up in absolute nothingness, up towards nothing ... [Prater, 1986, p. 15]

Throughout his life he was to love many women, through whom he sought what he'd lacked. But the ideal relationship for him was one in which the couple were able to leave one another alone to be separate beings. He inevitably succumbed to fears that he would be subsumed into nothing with a lover, or that she would require too much from him. Some recurrent images, often quite macabre, were of dolls with fixed smiles, and puppets with only the remotest possibility of movement to match their imagination: symbols of his instinctive rebellion against inauthentic modes of being that he felt intimate relationships made inevitable.

Poetry

Rilke often described himself as a paradox. His predominant pursuit in life was that of writing lyric poetry, but in a world dominated by masculine economic and technical skills. After leaving school he had been enrolled by his father at a commercial academy, which he stuck only for a time. It is apt that he was fairly rootless thereafter, and peripatetic in Europe: Vienna, Paris, and at last Switzerland.

In his twenties he had an affair with Lou Andreas-Salome, who took him on a visit to Russia, and also introduced him to psychoanalytic ideas. At that time he changed his name to the masculine, Rainer. Lou wrote an account of their relationship, saying "every man, no matter when I met him in my life always seems to conceal a brother" (Prater, 1986, p. 39).

Lou interpreted many of his anxieties and confusions. As Rilke put it, scientific psychoanalysis might perhaps banish the demons but would most certainly drive out the angels as well (Prater, 1986, p. 201). In 1912, with Lou's approval, he decided against undergoing analysis, even though he was at his most despairing and feeling blocked creatively.

Rilke's faith in life, as well as his awareness of death, was always strong, and even Schopenhauer's pessimism was unable to overwhelm him. But the sense of being an orphan was deep-seated and genuine, judging by the various poems evoking the delicate nostalgia of the isolated soul.

He married an artist, Clara Westhoff, whom he'd met at the Worpswede artistic colony near Bremen, and they had a daughter, but although he was always scrupulously concerned about their welfare, he ceased to live with them. He was fond of women generally and sympathetic to their artistic frustrations arising out of the requirements of family and society, and he had several other affairs throughout his life. Yet, ultimately, his need for solitude prevailed, especially during the period when he was writing *The Duino Elegies* (1912–1922) and the *Sonnets to Orpheus* (1922) (see Rilke, 1980).

Britton has written extensively on Rilke and his poetry as reflecting his inner world, so it is intended here only to draw from a few of Rilke's poems to try to give a sense as to some powerful feelings in him that may be seen as arising from his having been a replacement child. Britton sees it thus, "the phantasied identity with the dead baby sister had provided him with a location for a part of himself that wanted death, that wanted to live in the perpetual womb of the unborn" (Britton, 1998). The third *Duino Elegy* (1913) certainly delves with an uncanny sense into the vortex of prenatal origin.

Beginnings and endings were always intertwined in Rilke. There were two women's deaths which inspired great poetry from him, and I would suggest his mourning words for them are intensified by an early sense of his mother's early absence through incapacity to mourn and let go. First was his *Requiem* (1909) addressed to and for Paula Becker, a friend of Clara's at Worpeswede, of whom he'd been very fond. She was an artist who died young in childbirth, after a marriage of which he disapproved. There's almost an instruction that the dead one does *not* stay around, unlike the continual reflection in his mother's eyes.

> I have my dead, and I have let them go,
> and was amazed to see them so contented,
> so soon at home in being dead, so cheerful,
> so unlike their reputation. Only you
> return; brush past me, loiter, try to knock
> against something, so that the sound reveals
> your presence. Oh don't take from me what I
> am slowly learning. I'm sure you have gone astray
> if you are moved to homesickness for anything
> in this dimension. We transform these Things:
> they aren't real, they are only the reflections
> upon the polished surface of our being.
>   [From *Requiem for a Friend*, 1909; see Rilke, 1980, p. 73]

There was always the presence of absence at the centre of Rilke's life. Absence of a true mother's reverie; presence of something lost to her as well, and also mere narcissistic "surface" in her.

You who never arrived
In my arms, Beloved, who were lost
From the start,
I don't even know what songs would please you. I have given up trying
To recognize you in the surging wave of the next
Moment. All the immense
Images in me—the far-off deeply-felt landscape,
Cities, towers, and bridges, and un-
Suspected turns in the path,
And those powerful lands that were once
Pulsating with the life of the gods -
All rise within me to mean
You, who forever elude me.
     [From *You who have never arrived*, 1913; see Rilke, 1980, p. 131]

It is an absence that gives away the insufficiency in Rilke's self for which he turns back with yearning. The eighth *Elegy* links to his identification with the leaving Ismene–Eurydice/Rainer–Orpheus dichotomy, and shows why that myth came to be specially central to his psyche—the *Sonnets to Orpheus* (1922; see Rilke, 1980) were written, like a gift after the anguish of the *Elegies*, over a few days around the same time.

Who has twisted us around like this, so that
no matter what we do, we are in the posture
of someone going away? Just as, upon
the farthest hill, which shows him his whole valley
one last time, he turns, stops, lingers –,
so we live here, forever taking leave.
     [From the eighth *Duino Elegy*; see Rilke, 1980, p. 193]

In the *Sonnets to Orpheus*, completed five years before he died, he identifies now both with Orpheus in relation to Eurydice; and also Eurydice in relation to Orpheus (who represents the poet). These were inspired after the death of a young woman, Vera Knoop, whom he had barely known, a friend of his daughter. She had shown signs of becoming a great dancer, but then had fallen terminally ill. The poems perhaps also evoke his inner lost sister, sleeping in him.

And it was almost a girl who, stepping from
this single harmony of song and lyre,

appeared to me through her diaphanous form
and made herself a bed inside my ear.
And slept in me. Her sleep was everything:
The awesome trees, the distances I had felt
So deeply that I could touch them, meadows in spring:
All wonders that had ever seized my heart.
She slept the world. Singing god, how was that first
Sleep so perfect that she had no desire
Ever to wake? See: she rose and slept.
Where is her death now? Ah, will you discover
This theme before your song consumes itself?-
Where is she vanishing? . . . A girl, almost . . .
    [*Sonnets to Orpheus, I,* 2; see Rilke, 1980, p. 229]

Conclusion

The coming together of two elements: the integration of a lost sibling in the inner world and the attempt to cope with, if not repair, the impact of a grieving mother links the two writers that have been discussed here. As Green (1986) points out, "these sublimations reveal their incapacity to play a stabilising role in the psychic economy, because the subject remains vulnerable on the particular point, which is his love life". This seems to have been true throughout their lives of both O'Neill and Rilke, neither of whom, preoccupied with absence in their mothers, had fully resolved Oedipal issues, involving reconciliation to the primal scene.

Eugene O'Neill and his elder brother Jamie jointly carried the burden of the loss of the two-year-old Edmund. Jamie was the greater victim. Eugene was able, through his identification with his father, to use playwriting to separate himself over the years from both mother and then Jamie. Most of the biographies seem to gloss rather easily over the lost child, emphasizing much more the mother's addiction; as does O'Neill in perhaps his greatest play. But for Jamie the death was fatal, and Eugene paid his price in his relationships with wives and sons. It is significant that Eugene calls himself by the dead brother's name in *Long Day's Journey into Night*. Atonement or integrated hope? For O'Neill it was hard-nosed reality that was the passionate aim and achievement.

It is, of course, true to say that in assessing material one can find what one is looking for to suit a hypothesis, but Britton's assessment that Rilke was looking for a place to project his desire to return to the womb still leaves room for thinking about how that phantasy arose, and the poetry that is here presented is to suggest that his consciousness of being a replacement for his dead sister suffused his creative energies. He can certainly be said to have been "malignantly mirrored" (Britton, 1998, p. 56) by his mother. This led him to find close relationships taxing, and in the end unsustainable, as he felt they falsified his psychic quest. His poetry was his means of self-analysis, and through that he communicates the struggle he suffered to let his dead self go, symbolically to integrate his early deluded mother and haunting sister, and in the *Sonnets* to find his Orpheus; his inner strength and imagination as poet.

Andre Lussier (1999) writes about "The dead mother", and patients who have not been loved, which may be taken to mean being loved in the sense of being adequately contained.

> Not being loved means worthlessness: it leaves the child alone with the thought that it is better not to be alive than not being loved. . . . With my patients: unable to tolerate the idea of not being loved, they proceeded psychically to replace the actual world (mother) by an imaginary one, thus managing to avoid psychosis. [p. 155]

This would perhaps link with Kenneth Wright's (2000) interesting suggestion that the artist always lives on the edge of a no-mother abyss.

Nevertheless, in artistic terms both O'Neill and Rilke were successful psychically, in terms of transformation to the depressive position as represented in their work, without which they could not have so movingly affecting their audiences. The capacity to create artistically can be a crucial means for working through the pain and suffering of a bleak inner world, and it is hoped that these examples have shown this in quite differing ways. The artistic outcomes for O'Neill and Rilke range from tragic through to sublime, but, for both, the work certainly functioned as vital container.

References

Bion, W. R. (1962). *Learning from Experience*. London: Karnac.

Black, S. A. (1999). *Eugene O'Neill, Beyond Mourning and Tragedy*. CT: Yale University Press.

Britton, R. (1998). *Belief and Imagination*. London: Routledge.

Cain, A. C., & Cain, B. S. (1964). On replacing a child. *Journal of American Academy of Child Psychiatry*, 3: 443–447.

Commins, D. B. (Ed.) (1986). *Love and Admiration and Respect: The O'Neill–Commins Correspondence*. Durham: Duke University Press.

Etchegoyen, A. (1997). Inhibition of mourning and the replacement child syndrome. In: J. Raphael-Leff & R. J. Perelberg (Eds.), *Female Experience* (pp. 195–215). London: Routledge.

Freud, S. (1917e). Mourning and melancholia. *S.E.*, *14*. London: Hogarth.

Freud, S. (1920g). Beyond the pleasure principle. *S.E.*, *18*: London: Hogarth.

Freud, S. (1921c). Group psychology and the analysis of the ego. *S.E.*, *18*. London: Hogarth.

Gelb, A., & Gelb, B. (1964). *O'Neill*. New York: Harper and Rowe.

Graff, W. L. (1956). *Rainer Maria Rilke: Creative Anguish of a Modern Poet*. Boston, MA: Princeton University Press.

Green, A. (1986). The dead mother. In: *On Private Madness* (pp. 142–173). London: Karnac.

Klein, M. (1940). Mourning and its relation to manic depressive states. In: *The Writings of Melanie Klein*, Volume I, *Love, Guilt and Reparation and Other Works 1921–45*. London: Hogarth.

Lewis, E. (1983). Stillbirth: psychological consequences and strategies of management. In: A. Milunsky, E. A. Friedman, & L. Gluck (Eds.), *Advances in Perinatal Medecine*, Vol. 3 (pp. 205–245). New York: Plenum.

Lieberman, S., & Black, D. (1987). Loss, mourning and grief. In: A. Bentovim, Gorell Barnes, & A. Cooklin (Eds.), *Family Therapy: Complementary Frameworks of Theory and Practice* (pp. 251–265). London: Academic Press.

Lubin, A. J. (1975). *Stranger on the Earth: A Psychological Biography of Vincent Van Gogh*. St. Albans: Paladin.

Lussier, A. (1999). The dead mother: variations on a theme. In: G. Kohon (Ed.), *The Dead Mother: The Work of Andre Green* (pp. 149–162). London: Brunner-Routledge.

Manheim, M. (1982). *Eugene O'Neill's New Language of Kinship*. Syracuse University Press.

Meissner, W. W. (1992). Vincent's suicide—a psychic autopsy. *Contemporary Psychoanalysis*, *28*: 675–694.

Meissner, W. W. (1993). Vincent: the self-portraits. *Psychoanalytic Quarterly*, 62: 74–105.

Meissner, W. W. (1994). The theme of the double and creativity in Vincent Van Gogh. *Contemporary Psychoanalysis*, 30: 323–347.

Meltzer, D. (1973). Tyranny. In: *Sexual States of Mind* (pp. 143–150). Strath Tay, Perthshire: Clunie Press.

Meltzer, D., & Willams, M. H. (1988). Addendum 1—Interview with Adrian Stokes in *The Apprehension of Beauty* (pp 206–226). Strath Tay, Perthshire: Clunie Press.

Nagera, H. (1967). *Vincent Van Gogh*. CT: International Universities Press.

Nietzsche, F. (1927). *The Birth of Tragedy*. C. P. Fadiman (Trans.). London: Constable.

O'Neill, E. (1926). *The Great God Brown*. London: Nick Hern, 1995.

O'Neill, E. (1931). *Mourning Becomes Elektra*. London: Nick Hern, 1992.

O'Neill, E. (1945). *A Moon for the Misbegotten*. London: Nick Hern, 1992.

O'Neill, E. (1956). *Long Day's Journey into Night*. London: Nick Hern, 1992.

O'Neill, E. (1988). *Complete Plays, 1913–1920; Complete Plays, 1932–1943*. New York: Library of America.

Poznansky. E. O. (1972). The replacement child. *Behavioural Pediatrics*, 8: 1190–1193.

Prater, D. (1986). *A Ringing Glass. A Life of R. M. Rilke*. Oxford: Clarendon Press.

Rilke, R. M. (1980). *The Selected Poetry of Rainer Maria Rilke*. Stephen Mitchell (Trans.). London: Picador.

Rosenfeld, H. (1965). On drug addiction. In: *Psychotic States* (pp. 128–143). London: Karnac.

Rosenfeld, H. (1987). *Impasse and Interpretation*. London: Tavistock/ Routledge.

Rowe, J., Clyman, R., Green, C., Mikkelsen, C., Haight, J., & Ataide, L. (1978). Follow-up of families who experience a perinatal death. *Paediatrics*, 62: 166–170.

Sabbadini, A. (1988). The replacement child. *Contemporary Analysis*, 24: 528–547.

Segal, H. (1991). *Dream Phantasy and Art*. London: Tavistock/ Routledge.

Sheaffer, L. (1973). *O'Neill: Son and Artist*. London: Paul Elek.

Steiner, J. (1993). *Psychic Retreats*. London: Routledge.

Wright, K. (2000). To make experience sing. In: L. Caldwell (Ed.), *Art, Creativity, Living* (pp. 75–96), London: Karnac.

PART II
CLINICAL THEORY

CHAPTER SIX

Sibling trauma: a theoretical consideration

Juliet Mitchell

I n 1928, introducing the topic of psychoanalysis and siblings to
the American Psychiatric Association, Oberndorf claimed:

> The very presence of the second sibling, irrespective of age or sex,
> creates an entirely different and determining environment and one
> finds it not infrequent that the one sibling so centres his interest
> upon the other that this relationship almost literally represents all
> the world to him . . . In the very early years of child life, the sibling
> relationships may quite overshadow anything else in the environ-
> ment. [Oberndorf 1928, pp. 1013, 1019]

One colleague, a Dr Gregory, raised a question to open the
discussion. He asked for an opinion on a patient with murderous
hatred of her mother. The President-Chairman questioned the relevance to the siblings. Dr Gregory could not discover the relevance
and Dr Oberndorf was left describing the hatred that succeeds
fantasies of maternal incest—the Oedipus complex. There was no
other discussion; siblings, as far as one can tell from the report,
were not mentioned.

There are good theoretical and doubtless good *ad feminam/ hominem* reasons for the difficulty in sustaining a place for siblings in our understanding of unconscious psychic life—the task of psychoanalysis. Indeed, the problem is more general: by and large within the social sciences in general, and certainly within all the postulates of psychoanalysis, our theoretical models of relationships and of meaning embrace only a vertical dimension and lateral relationships structured along a horizontal axis have to be read off this.

This chapter is an attempt to open up the question of a theoretical model of sibling–sibling relations from the perspective of psychoanalysis. That we do not have one is well-recorded. Colonna and Newman noted in 1983:

> Many hours are devoted to the [important role of siblings] in the analysis of patients, but the literature does not accurately reflect this. . . . If one compares the extensive literature on the parent–child relationship, the role of early object-relations, and the many reexaminations of the Oedipus complex . . . with the few papers focused directly on siblings, it becomes apparent that the reasons for this neglect require an explanation. [Colonna & Newman, 1983, p. 305]

I am concerned not with the presence or absence of publications addressing siblings, but with the fact that the topic comes and goes. I believe this is because we do not have a theoretical model: descriptions and observations that do not develop such a model have a limited shelf-life. The fact that siblings insist on returning for explanation may be because there is some change in the social basis that gradually and unevenly is being reflected in our mental constructions (Mitchell, 2004); alternatively or additionally, it may be because their persistent presence goes on demanding its own model of explanation. Although the first question is extremely interesting, it is this latter possibility that is my focus here.

Against the insistence of siblings, arguments for their subservience to the Oedipal-castration vertical model or to the pre-Oedipal area are strong. They have been resistant to all but different relational models coming particularly effectively from group psychoanalysis (Brown, 1998; Brunori, 1998; Hopper, 2003). It seems to me the question of an independent paradigm that would offer a causal role in psychic life to siblings is very much an open one still.

The vertical model of psychoanalysis revolves around the twin poles of trauma and desire: desire for the mother that is eliminated through the threatened trauma of castration. The bisexual child, girl or boy, is identified with its own phallus at the moment when it grasps that there are people (women) without such an "identity". I am not concerned here with the rights or wrongs or variations of this theoretical explanation of the structuring of unconscious mental life. I am asking only: is it possible to envisage an equivalent of the horizontal plane for the laterality of siblings? To examine this here, on this occasion, I concentrate on what I consider to be the specific psychoanalytic meaning and implications of trauma, leaving desire for another day. I am not attempting to contribute to the extremely rich literature on trauma. My aim is briefly to specify the place of trauma in psychoanalytical theory in order to ask whether siblings have a place, or what place they have, there.

The birth of a sibling is frequently described, both colloquially and in the psychoanalytical literature, as "traumatic" for the older child, particularly the toddler at the height of his/her phallic omnipotence: ". . . the mother's pregnancy and the sibling's birth may act as a traumatic stimulant *if* internal or external conditions disturb the child's reaction to these 'average, expectable events' " (Volkan & Ast, 1997, p. 13, my italics). A model of the kind I am seeking must make use of some generalizable factor if it is to involve causality. Thus, if sibling birth does not need to be "traumatic", as Volkan and Ast imply, then there is nothing of use here for such a model.

However, before accepting this variability of the traumatic effect, we need further to define trauma. I suggest we want a grid (not in Bion's sense) to express the widespread use of "traumatic" along a range of implications. That by Volkan and Ast above I shall call a "weak" use; it is descriptive but not determining. This does not in any way imply its unimportance, simply its status as a model-provider. Weak trauma could influence the shape of the psychopathological and of character, but not be influential in causing aspects of them to come into being. The weak use of trauma could be easily supplanted by the terms "shock" or "disturbance". The "strong" use of trauma, by contrast, can only mean "trauma" and thus it has a specific limited meaning. I believe, however, that there are differences within the "strong" trauma that are relevant to model-building.

A psychological trauma in the strong sense is like a physical trauma—a shock or wound that because of its excessive strength breaks through a surface. Here it breaks through not the skin or muscle to something within, but the psychological barriers that are in place. The implosion releases unbound energy within the organism. This, and its implications, are referred to by a "trauma" in general in its "strong" sense.

In the weak sense, as indicating extreme difficulty, trauma can be viewed as part of development; this is not so with strong trauma. The strong trauma does not change or develop, it is absolute for all time; it cannot be repressed or defended against. Time heals simply because the space the trauma occupies gets smaller and smaller as life's other experiences crowd in around it, as human kindnesses reassure the sufferer that they are loved and their life matters. As Elizabeth Barrett Browning recalls on the birth of her brother in "Sonnets from the Portuguese";

> Betwixt me and the dreadful outer brink
> Of obvious death, where I, who thought to sink,
> Was caught up into love, and taught the whole
> Of a new rhythm. [quoted in Earnshaw, 1995, p. 23]

However, the "strong" trauma is always there and will, for example, emerge again and be "reused" if there is another trauma in later life.

There is a necessary further characteristic of "trauma" if its understanding is to function as a building block of a possible model—can the trauma, like that within the castration complex, be a key part of the structuring of psychic life. I can only provisionally describe such a trauma as a trauma within a complex. For the trauma to be part of a complex that sets up unconscious life, it must derive not from nature (to which it may refer) but from culture. This sets up a key distinction within "strong" trauma. An earthquake may break through psychological barriers—but the law that prohibits incest, even though it is realized through nature, is man-made. The castration complex is the example: the trauma is when the small child realizes that the most important person in its world—the mother—has not got a penis and this applies to half the human race. Of course, women are not really castrated, but this natural state is classified as castration. If prohibition on incest is infringed, a strong trauma results—but it is more than this because the perception of the absence of the penis is itself already traumatic, the trauma has already occurred and, given the timelessness of trauma, will repeat itself to some degree throughout life.

Notoriously, Freud first considered some psychopathologies, most particularly hysteria, were caused by the delayed effects of a father's seduction of his young child. In the sense of understanding the mechanisms of unconscious processes, psychoanalysis came into being when this proposed particular trauma instead was viewed as a trauma that arose because a social law might be infringed not by the actual abuse of the parent but by the incest of the child in fantasy.

In reality after the First World War, with all the questions it threw up around the issue of traumatic neurosis, Otto Rank returned to the first notion of trauma, only this time proposing the trauma of actual birth. He proposed that our psychic life *in toto* was a response to the trauma of birth. He developed a common theme— that birth is experienced with so great a degree of anxiety that all later anxiety attacks and, hence, all neuroses, are efforts to abreact this primal anxiety; all struggles are struggles to return to the first "safe" mother of before birth. Trauma is here equated with excessive shock and therefore is being used with a weak meaning.[1] Rank was concerned not with the trauma but the resultant anxiety. In response, Freud reviewed the question of the danger (the "trauma") that occasions the anxiety as well as the nature of anxiety itself.

All the literature on siblings confronts us with the importance of trauma in the weak sense of the word—something that can be overcome in the course of development. What we need to know first is whether the arrival, real or imagined, of a new baby is a trauma in the weak or strong sense. The list of problems of sibling reception includes eating disorders, phobias, bed-wetting, imaginary companions, hatred, violence, "false selves", serious illnesses, night horrors, and terror of death. As a very active paediatrician, Donald Winnicott, the psychoanalyst, realized how prevalent or how exacerbated was the toddler's illness when a new baby was born (Winnicott, 1931). I greeted my own brother's birth with scarlet fever. Are these cross-culturally recorded illnesses (Mitchell, 2003) the response to a bad experience (weak trauma) or the result of a strong trauma? Many parents argue that their child has had no adverse response to the sibling. Until thinking about siblings, I had experienced my own illness, not the advent of my brother, as traumatic. Many parents are of the same opinion. Parents do not want to know. In her autobiography, Jungian analyst Judith Hubback tells how

> My aunt Rhona, my grandparents' third daughter, had what I thought was a bad squint, which I noticed when she came to visit my own family on some occasion. I was told, it seemed to me belatedly, since my mother had often talked about her childhood, that Muriel, the second girl, had pushed Rhona off a wall they had climbed onto. She had fallen onto a holly hedge, and lost the sight of her eye. The story illustrates how a tragic event, resulting from fairly ordinary childhood aggression between sisters, had to be concealed. [Hubback, 2003]

If sisterly "tiffs" result in blindness, turning a blind eye is likely. But is this just a somewhat extreme example of a normative denial? Does our parental reluctance translate into our clinical and analytical refusal to take the strong trauma of the sibling and its implications for incest and violence seriously enough? Just as when we were children, and we did not want to know about the sibling's arrival, so as adults we do not want to know about either our own murderousness nor about that of our own children. If there is denial we are looking at a strong trauma with all that it implies.

Winnicott describes the crazed and ill pre-Oedipal toddler as "utterly normal" and, like war-traumatized soldiers, indeed she/he is. She/he has been just knocked temporarily off-kilter. The child would be suffering from a traumatic (strong sense) neurosis caused by an actual event. However, the recurrence of these illnesses in puberty and adolescence must make us ask whether they are not responses to trauma not only in the strong sense but also in the "complex" sense of the term.

The grid so far suggests a primary division into weak and strong trauma and then a further division within strong neurosis into actual or traumatic neuroses and complex or psychogenic neuroses to which, to date, only the castration complex has laid claim.

How can we establish whether or not we are dealing with a traumatic/actual or psychogenic neurosis within the strong trauma? In 1920 Freud had observed the small child try to master the trauma of helplessness he felt when he was left by his mother. His game of enacting her departure and return was compulsively repetitious (Freud, 1920g). This repetition is the mark of the trauma facing the engagement of automatic "biological" anxiety and ego-anxiety: the unbound energy released by the trauma within the organism produces an involuntary, automatic anxiety, the ego tries to get hold of this anxiety to bind the unbound energy and to use the anxiety as a warning signal to prevent the trauma happening again. The compulsion to repeat marks a trauma in the strong sense. The question then would be whether the compulsion to repeat the trauma could be found in traumatic sibling relations along a horizontal axis. I believe it can. I shall illustrate this before going on to consider the organizational "complex" aspect of a strong trauma and its distinction from actual/traumatic neurosis.

The psychological illnesses of childhood have either implicitly been understood as weak trauma or as "actual neuroses", or inter-preted as psychogenic but caused by Oedipal-castration problems. In looking at the trauma—both actual and psychogenic—through its expression as compulsively repeated, I am looking at strong trauma and asking whether it is understandable horizontally. The childhood maladies could be a response to a weak trauma and therefore a part of development; if they are compulsively repeated, they are strong trauma and not subject to development.

In an unusual, indeed quirky, book that can plunge the reader back into Wilhelm Fliess's theories of periodicity, Australian psy-chiatrist and psychotherapist, Averil Earnshaw argues for what she calls "Family" as opposed to "Clock time" (Earnshaw, 1995). Her title, *Time will Tell*, and subtitle, "What was I doing at my child's age now? What happened to my parents at this time in their lives?", explain her theme. We repeat crises across generations: "We need to connect ourselves in ages with our parents, and with our children. Failing this, we find ourselves doing strange things, falling ill, and involving other people in our personal dramas" (*ibid.*, p. 13). Earnshaw's material is fascinating. From the fifty-one lives of famous people that Earnshaw recounts (they include Freud and Jung) I shall select Sylvia Plath as certainly extreme, but also typical.[2]

- When Sylvia, the first of two children was born, her mother was twenty-six. Sylvia gave birth to Frieda, the first of her two children when she was twenty-seven.
- Sylvia's mother, Amelia, gave birth to her second child, Sylvia's brother, Warren, when she was twenty-nine. Sylvia gives birth to Nicholas, Frieda's brother, when she is twenty-nine. Sylvia and Frieda were two and three-quarters and two and a half respectively when each of their brothers was born.
- Between Frieda's and Nicholas's births, Sylvia had a late miscarriage and an appendectomy—as though awaiting to be twenty-nine to give birth?
- When Frieda was three and Nicholas aged one, Sylvia committed suicide.

Earnshaw discovers innumerable age "coincidences" of this kind. She speculates about the possible inscription of DNA, about telepathy, and finally settles for an explanation that we have to live in our lives what our parents repress from their knowledge of their own lives. But what evidence is there that Sylvia's mother (Amelia) was repressing something relevant? Of her own life, Earnshaw writes: "When I had reached my mother's age when my young brother was born, I was the one who became ill. My mother remained well. Why?" Siblings, I consider answer this question for Earnshaw as for Plath.

I suggest that the coincidental dates across generations are fun signposts but not the issue. The issue is the compulsive repetition of a trauma. If we look at the experience of a trauma, it is of the annihilation or "death" of the subject. Suffused by the unbounded energy, overwhelmed by automatic anxiety, "me" is wiped out, for the moment at least. While making use of the coincidences of ages, the substantive enquiry should be about this "death" and its inverse in creativity:

- Sylvia identifies with her mother and "creates" a girl like herself.
- A new baby, however, "reminds" her of that new baby when she was two and three-quarters: her brother, Warren.
- She is very ambivalent about babies: narcissistically loving the replica of herself (Sylvia/Frieda); hating the one who replaces her (Warren/Frieda).

- She miscarries; something goes wrong inside, her appendix.
- Nicholas is born.
- Sylvia kills herself.

Read through death, this is the psychic trajectory of the sibling with the sibling. Earnshaw quotes Plath: "A baby. I hated babies. I who for two and a half years had been the centre of a tender universe felt the axis wrench and a polar chill immobilise my bones. I would be a bystander" (p. 126).

It is Earnshaw, not her mother, who becomes ill because it was the little girl who became ill originally. When fifteen months old, Earnshaw had nearly died of gastro-enteritis: sitting on her mother's lap, she would have been very aware that something was wrong with her mother's swollen belly, which three months later turned into her brother. Earnshaw was haunted by her own imminent or "already-taken-place" death throughout her childhood: her older brothers' ejected her from a fast-moving pram; her mother conceived her younger brother when she was three months old. Like Winnicott's patient, the Piggle, or any other small child, she did not know what she felt or who she was, *she* was no one (see Mitchell, 2003):

> The mother said that there had been a great change toward ill health in the Piggle recently. She was not naughty and she was nice to the baby. It was difficult to put into words what the matter was. *But she was not herself. In fact she refused to be herself and said so: "I'm the baby"*. She was not to be addressed as herself. She had developed a high-voiced chatter which was not hers. [Winnicott, 1978, p. 13, my italics][3]

The dethroned child makes a shallow or "hysterical" identification with the mother, who should protect her from traumatic helplessness, and with the new baby who is being thus protected. In later life when compulsively re-enacted, this therefore will be intergenerational. The age coincidences are the unconscious numbers game of these identifications. They are not the point. I suggest that our love of coincidences misleads us into seeing this repetition only along a vertical axis. The serious trauma of being "not oneself", "beside oneself", "out of one's mind" is a lateral dynamic and compulsively repeated can have the seriousness of the original experience: Plath commits suicide.

Plath miscarried her second child. Her first, Frieda, will have unconsciously been both herself and her brother. A small-scale study conducted in New Haven, Connecticut of interviews with mothers found that a majority of mothers thought of their first-born as a re-edition of their brother or sister. Earnshaw found that most of the creative people she read about, produced their creations at the same age as the same-sex parent procreated or conceived them. Again, the point is not the age, but the interplay of creativity and annihilation. A first child will be both oneself and one's sibling— the latter annihilates but one was also missing at the "primal" scene of one's own conception.[4]

That her first child would have unconsciously recalled her brother may well have accounted for Plath's difficulty in conceiving her second child—unconsciously she was still living the traumatic experience of Warren, the second child's birth. Like her own daughter, until that moment she had been unique. Her brother displaced her, traumatically making her feel she was only a bystander at the cot-side of life that he had come to represent in her place. As a two and three-quarter-year-old child who had lost her place and her identity, she identified herself with the salient others, with her mother and with the baby brother, the first a vertical, the second a horizontal, identification.

Plath would have identified with the baby. But it was a baby she wished dead. Identified, then, with a dead baby, she miscarries, and then becomes ill with something wrong inside her (appendicitis) in an identification with a hated foetus. We learn that when her brother Warren was born she had become both a terrible "trouble-maker" and a "false-self", acting as a perfect little wife to her father—"not herself", the self which was displaced, traumatized, "dead". Simultaneously, she became the loved brother whom she wanted dead. In a version of a classical hysterical identification (see Freud, 1926d)—you want to be your baby brother; well, be your baby brother—he is a brother you want dead, be a dead baby. When her own live son is born she feels as she did as the little girl when her live baby brother arrived—she experiences herself as doubly dead— dead because Warren has replaced her, dead because she wants to be the Warren she has imaginatively killed. She kills herself.

It would seem from these observations that it is possible to consider that the compulsively repeated trauma of the sibling birth is a "strong trauma"—the compulsion indicates its status: what is repeated is the traumatic annihilation of the subject through the sibling who replaces it. For her pilot survey, the central question Earnshaw asked her hundred randomly selected interviewees enabled her to calculate the year when her respondent had "reached the same-sex parent's age when the next child was born"—what is significant is not the age but the repetition of a strong trauma. Four out of five of the biographies of the famous lives Earnshaw studied demonstrated this. The compulsion to repeat the trauma may well choose, but it also may not, a date that coincides with the original hysterical identification by the displaced child with its mother and with the new baby.

What we are witnessing in Earnshaw's minefield of examples, is the repeated continued presence of the sibling birth and hence a strong trauma. A strong trauma, is not, however, necessarily an "organizing" one. It could, so to speak, still be picked up and used by the organizing function of the castration complex that succeeds it. I have previously initiated the question of whether or not it is the castration complex or something else as well, using hysteria (Mitchell, 2000) and, much more briefly, psychopathy (Mitchell, 2003). Here, to illustrate the argument, I shall turn to panic attacks which, according to a recent commentator, Franco de Masi (de Masi, 2004), have replaced hysteria in diagnostic popularity. I would argue that a panic attack is an expression of the repetition of a strong trauma—real or imagined.

In conjunction with thinking clinically, I will use de Masi's account of panic attacks simply as material to ask the question about siblings and trauma (not, of course, de Masi's question). I want, however, just to highlight one aspect: in de Masi's account, he describes how what is feared appears, in fact, to have already taken place. This is the same formulation as Winnicott's threatening future catastrophe having already occurred in the past. The patient, as in a delusion, lapses into nameless dread (de Masi/Bion). What has already taken place is the annihilation of the subject, his own psychosomatic death. When recently I asked an ex-soldier what had terrified him most, the answer came: "Being strafed by friendly fire." Psychoanalysts and others usually stop here, as this typical answer is taken to indicate the crucial removal of those who should protect one, typically parents. They have become attackers. I am more interested in the next response: Question: "Did you think you were about to die?" Answer: "I thought I was already dead."

The panic attack or an actual new trauma repeats an old one *that is still there*. One is already dead. De Masi records the same "already dead" in the panic attack.

De Masi notes two stages to the panic attack—the first psychological, the second an uncontrolled somatic anxiety:

> patients will identify any unusual signal (a heart palpitation, a muscle ache) until, in a frenzy of anxiety, their imagination will end up construing the danger that sets off the sense of fear. It is this psychic–emotive component that, if not stopped, will lead into a fall into somatic terror. [De Masi, 2004, p. 313]

I believe this sequence reverses the order of the trauma, which strikes first somatically and then records the ego's desperate struggle to get hold of the overwhelming anxiety. If so, the panic attack will itself—like hysteria—be a part of the latter effort.

Of the panic episode De Masi writes:

> It is like a repetitive micro-delusion exposing the patient to a concrete experience of dying, suddenly facing him with a "nameless dread" and provoking in him that fear of annihilation, biological as well as psychological, that has the power of destructuring the mind and damaging any sense of existential continuity and integrity. For such a destabilising effect to occur, the trauma must be experienced in conditions of total loneliness and impotence. [*ibid.*, p. 321]

The nameless dread, the catastrophe, the loneliness of the trauma are usually taken to refer to the earliest helplessness of the neonate. Freud's response to Rank's proposal of trauma of birth can be fitted in here. Freud notes the trauma (strong sense) causes overwhelming biological anxiety, then the emergent ego's effort to get hold of it as a warning; the salient feature is "helplessness". Bion has probably produced the nearest thing we have to a theoretical model of this earliest universal stage. What concerns me with any account of the neonatal psychic experience is not that it has to be a hypothesis but that it does not (perhaps it cannot) take account of social laws. I would suggest that it is when this earliest trauma of helplessness is repeated in the context of sibling birth that social laws impact on drives and desires to affect the structure of unconscious mental processes. These laws will affect giving birth (Mitchell, 2003); sex (desire) and violence (trauma). It is these laws that will set up the dividing line within strong trauma between actual trauma leading to traumatic neurosis and psychogenic, "complex" organizing trauma.

Before taking further the understanding of sibling trauma at a theoretical level, I want very briefly to look at three aspects of one human phenomenon that can be used to consider the question of social law and human drive/desire. These are the social constraints on first, parental violence; second, warfare; and third, rape and domestic violence. All indicate that there would seem to be a desire for violence and a prohibition against it.

First, parents: at one end of the scale we have child abuse, at the other what is considered legitimate punishment. The parent must want to commit some act of violence. Of mothers, Winnicott, trying to rescue the baby from Klein's attribution of primal envy, wrote that he *knew* the mother's hatred came before that of her offspring. The considerations of maternal ambivalence or primary preambivalence have a long history; but from both parents their uncontrolled or controlled violence is cross-culturally notable, although in greatly varying degrees. This violence is intergenerational and can be explained as the failure (abuse) or success (punishment) of the parent in internalizing a protective/punishing superego following the castration complex and growing up to put it into practice. But there may not be only this vertical violence operating in this scenario. We can use the increasing number of child-headed households that are coming into being as the world's poor and rich grow further apart to ask if there is not also a sibling dynamic in play in the parents' hating-violence. "The Mother" is a fictional account of a little girl in Bombay.

> I have been looking after my younger brothers and sisters since I was five years old. I can proudly say that I have brought up all my brothers and sisters, because what with Mother's pregnancies and the many mouths to feed, both Mother and Father have had to work hard, so that we have something to eat at the end of the day.

I walked him. I sang to him. I talked to him. But he would not stop crying, and I was tired of carrying him and wanted to throw him on the pavement. I just wanted to rest on my quilt for a while and run on the streets like a bird, without the burden of any of my brothers or sisters.

At the end of the day my brother was crying so much that pedestrians were telling me to take care of him. I was so angry with him that I threatened to throw him under the bus. But it was of no use. He seemed to be crying much more than before, so I also sat down on the ground and cried with him.

I was frightened, as he seemed to get the hiccups and looked as though he was fainting. I thought I had killed my brother.

I wanted my mother, but did not know where she was. Then I did what my mother would have done to stop him from crying. I opened my blouse and gave him the nipple of my yet unformed breast. He stopped crying and looked up at me. He did not know the difference, and I was crying like my mother. [David, 1999, 105–108]

The social sibling care among the wretched of the earth would spell out as the psychological care and play-acting "little mother" of the Western world. Every mother and every father too, had or expected to have a younger sibling. A child-mother may wish to throw the baby under a bus, disciplining is scarcely allowed her until she is a biological or an adult parent. Although we must always remember that in *Great Expectations* it was Pip's older sister who brought him up "by hand". Every parent expresses or controls his/her own sibling violence, his/her simultaneous love/hate, for "It is a curious subject of observation and enquiry whether hatred and love be not the same thing at bottom. Each, in its utmost development, supposes a high degree of intimacy and heart-knowledge" (Hawthorne, 1850, p. 212).

Second: warfare. Despite all Oedipal explanations, warfare would seem to me so obviously a lateral scenario. It is predominantly male–male violence, and runs from the not- sanctioned destruction, as with terrorism, via Antigone's two brothers, Polynices and Eteocles, to the sanctioned so-called "legitimate war". Abu Graib is a recent reminder that this violence, abusive or legitimate, can be heterosexual, too. As with parental punishment, where the law is specifically placed will be culturally variable: one man's legitimate warfare is another man's terrorism and vice versa. The point here is that it, too, is on a continuum from asocial abuse to sanctioned violence, hence a social law must intervene to demarcate the two.

Third: rape and domestic violence. Here again the lateral dimension makes good sense: there is widespread sibling incest and big brothers attack little sisters and in the end even small brothers may be the stronger. Crucially, historically and cross-culturally versions of both sexual rape and domestic violence are sometimes sanctioned. What is abuse to us is punishment in other cultures. However, the main point here is that we are once again on a continuum from abuse to permission; something is prohibited, something allowed.

A social prohibition is psychically all-important. In attempting to restrict the desire and the representation of the drive—in this case to kill, the social prohibition ensures that this representation will be repressed (or otherwise defended against). This means that it will be disallowed from within, not from an external rule. But it will also mean that the repressed will return and a psychic conflict ensue, producing symptoms such as those we see attached to sibling relations. Because war has been understood only on a vertical Oedipal–castration model, its violence is understood as a regression to the pre-Oedipal. But this is to fail to see that war is not only the unruliness of say, a pre-Oedipal anal-sadistic phase, it is also the conflict between internalized laws against killing and the return of the repressed ego-orgasm in the ecstasy of liberated murder.

Most accounts see violence and wars as a survival of savagery—of the naked ape of our unsocialized pre-Oedipal infancy. This cannot be entirely or even mainly correct. For wars, although their traumatic effects are exactly what breach symbolization, nevertheless are themselves, just as much as peace, the objects of symbolization.

In his epic chronicle of the Mediterranean world (1949), Fernand Braudel opened his chapter "Forms of War" with the observation:

> War is not simply the antithesis of civilisation. Historians refer constantly to war without really knowing or seeking to know its true nature—or natures. We are as ignorant about war as the physicist is [ignorant] of the true nature of matter. [p. 836]

As Braudel points out, the artefacts of war are as much a part of civilization as are those of peace. There is no simple regression to barbarism, simply a line across the continuum of violence. What we need to understand is the dialectical relationship between different forms of war—why sometimes crusades, sometimes "cold" wars, world wars, terrorism, piracy, and so on?

The strong trauma is of an annihilation of the narcissistic ego, the trauma will come again, be replenished, be imagined—in new trauma, in aspects of psychopathology, in compulsively repetitive behaviour, in the cruel theatre of the panic attack. But new life is also exciting, lovable, and the murderous hate that succeeds the traumatic annihilation contains both infantile love/sex and violence. Otherwise, there is a masochistic turning around on the self, as in Plath's melancholia of suicide, when no one is there psychically for the sufferer, not even her own two small children.

The strong, unrepresentable trauma that makes meaningful the social prohibition is the danger to the subject if the outgoing violence to the newly discovered "other" is not controlled. You may not (or at least only sometimes) kill your brother or your sister. If you do—you too will be killed (Polynices and Eteocles) as you already have been in the psychic death (the first stage of the trauma) occasioned by the other's arrival. Because there is desire, drive, and social prohibition, the prospective trauma of murdering and being murdered is made real by the already psychically experienced annihilation on the other's birth or prospective birth. Psychological conflict, with all its symptoms, ensues; these can be turned back to their representations and made conscious. We have here a "complex". As such, it must be available to everyone: the only child, the last child, is no more exempt than the older child. Yvonne Kapp, the second and last child, was ten years old when she imagined her mother (ill with appendicitis) was pregnant:

> ... all this time some unborn brother or sister of mine had been lying under my mother's heart and she never told me. I felt betrayed and, at the same time, a feeling I had never before experienced, an emotion so powerful and so violent swept over me that I thought it must destroy me. There was a strange tightening in my belly and a dreadful weight or terror and hatred of I knew not what.

This anguish, now fastened upon me like some gnawing animal, was intensified by the blazing heat of those days from which, like the pain, there was no escape. What I went through then, concentrated into little more than a few days, was a lifetime's savage and ungovernable jealousy of a younger sibling. That torment remains in essence indescribable, but it poisoned every waking moment. I did not know, of course, that it was jealousy, but I did know that in some horrible way my feelings were shameful and this added an overwhelming sense of guilt to my burdened spirit. [Kapp, 2003, pp. 38–39]

It is a strong trauma. If we turn back to the original observation of the small child mastering his mother's absence in what has become the famous, compulsively repetitious game with a cotton-reel, we can observe it has two dimensions. The thrown-away and retrieved cotton-reel represents the mother. But the child also plays at appearing and disappearing in the mirror. The first game is inter-generational, vertical; the second, lateral, horizontal. The compulsion to repeat indicates a strong trauma that can be a along a vertical or horizontal axis.

However, the disappearing infant subject itself is not being anni-hilated as a result of a social prohibition except in the sense of the cultural necessity to give up its sense of narcissistic totality. This I will call "customary".

When both the Oedipus complex and the sibling arrive the social law threatens to destroy the subject if she/he persists in her/his desire—the desire for incest with the sibling as a repetition of the subject (narcissistic love) and for murder of the sibling if it is not the same as the subject. The trauma that makes real the threat of the social law is the annihilation of the body-ego when the sibling arrives or is expected. The presence of the sibling is the absence of the subject, and this "knowledge" of being annihilated underlies the trauma that makes real the prohibition on violence, the social law that says "thou shalt not kill" (on the whole) those who are classed as siblings.

The customary demand to give up the omnipresence of the mother and of the "self" produces a strong trauma that is evidenced in its compulsive repetition. The law against sibling incest and murder is a prohibition on a social desire that is made real by the trauma of annihilation; again, a strong trauma, and this time a part of an organizing complex. In child-punishment, rape and domestic violence, warfare, what breaks through as "abuse" is the prohibited desire. It is the wish to kill that returns from repression as can be witnessed in the ease with which the legitimated violence spills over into abusive excess. This can be directed to the self, as with Plath's suicide, or to the other—both demand that one thinks laterally. When the effects of the trauma of war persist through the lifetime of the sufferer (Showalter, 1997) we are likely to be looking not only at the horrors the victim experiences, but at the bursting through from unconsciousness of the horrors he wanted to inflict, but would normally have not been allowed to by his own superego.

Although it can be a weak trauma as well, the replacement of the subject by the sibling and the violence it unleashes would seem to be a strong trauma ranging from the actual through the customary to the lawful or organizationally complex and embracing all three strong dimensions. It is the latter that can lay claim to providing a possible model of the horizontal axis, which contributes to the construction of unconscious processes.

Furthermore, there seems some justification for seeing the sibling trauma as not exactly equivalent but as an analogy to the castration trauma and not to Otto Rank's trauma of birth (Rank, 1999). If so, this is a trauma whose threat "enforces" the laws against the violence that we as siblings so ardently desire. It is an "organizing" trauma. While it is enacted or compulsively repeated it cannot be understood; if it cannot be understood then there can be no ethics in which we respect the other and ourselves as other to that sibling other.[5] For this reason, above all, we need to know whether or not we have here a possible way of conceptualizing an autonomous model for lateral relations along a horizontal axis.

Notes

1. Birth could be used for a strong trauma in that who is allowed to give birth is culturally prescribed. The experience of birth could then be used to give meaning to the prohibition, but this was not Rank's point (Mitchell, 2000).

2. The *raison-d'être* of psychoanalytic theory is that psychopathology is useful to understand so-called normality as it offers normal processes writ large or in bright colours. This is why Plath is useful.

3.   There will also be a mimetic element to the toddler's illness: the parturient mother goes to hospital or, if giving birth at home, must seem to the child to be undergoing something like death pangs. This can be repeated in hysteria and the couvade.

4.   Because of the shibboleth of the Oedipus complex, Freud was at great pains to insist on the importance of the primal scene, not the sister, in the case of the Wolf Man (see Mitchell, 2003).

5.   This, without reference to siblings, is what Sergio Benvenito (2004) argues the moral masochist is without.

References

Braudel, F. (1949). *The Mediterranean and the Mediterranean World in the Age of Philip II*. Harper Collins, 1992.

Brown, D. (1998). Fair shares and mutual concern: the role of sibling relationships. *Group Analysis, 31*(3): 315–326.

Brunori, L. (1998). Special Edition: Papers from the siblings workshop. *Group Analysis, 31*(3): 305–314.

Benvenito, S, (2004). Freud and masochism. *Journal of European Psychoanalysis, 16*:

Colonna, A. B., & Newman, L. M. (1983). The psychoanalytic literature on siblings. *The Psychoanalytic Study of the Child, 38*: 285–239.

David, E. (1999). *By the Sabarmati*. Harmondsworth: Penguin.

De Masi, F. (2004). The psychodynamic of panic attacks: a "useful integration of psychoanalysis and neuroscience". *International Journal of Psychoanalysis, 85*(2): 311–337.

Earnshaw, A. (1995). *Time Will Tell: What Was I Doing at My Child's Age Now? What Happened to My Parents at This Time in Their Lives?* Glebe, Australia: A and K Enterprises, Printed Fast Books.

Freud, S. (1920g). Beyond the pleasure principle. *S.E., 18*. London: Hogarth.

Freud, S. (1926d). Inhibitions, symptoms and anxiety. *S.E., 20*. London: Hogarth.

Hawthorne, N. (1850). *The Scarlet Letter*. Boston: Ticknor, Reed, & Fields [reprinted Florence: Quinti Classics, 2001].

Hopper, E. (2003). *Traumatic Life in Groups: The Social Unconscious: Selected Papers*. London: Jessica Kingsley.

Hubback, J. (2003). *From Dawn to Dusk*. Wilmette, IL: Chiron.

Kapp, Y. (2003). *Time will Tell*. London: Verso.

Mitchell, J. (2000). *Mad Men and Medusas: Reclaiming Hysteria and the Effects of Sibling Relations on the Human Condition*. London: Allen Lane and Penguin.

Mitchell, J. (2003). *Siblings: Sex and Violence*. Cambridge: Polity.

Mitchell, J. (2004). Procreative mothers (sexual difference) and child-free sisters (gender): feminism and fertility. *European Journal of Women's Studies*, 11(4): 415–426.

Oberndorf, C. P. (1928). Psycho-analysis of siblings. 84th Annual Meeting of the American Psychiatric Association, Minneapolis, June 1928, pp. 1017–1019.

Rank, O. (1999). *The Trauma of Birth*. London: Routledge.

Showalter, E. (1997). *Hystories: Hysterical Epidemics and Modern Culture*. London: Picador.

Volkan, V. D., & Ast, G. (1997). *Siblings in the Unconscious and Psychopathology*. Madison, CT: International Universities Press.

Winnicott, D. W. (1931). A note on normality and anxiety. In: *Through Paediatrics to Psycho-Analysis*. London: Hogarth, 1975.

Winnicott, D. W. (1978). *The Piggle: An Account of the Psychoanalytical Treatment of a Little Girl*. London: Hogarth Press and the Institute of Psychoanalysis.

CHAPTER SEVEN

The idealization of the twin relationship

Vivienne Lewin

S iblings have an important place in our inner world. Twins are siblings of a distinctive kind and, while their relationship is at least as important as those of other siblings, the twin relationship also poses problems for the developing twins, difficulties that are unique to twins. The early dyadic and triadic relationships of the infant with its parents are disrupted by the presence of a twin. For all parties, the presence of two infants of the same age complicates the dynamics by creating an extra set of relationships to negotiate. Twin infants have to negotiate the triangular relationship between infant, mother, and father; and also the relationship with the other twin and the awareness of the other twin's relationship with mother, father, and with itself. For twins the early dyadic stage is essentially another triangle from the start.

Twins seem to fascinate us and I hope to explore the reasons for this. I have found it interesting that on many occasions, as soon as I have mentioned in conversation that I was writing about twins, the person I was talking to seemed to feel compelled to tell me an anecdote or story about twins, excited by some aspect of the twin relationship. Most often this interest has related to the uncanniness of two people who look so similar, or to the extraordinary, even apparently telepathic, communication between twins. Rank (1971) has written about our sense of the uncanny when we see two people who look the same. He explores the significance of "the double" in mirrors, shadows, and phantasies. He suggests that the concept of the double is linked with death—that by duplicating oneself we hope to avoid the inevitability of death. Fanthorpe (2000) refers to "the strangeness of the other who looks the same".

As a recent example of my being offered stories about our fascination with the sameness of twins, a neighbour (anonymously) put through my door a newspaper article from the *Evening Standard* about a pair of twins who each underwent extensive plastic surgery to make them look more alike (Prigg, 2004). These monozygotic (same egg) twins disliked the differences between them, particularly as they were frequently referred to as the "ugly twin" and the "pretty twin". The surgical remodelling minimized these differences, as a result of which the twins claim to have been brought "closer together than ever". The twins subsequently moved into the same home. Rather than being able to enjoy the difference that might have brought each twin sister a sense of individuality within the twin relationship, they sought sameness. This demonstrates the narcissistic aspect of a twin relationship, the seeking of other as self, and of self in the other. The idealization of sameness obliterates difference and the value of difference, and denies the need for an individual sense of self. Perhaps the need for sameness in these twin sisters was exacerbated by the splitting that seemed to define each twin. If the "ugly twin" was deemed to carry the "bad" aspects, while the "pretty twin" had the "good" ones, they might have felt that only by bringing the two selves together as two halves of a unit could the split be lessened. They enacted this by creating superficial sameness through surgery, and by moving in together. It seems they did not feel it was possible to redistribute the projected qualities of goodness and badness between them in a way that could be integrated into each individual personality.

When I first started my research on twins, I came across an account of the extraordinary similarities that had been observed between twins who had been separated at birth and reared apart, and then reunited as adults. This research was initially conducted by Tom Bouchard Jr (Wright, 1997). Like so many others, I was fascinated to read of these uncanny accounts, and pondered about the underlying implication that the way we are, our identity, all lies in our genes. The study was called the Minnesota Study of Twins Reared Apart. (I will say more about this below.) This excited research on twins is the sort of material that really feeds our fascination with twins. We want to find an uncanny sameness in twins, particularly in monozygotic twins. It seems to satisfy a deep longing in us.

I want to give another example of our fascination with twins and how this blends with the reality of twin development. Elvis Presley was a twin. Apparently, his twin brother Jesse was born dead, and the family have recounted stories about their surprise at the emergence of a second live baby. Dundy (1985) has written a biography of Elvis and his mother. I have used her book to illustrate both the idealization of twins (and, of course, the idealization of Elvis) and the reality of the enduring nature of the twin relationship in the internal world and its manifestations in all aspects of life. Dundy writes:

> Elvis was born a twin. . . . The fact that the mystery of death was attendant at his birth, that the very beginning of his life marked the end of his brother's, affected him throughout his life in a way that people who are not twins would find hard to understand. [Dundy, 1985, p. 67]

It is true that the death of Elvis's twin would most likely have been an important issue in his developing sense of self. Whatever residual sensory memory Elvis would have had of his twin *in utero*, the birth stories told by his parents and family would certainly have enhanced his sense of himself as a lone twin. However, Dundy then goes on to discuss the mystery of such twin bonding, citing the above-mentioned studies of twins reared apart and the apparent extraordinary similarities in the details and particularities of the lives of the separated twins. These studies have now been largely discredited. Joseph (2004) has examined twin studies and the erroneous conclusions based on some of the research. I mention it here because I think our fascination with twins might lead us to make assumptions about the genetic aspects of development based on unsound experimentation using the twin method and what Joseph calls the "gene illusion". Joseph suggests that these studies are skewed by many factors, including researcher bias; the possible omission of pairs of twins separated at birth who might turn out to have no greater similarities than any other people; the amount and quality of contact between the twins before the study was conducted; and any vested interest the twins themselves might have had in appearing so alike. The fundamental issue that is not addressed by these studies is whether factors other than genetic identity have contributed to the observed similarities.

Twins are usually divided into two distinct groupings: monozygous or same-egg twins, and dizygous or different-egg twins. Thus, monozygous twins originate from one egg that splits at a very early stage into two embryos. Dizygous twins are the result of the simultaneous fertilization of two eggs. The twin method of research relies on the assumption that monozygous twins have identical genes, while dizygous twins have a genetic similarity no closer than that of other siblings. The suggestion that monozygotic twins have identical genes has been somewhat overemphasized in the nature–nurture debate. Gringras and Chen (2001) have reviewed the scientific research on twins. They conclude that monozygotic twins do not have exactly identical genes. Although both twins develop from the splitting of one egg, both genetic and physical differences occur in monozygous twins as a result of various factors, including intrauterine effects, mutations in the genes, and epigenetic modifications within the chromosomes (chromosomes that are chemically altered after formation). The development of each twin will be affected according to which genes are activated, and this is altered by both environmental and hormonal factors. Our genes provide us with the potential for development within certain parameters, but the direction that development takes would depend on other factors. Hence the differences we observe in monozygous twins in both appearance and personality.

It is evident to anyone who is a twin or has known or worked with twins that no two twins are truly "identical", and I will therefore refer to twins according to their zygosity rather than using the terms "identical" and "fraternal". (I think these terms are useful only as regards the nature of the twinning processes that occur between the twins, either seeking sameness or allowing difference.) Whether mono- or dizygotic, the processes of twinning occur between twins to variable degrees. The nature and degree of the twinning processes within each pair of twins will affect the development and the nature of the twin relationship. It is important to note that twinning processes are not unique to twins. They also occur between infant and mother; and between singletons and other siblings, younger or older. I will talk later about our earliest twinning experiences.

To go back to Elvis, as Dundy (1985) notes, twin bonding is indeed an important factor in the twin relationship. Twin bonding is the result of various developmental and emotional factors including the closeness of the twins in age and the way in which this affects the relationship between the twins and their relationships with the mother and father. Where twinning processes between the twins is extensive, the twin bond will become both central to development, and would also limit the development of a separate identity for each twin, leading to a more enmeshed twinship. The twin relationship is powerfully represented in the internal worlds of the twins, and the internal twinship is enduring. It is not, however, a mystical bond of an order unknown in other relationships. As I will discuss later, I believe the tenaciousness of the twin bond has its roots in the infant's earliest relationship with its mother.

Dundy (1985) links Elvis's preoccupation with gazing at himself in mirrors as a teenager with Narcissus's gazing into the stream looking for the image of his dead twin. Pausanias tells a story about Narcissus that is contrary to the popular myth of Narcissus dying at the stream, unable to relinquish the reflection of his own beauty. Instead, Pausanias suggests that Narcissus gazed into the stream to comfort himself for the death of his twin sister. Narcissus knew that the image he saw was a reflection of himself, but it was so similar to his lost twin's image that seeing it comforted him. Here we see again the linking of mirrors, reflections, and doubles with death, as suggested by Rank (1971). It may be that Elvis, like Narcissus, looked and longed for his dead twin; but we also know that teenagers have a predilection for gazing at themselves in mirrors.

Dundy notes that Elvis's middle name was Aron, while that of his dead twin was Garon. (It is another feature of our fascination with twins that they are so often given very similar or rhyming names.) The death of a twin at birth generates a confusion of feelings in an immature infant. These feelings would include a sense of loss, guilt at survival when the other twin has died, but also feelings of triumph in survival and triumph over the dead twin. The task of dealing with this loss is made more difficult for the infant by the fact of its emotional immaturity. The infant has not yet developed the capacity to mourn its lost twin. Woodward (1998) suggests that the ability to mourn is linked with the capacity to verbalize, and that before this capacity develops, the infant twin survivor will have difficulty dealing with its loss. Apparently, Elvis always signed his name as Elvis aron Presley; that is, his middle name had a lower case "a" instead of a capital letter. Dundy suggests that he did so to leave space for the missing G in his twin's middle name "indicating how strongly Elvis felt his twin's absence" (Dundy, 1985, p. 69).

Dundy goes on to develop this theme. She suggests that Elvis's survival in the face of his twin's death created in him a sense of power, and that all his life he was engaged in a conflict between powerfulness and powerlessness. "Elvis might relate to friends and lovers with the intimate dependency of a twin looking for his other half—but he would always be the dominant one" (Dundy, 1985, p. 69). Thus, Dundy is illustrating the way in which the enduring nature of the internal twinship is expressed in all other relationships. The death of his twin and the internal representation of this twinship would, of course, also have been affected by Elvis's relationship with his mother. A mother faced with the need to welcome a live infant at the same time as she mourns a dead one has a difficult task. The surviving twin would always remind her of the dead baby and so the life and death twinning would endure in the minds of both mother (and father) and the surviving twin.

Elvis was apparently obsessed with comic books in which, like so many boys, he identified with the heroes. He kept all his comics in meticulous order, and even retained them as an adult. The comic book characters that most interested Elvis were those that had a dual personality. In these heroes there is a twinship that resides within one person (as it does in a twin whose other twin has died), the one side of the twinship being powerful, the other powerless. For these comic characters, the powerful self was always a secret self and the powerless one dull, crippled, or weak.

Among these comics were Captain Marvel and his alter ego Billy Batson; Batman and Bruce Wayne; Superman and Clark Kent; Spirit and Dandy Colt; and Plastic Man and The Eel. Apparently Billy Batson (Captain Marvel's alter ego) even had a twin sister,

Mary, who also had a twinned powerful alter ego called Mary Marvel. Dundy claims that Elvis modelled himself primarily on another comic book twinned hero, Captain Marvel Jr, who had a twin self called Freddy—a poor, crippled newsboy. She refers to Elvis's "twin-fusion" (Dundy, 1985, p. 71) with Captain Marvel Jr and wonders whether Elvis felt crippled by his twin's death. She also notes that the powerless twin, Freddy's, surname was Freeman, echoing Captain Marvel Jr's ability to fly high over the earth. I have found that it is not uncommon when a twin has died at birth for the surviving twin to believe that the dead twin has been freed by death, leaving the surviving twin to suffer both the difficulties in mourning the loss of the other twin and the exigencies of life. Dundy suggests that Elvis so identified with his comic hero that he adopted Captain Marvel Jr's hairstyle, black hair with a lock falling forward, and his stance, standing with legs astride. Elvis even used the striking lightning emblem that appeared each time that Captain Marvel Jr emerged in the comic in his personal jewellery and as the emblem on his private plane. Again, we need to be wary of making links that are too simple. The lightning sign is very common in all sorts of graphic displays, and is not necessarily connected with Captain Marvel Jr.

What about Elvis's relationship with his mother? It is clear from the book that Elvis's mother, Gladys, came from a very poor and deprived background, and was intensely possessive of her surviving twin son throughout his life. Dundy describes Gladys' "passionate concentration which deepened into a powerful intensity when her son was not there" (Dundy, 1985, p. 73). Gladys could not bear to be parted from her son even when he was an adult. We discover that Gladys's mother and grandmother had also died in the year of Elvis's birth and his twin's death. All these losses would have affected Gladys's relationship with her surviving son. It does seem that powerful twinning processes developed and persisted between mother and son, based not only on the death of Elvis's twin brother, but also on circumstances that made the ordinary separateness between infant and mother more difficult to attain.

Where twinning processes are extensive, whether between twins or as seem to have occurred between Elvis and his mother, separateness poses a threat to the identity of each "twin". The twins feel themselves to be inseparably bound to each other and feel that their psychic wholeness would be damaged or destroyed by separateness. Dundy notes that at his mother's graveside, Elvis cried out "Goodbye, darling, goodbye. I love you so much. You know how much. I lived my whole life for you . . . Oh God, everything I have is gone" (Dundy, 1985, p. 347). The unconscious narcissistic elements of the twinning are very powerful.

In my recently published book, *The Twin in the Transference* (Lewin, 2004), I wrote about an account by George Engel of a twin relationship and the surviving twin's anniversary reaction to his twin's death, based on unconscious factors (Engel, 1975):

> Engel's anniversary reaction to his twin's death after a heart attack is an expression of how powerful this unconscious narcissistic entanglement in twins can be, a persistent element at the core of a more healthy twin relationship. Although Engel seems to believe that he and his twin had dealt with their rivalry, had tamed it to manageable proportions by establishing an equivalent mutual aggression and developing a complementary relationship, it seems that unconscious elements prevailed. After his twin died, Engel waited with a sense of prescience for his own equivalent heart attack. This occurred one day short of 11 months after his twin had died. His immediate reaction was one of relief—he no longer had to anticipate the heart attack, "the other shoe had fallen" (Engel, 1975: 25). He could now exonerate himself of the phantasied crime of killing his brother and the associated guilt (indicated in a phantasy that he experienced while in hospital). Engel had recognised his murderous wishes towards his twin brother, but he had not escaped the twinship. In the Judaic tradition, the period of mourning is exactly one day short of 11 months, and Engel's heart attack thus did indeed occur on the anniversary of his twin's death. In so doing, it phantastically united him with his twin again, recreating their narcissistic bond. The power of the unconscious phantasy of oneness with his twin showed itself with force and accuracy. [*ibid.*, p. 68]

Along the same lines, it is interesting to note that Elvis was forty-two when he died, the same age that his mother claimed to be at her death. (She was actually forty-eight, but had hidden her true age.) Elvis's twinning with his mother would have made her death all the more unbearable to him. We might also interpret his extreme distress at her death as the reliving of the death of his twin, an event that apparently haunted him all his life.

I have found the material about Elvis interesting, not just because it is about a man who is something of an idol for millions of people, but also because of the recurring twin theme, both the idealization of twins and the reality of the enduring nature of a twin relationship. It is an example of our fascination with twins, and the ways in which we seek to emphasize the idealized twinning between them. Dundy positively fishes out twinning themes in Elvis's life. As an example of Elvis's eternal twinning, Dundy traces the number of twins that are featured in Elvis's films. She writes with reverence and excitement not only about Elvis, but also about his twinship with both his dead twin and his mother. It is true that a twin relationship endures throughout the lives of the twins, even after one twin dies. The twin relationship is a primary relationship, on a par with the parental relationships in terms of its develop- mental importance. However, I think that the idealization of twins and the wish to attribute magical qualities to the twin relationship has other roots, as I will now explore.

The perceived closeness of the relationship in some twins and the intimate understanding between them is something we all long for. Twins have frequently been observed to use a private language in their communications with each other (crytophasia). The private language of twins is usually a distortion of ordinary language, and it may also consist of made up words, signals, and gestures. Here is a quote from a twin writing in a student magazine:

> Growing up alongside a peer causes such mysteries as "twin babble," a private language created between twins that are learning to talk. One of these words was "picky," which was our term for soda. Our disposition to talk in our own private language was so strong in fact that our mother had to refuse us our requests until we used the correct, English word.
>
> Since our birth it has been evident that my sister and I share our own private world that has never needed to include anyone else. Even though the days of twin babble are long gone, we still have conversations consisting of two words, none finished sentences, that only [we understand]. When we are alone, we are content with one another's company. Silence is comfortable, and the topics of conversation are endless. We rarely talk about other people's lives because they have never interested us since we became accustomed to talking about topics that pertain to life from an early age. It's

difficult to understand what you will never experience, but people
are always trying to uncover the mysteries of twins. [Hillary S,
2004]

Thus, Hillary S describes very clearly the closed system created
by some twins in their twinship, one in which their secret language
is used not only to communicate intimately with the other twin, but
also to exclude anyone external to the twinship. The intimate
communication between twins is sometimes attributed to telepathy.
However, I understand that tests to establish whether or not twins
communicate telepathically have concluded that, while they do
sometimes have an unusually close degree of understanding, this is
due to non-verbal signals and their private language rather than to
any telepathic contact (Wright, 1997). I believe that the closeness of
communication between twins resonates with us for a reason that
is central to our idealization of twins—that is, a longing for perfect
understanding as is perceived to happen between twins.

The longing for perfect understanding and our fascination with
twins originate in an infant's earliest experiences with its mother.
Klein (1963) suggests that the close preverbal contact between the
unconscious of the mother and that of the infant creates an experience of complete understanding without words. However, this
"perfect understanding" is intermittent. Mother is not always there,
and she does not always get it right. She would at times be tired or
pre-occupied. Even at times when the infant has been satisfied,
persecutory/paranoid anxieties would arise. The inevitable and
irretrievable loss of an understanding without words creates an
unsatisfied longing and leads to a sense of internal loneliness. As
Klein notes, the integration of the good and bad breast, and the
good and bad aspects of the self can never be securely established.
Some polarity between the life and death instincts persists. As a
result, "complete understanding and acceptance of ones own
emotions, phantasies and anxieties is not possible and this continues as an important factor in loneliness. The longing to understand
oneself is also bound up with the need to be understood by the
internalised good object" (Klein, 1963, p. 302).

This longing is expressed in the universal phantasy of having a
twin. The infant creates a phantasy of the breast (the maternal function) using the processes of splitting and projective identification, in

the hope of finding again the understanding without words. Thus the phantasy breast is a twin of the infant, created by the projection of aspects of the infant itself. The phantasy twin represents those parts of the infant that have not been understood, and which the infant is longing to regain. Bion (1967) suggests that the breast is the infant's first imaginary twin. The creation of this phantasy twin-breast provides the infant with the illusion of attaining the desired perfect state of mind. Thus, the experience of being understood without words is at the heart of the ubiquitous longing for a twin.

The processes of twinning, that is the creation of the other as self, may be used in the search for understanding, as in the relationship of the infant and the breast, described above. However, twinning may also be used to try and rid oneself of unwanted aspects of the self, splitting off these undesirable parts and disowning them as belonging to the other. The twinning processes between the infant and the breast are echoed in the twinning processes between twins themselves in both the above modes. Thus, twins engage in twinning processes between them as the infant does with its mother, the other twin being perceived as either providing perfect understanding (as exemplified by Castor and Pollux in an idealized twinship) or as carrying the unwanted dissociated aspects of the self. In this latter situation, the other twin represents the hated aspects of the self and is felt to be alien and undesirable. (The rivalry and hatred between Jacob and Esau are examples of this.)

Thus, in addition to the companionable twinship that is so important to the twins, each twin may also perceive the other twin as the embodiment of the breast-twin. Two factors thus account for the enduring nature of the twin relationship and for the idealization of the twin relationship both by the twins themselves and by outsiders. The overlay of the breast-twin and the actual twin, and the importance of the actual twin as a primary object, together create an indelible internal twinship.

In childhood, many children "find" an imaginary companion to whom they relate as if they were actual friends. The imaginary companion essentially represents aspects of the child, and is therefore a phantasy twin of the child. Twinning and the processes of splitting and projective identification are central to the creation of a phantasy twin or imaginary companion in childhood, as they are in the infant. However, the creation of an imaginary childhood twin

or companion is a more conscious affair. The child knows it has
created its imaginary companion, and may use it in various ways.
The imaginary twin may help the child combat loneliness at the loss
of mother to a younger sibling (Burlingham, 1945). It may provide
the child with the illusion of greater strength and power. In being a
repository for the split-off parts of the child, the imaginary companion may serve either a defensive or an organizing function. In the
organizing mode, the imaginary twin may be used as a temporary
alter ego that will later be integrated into the child's psyche. In
defensive mode, the imaginary twin would remain a split-off part
of the child and would cause developmental problems (Nagera,
1969). Thus, the twinning processes in the infant are unconscious
and persist to a greater or lesser extent throughout life whether the
infant is a singleton or a twin. In contrast, an imaginary childhood
companion usually fades when the child feels more able to tolerate
the split-off aspects of the self and integrate them into the developing ego. Occasionally, an imaginary childhood twin or companion
persists into adulthood, and this would be indicative of a developmental difficulty.

It is important in considering twin relationships to distinguish
between the two aspects of the twinship. On the one hand there are
the "special" aspects of the relationship between twins that are the
result of the unparalleled closeness and companionship of the
twins. On the other hand, the more narcissistic elements of the
twinship may result in the idealization of a twin relationship that
seems to exemplify and embody an understanding without words.
In the former, companionable type of relationship, the loss of the
twin-breast is acknowledged, and the lost ideal object is mourned
and relinquished (although never completely, hence our ubiquitous
longing for perfect understanding). In the latter, the ideal twin-
breast becomes concretely identified with the other twin, and the
recognition of the loss of perfect understanding is evaded. This may
lead not only to an enmeshed twinship in which each twin feels
dependent on the other twin for its identity, indeed for its survival;
it also creates a relationship in which the twins feel trapped.

Both mother and a twin may become primary objects for twin
infants. Where the mother is used predominantly in development,
the infant will internalize a good integrating object by introjecting
the maternal function. This good internal object will serve as the

core of the developing ego. Alongside this will be the internalized twin relationship as an important and indelible internal object relationship, but one that does not replace the maternal object relationship. However, in other situations, whether due to maternal neglect or absence, or to the infant's limitations in its capacity to use mother's help, the infant twins may turn to each other for their developmental needs. The internal twinship would then be the predominant object relationship. However, as the twins are equally immature, they would not be able to provide each other with a sufficiently containing object, one that would enable and allow them to grow towards separateness and individuality, as would a maternal object relationship. While older siblings may provide some greater degree of containment, the lack of generational or even sibling age difference in twins would be a limiting factor in this regard. The result would be a lasting twinship of a narcissistic kind.

A degree of narcissistic twinning remains as a residue in all twin relationships, including those where there has been a greater degree of development of individual identities in the twins. There is also another source of confusion in the development of a sense of self for twins. The closeness in age of the twins will affect not only their relationship with each other, but also mother's (and father's) relationship with each of them. The narcissistic twinning and confusion of identity between the twins may be reinforced by each twin's experience with mother and father, especially where the twins are so similar that it is difficult for the parents to distinguish between them. The parents' feelings in relation to each baby might, so to speak, be directed at the "wrong" infant. The twins may then have the experience of having to take in something that belongs to the other twin, creating a sense of a sharing of self with the other twin. This interference in, or a lack of, containment, would lead to a further confusion of identity as the infant twin's communication with mother seems to have been misunderstood or misdirected.

The parental attitude towards each twin would have powerful effects on it. Bettelheim (1955) describes the way in which twins he was treating in his school were "turned into" the "good" or "bad" twin as a result of "neurotic" projections from their parents. This transfer of projections between one child and the other occurred only with twins, not with other children in the family. He notes that when the delinquent child had been rehabilitated during his stay at the school, the other, previously "good", twin started to display the symptoms of neurosis projected by the parents.

> In both these situations, as the "bad" delinquent twin became reha-
> bilitated during his stay at the School, the previously "good"
> sibling slowly turned into the "bad" one. In these cases, where both
> children probably had very similar life histories, neurotic attach-
> ments and needs were seemingly more readily transferred from
> one to the other. Even then, however, the neurosis or delinquency
> of the "good" twin who turned "bad", though of the same type,
> was relatively mild compared with that of the twin placed in the
> School. Apparently the original "bad" twin shielded his twin sib-
> ling during their earlier years from the full impact of parental
> neurotic involvement. When, on removal of the "bad" twin, these
> neurotic feelings were directed against the one remaining at home,
> the latter met this crisis with a personality much better able to with-
> stand it, because of his previous more fortunate life experience.
> [Bettelheim, 1955, p. 492]

Although Bettelheim refers to the "very similar life histories" of the twins concerned, he goes on to point out that the twins' experi-ences in relation to the parents were actually different, and further-more that this had an enduring effect on the capacities of the children. The twin that had had the better start with his parents was more able to tolerate the parental projections without too great a disturbance. So again we see that the idea that twins are exposed to exactly the same developmental factors through their shared envi-ronment does not hold true. Each twin has its own unique experi-ences within the family environment and, as a consequence, each will have an individual pattern of psychic development, whatever the degree of overlap described above. The twins may distribute qualities between themselves either within an enmeshed system, keeping the twins bound to each other, or in a more separate twin-ship, sometimes through the development of complementarities to each other.

The creation of a phantasy twin as described above is a narcis-sistic affair. The processes of splitting and projective identification may operate between parts of the self, creating an internal twin pair, or between the self and an external object—either the mother–breast or the other twin. The creation of a phantasy twin would be part of normal development as the infant engages with its mother. As a result of maternal containment the infant would gradually relinquish this idealized twin and develop towards an individual and separate identity. In the presence of a twin, the process is more complex and may be more problematic. The inter-action with the other twin, who is always present in the mind of both mother and baby, adds an additional dimension to the development and the internal world of the infants. Where the twins engage with each other in extensive mutual projective and introjective identification there will be a blurring of individual boundaries between them and the twinship itself may become a narcissistic system encompassing both twins. The other twin may come to be perceived as an embodiment of the phantasy twin as a narcissistic twin system evolves.

An omnipotently fused narcissistic relationship of the kind described by Rosenfeld (1964) may exist between twins. The self becomes so identified with the incorporated other twin that all sense of a boundary between self and twin, and of an identity separate from the other twin, is denied. The twins may believe that the twinship offers them a self-sufficient system and that they have no need of any other objects. The enmeshed narcissistic twinship may then be used as a psychic retreat (Steiner, 1993). The twinship retreat may offer apparent safety from unbearable anxiety associated with development towards the depressive position and separateness for each twin within the twin relationship. However, alongside the apparent safety offered by the psychic retreat, the twins would feel trapped in the narcissistic twinship. Emerging from the psychic retreat would confront the individual twin with anxieties of an intense and possibly psychotic nature. In the extreme, this may result in a sense of fragmentation of the self. The lack of maternal containment, whatever the cause, would be a potent factor promoting the use of the twinship as a psychic retreat.

The use of such a twinship retreat would enable the twins to avoid an experience of dependence on a maternal object rather than the twin. The inter-twin dependency would predominate, frequently excluding the mother. However, it is dependence on a maternal object that would enable the twins to develop separately within the twin relationship and free them from the enmeshed twinship. In therapy or analysis, the analyst would be perceived as a twin in all the manifestations of the twin relationship. This provides the analyst with vital information about the twin patient's internal world of relationships and formative experiences. An analysis of the twin transference relationship is essential to the successful resolution of the transference relationship and the analysis. While the patient may perceive the analyst as a twin in the transference relationship, the capacity of the analyst to use her understanding of the twin transference is a parental function. However, the patient may avoid any recognition of a parental transference relationship with the analyst and may instead use the analytic twinship as a retreat to avoid a developmental (parental) relationship with the analyst.

The idealization of the twinship may then be enacted in the analytic relationship, as the analyst becomes the transference twin instead of analysing it. The sense of the "specialness" of the twinship will become manifest in the enacted analytic twinship, as the analyst colludes with the twin patient to avoid the painful developmental realizations of difference and discord, smallness and dependency; and the loss of the ideal twin-breast.

The overvaluation of the twin relationship would lead to the creation of a narcissistic system in which the twins may be bound by either loving or hating feelings (Rosenfeld, 1971). In narcissism, there is withdrawal from external object relationships to an identification with an idealized internal object, either in love or hatred. For twins, the loving internal object may be the internal twin. Castor and Pollux represent the loving or libidinal aspects of the narcissistic twin system. They were twins born to Leda after she was seduced by Zeus, disguised as a swan, and she was also pregnant by her husband, Tyndareus. Pollux was a god and Castor mortal, thus embodying the splits between twins. They formed an impregnable "loving" twinship, acting together to inflict terrible injuries on their enemies. They remained inseparable, even after the death of Castor, and lived forever alternately in the heavens and the netherworld. The loving narcissistic element of twin relationships is commonly encountered after one twin has died. The surviving twin feels incomplete, and longs to be reunited with the other twin rather than mourn the loss of the twin.

Where the destructive narcissistic forces in the twinship are idealized, rather than the loving ones (Rosenfeld, 1971), the twins would become bound together in mutual hatred. The internal twin-ship would be a destructive narcissistic organization that opposes any contact with a loving external object relationship. The murder-ous feelings between the twins would be played out between them, rather than directed outwards as it was with Castor and Pollux. A twinship based on these processes would be developmentally damaging to both twins. It is likely that one twin would not only be dominant, but would also keep the other twin in thrall using threats and propaganda to maintain this order. The Gibbons twins described by Wallace (1996), and Bill and Bert described by Burling-ham (1963) are both examples of a destructive narcissistic twinship in which the twins can neither live harmoniously together, nor apart. When together, their murderous aggression is played out. When apart, they feel incomplete and fear disintegration.

The narcissistic twinship may be psychotic in nature. Potash and Brunell (1974) describe monozygotic twin sisters who were locked in a *folie à deux* of a shared delusional world. The authors suggest that the twin sisters used this delusional system in order to cope with abusive parents, but that the psychotic twinship rendered them inseparable. They were visually paranoid, highly disturbed, and entertained suicidal thoughts. They supported, believed, and identified with each other's delusions. The twins were hospitalized in order to both separate them and to keep them safe while they received multiple–conjoint psychotherapy with a male and a female therapist. Through this work, each twin discovered a safe setting for the expression of "dangerous" emotions, and began to discover that her anger did not harm her dependent twin. As a result they no longer felt the need to deflect their hostility into a delusional system. The twins were able to separate, as they discovered that it was safe to be an individual, and "each learned that she had her own ideas, beliefs, and interests that could be shared without the other having to accept it as her own reality."

We might think of the sense of self as cohering within a psychic membrane/skin (Bick, 1968), so that an individual has a more or less cogent idea that "this is me". This process is more complex for twins, for whom there is likely to be a greater or lesser degree of overlap with the other twin in terms of a sense of identity both within and outside the twinship. As described earlier, the sense of self develops within the intimate relationship with mother and father. Where a twin is always present in the minds of both infant and parents, there is likely to be some overlap between the twins in which the sense of self is to a greater or lesser extent shared, or the boundaries less clear.

The issue of separateness and separation from the other twin is central to both development and analytic work with a twin. By this I do not mean separation leading to the ending of the twinship. The twin relationship is an enduring, indeed, a valuable and an ineradicable, object relationship. Instead, I believe that it is possible to enable a twin or twin patient to find separateness and individuality within the twin relationship without either denying the importance of the twinship or psychically murdering the other twin. This development might be characterized as the twinning processes changing from those of an "identical" twin to a "non-identical" twin, a change from a more narcissistic twinship to one that is more object-related.

Following Rosenfeld's (1987) ideas about thick and thin-skinned narcissism, Britton (2003) writes about the thickness or thinness of the psychic membrane in narcissistic individuals and the way in which this affects the nature of their relationships with others, particularly in his countertransference experiences in analysis. In intimate relationships, such as marriage and analysis, an individual negotiates the shared psychic space. The experience of being in that psychic space with that individual and the quality of the negotiation of the space is determined by the nature of the psychic skins of the participants.

I have suggested (Lewin, 2004) that twins who are enmeshed jointly occupy a psychic skin. It is as if the psychic membrane between them is thin and easily penetrated, so that they are highly responsive to each other, leading to the impression that they share an identity. The psychic envelope around the twins is thick, isolating the twins from the outside world. The twinship becomes the most highly charged and important relationship. Within this narcissistic system, the twins negotiate the shared psychic space according to the way they have formed an individual identity in relation to the other twin. As Piontelli (2002) has observed of the behaviour of twins, starting from their time *in utero*, the pattern of relating and the nature of the relationship between twins are enduring.

The birth stories for twins are redolent with ideas about the shared space—fighting for space in the womb, one twin taking too much space, the approach/avoidance patterns of the foetuses in relation to each other. The emotional space twins have to share by virtue of their identical age and the sharing of the environment in the crucial early years in a way that no other siblings do, will be re-enacted within all their intimate relationships. This is particularly so within the consulting room, where the analyst becomes the analytic twin in all its many aspects.

It is my experience that a twin patient at the more narcissistic end of the continuum may occupy two overall positions.

1.   The analyst may be excluded from the twinship, kept outside the thick psychic twin envelope, and regarded as irrelevant. This would fit with what Britton (2003) refers to as a thick-skinned (schizoid) narcissist. The patient appears to be solely and intensely preoccupied with the other twin, in loving or hating mode, while the analyst is treated as an unnecessary parental figure. In this situation, it is not uncommon for the patient to end treatment when the twinship membrane is pene-trated by the analyst.

2.   The analyst may be over-included in the twin patient's world, as if she is an analytic twin in an enmeshed twinship with the patient. The patient fights to occupy the psychic space in what at times seems to be a life and death struggle. There is no room for separateness of any degree and the analytic space is oblit-erated by the patient. This may take the form of outpourings that fill the session, leaving no space for thinking, or what appears to be an emotionally charged fight expressed either in silence or verbal aggression. The patient seems to experience any independent thought by the analyst as an attempt by the analyst to intrude and take over his/her mind, to occupy all the space. Likewise the analyst feels grossly intruded upon in a way that may paralyse analytic activity.

Typically, for these thin-skinned twin patients, the ordinary difficulties of everyday life seem to take on giant proportions that threaten the patient. It is as if the attacking twin is all around them. It is interesting how frequently these patients arrive late for sessions because, in all sorts of ways, life has made it too difficult for them to get there on time. The patient will anxiously and angrily describe the details of their apparently horrendous journey and the unfairness of the world. There is a pervasive sense of someone being to blame, leading either to profuse apologies by the patient or to a sense of the analyst being to blame for the difficulty of the journey. The persistent complaint is that the patient feels that the analyst is useless in removing her pain and/or that the analyst is a hostile invader causing her more pain. The patient fills the consulting room and the analyst's mind with her angry pain and distress about her life, past and present. The analyst feels obliged to listen to the painful story, but feels pinned down, invaded, overwhelmed, and sometimes suffocated by the awfulness the patient is describing. The patient's mood seems larger than life and all pervasive. It is as if there is no helpful internal parent, only a twin–analyst who functions as a receptacle for the expulsion of unbearable experiences.

These modes of relating may vary for each patient at times, but it seems that one or the other tends to predominate.

In conclusion, the nature of the twin relationship will be determined by many factors, including heredity and the way in which each twin of a particular genetic disposition negotiates the primary relationships with mother, father, and the other twin. Each twin has a dual task of forging a personal identity through individual psychic development, and of negotiating the twin relationship, maturing from the more narcissistic end of the spectrum to a twinship of both separateness and togetherness. In a twinship at the more narcissistic end of the spectrum, intense twinning processes hamper the recognition and experience of the "otherness" of the other twin. Instead, the unity of the twinship is idealized in denial of the recognition of "otherness" of each individual twin. The idealization of the twin relationship is based on essential internal loneliness that leads to a ubiquitous longing for a twin, a longing that emanates from the infant's earliest preverbal experiences with its mother.

References

Bettelheim, B. (1955). *Truants from Life (The Rehabilitation of Emotionally Disturbed Children)*. Glencoe, IL: The Free Press [reprinted in paperback by Simon and Schuster, 1964].

Bick, E. (1968). The experience of the skin in early object-relations. *International Journal of Psycho-Analysis, 49*: 484–486.

Bion, W. R. (1967). The imaginary twin. In: *Second Thoughts. Selected Papers on Psycho-analysis* (pp. 3–22). New York: Jason Aronson.

Britton, R. (2003). *Sex, Death and the Superego. Experiences in Psycho-analysis*. London: Karnac.

Burlingham, D. T. (1945). The fantasy of having a twin. *Psychoanalytic Study of the Child, 1*: 205–210.

Burlingham, D. T. (1963). A study of identical twins—their analytic material compared with existing observation data of their early childhood. *Psychoanalytic Study of the Child, 18*: 367–423.

Dundy, E. (1985). *Elvis and Gladys. The Genesis of the King*. London: Weidenfeld and Nicolson.

Engel, G. (1975). The death of a twin: mourning and anniversary reactions. Fragments of 10 years of self analysis. *International Journal of Psychoanalysis, 56*: 23–40.

Fanthorpe, U. A. (2000). Sightings. In: *Consequences*. Calstock, Cornwall: Peterloo Poets.

Gringras, P., & Chen, W. (2001). Mechanisms for differences in monozygous twins. *Early Human Development, 64*: 105–117.

Hillary S. (and Heather S) (2004). from the Fall Mountain's Student Magazine, *Mountain Expressions*: http://www.fall-mountain.k12.nh.us/english/mtexp2/twin.htm, 11/05/04, 11pm.

Joseph, J. (2004). The gene illusion. *Human Givens Journal, 10*(4): 12–19.

Klein, M. (1963). On the sense of loneliness. In: *Envy and Gratitude and Other Works* (pp. 300–313). London: Hogarth, 1980.

Lewin, V. (2004). *The Twin in the Transference*. London: Whurr.

Nagera, H. (1969). The imaginary twin companion—its significance for ego development and conflict solution. *Psychoanalytic Study of the Child, 24*: 165–196.

Piontelli, A. (2002). *Twins: From Foetus to Child*. London: Routledge.

Potash, H., & Brunell, L. (1974). Multiple–conjoint psychotherapy with folie à deux. *Psychotherapy: Theory, Practice, Research*; 270–276. Quoted by Sharon, I., Sharon, R., & Eliyahu, Y. (2004). Shared psychotic disorder. EMedecine.com, Inc. 16 February, 2004.

Prigg, M. (2004). Twins in £40,000 makeover . . . to look more alike. *Evening Standard*, Thursday 6 May.

Rank, O. (1971). *The Double. A Psychoanalytic Study*. H. Tucker (Ed. and Trans.). Chapel Hill, NC: The University of North Carolina Press.

Rosenfeld, H. (1964). On the psychopathology of narcissism: a clinical approach. *International Journal of Psycho-Analysis, 45*: 332–337.

Rosenfeld, H. (1971). A clinical approach to the psychoanalytic theory of the life and death instincts: An investigation into the aggressive aspects of narcissism. *International Journal of Psycho-Analysis, 52*: 169–178.

Rosenfeld, H. (1987). *Impasse and Interpretation*. London: Tavistock.

Steiner, J. (1993). *Psychic Retreats. Pathological Organisations in Psychotic, Neurotic and Borderline Patients*. London: Routledge.

Wallace, M. (1996). *The Silent Twins*. London: Vintage.

Woodward, J. (1998). *The Lone Twin. A Study in Bereavement and Loss*. London: Free Association Books.

Wright, L. (1997). *Twins. Genes, Environment and the Mystery of Human Identity*. London: Phoenix.

CHAPTER EIGHT

The influence of sibling relationships on couple choice and development

Elspeth Morley

Introduction

T wo recent books (Coles, 2003; Mitchell 2003) have generated excitement in the field of psychotherapy in drawing to our attention the extraordinary absence of focus in the psycho-analytic literature on the *lateral* relationships of siblings/peers compared with the cornucopia of concentration on *vertical* parent–child relationships. Excitement and, indeed, controversy. Are there universal principles governing the lateral which can take their place alongside the vertical? Are they the *same* principles in a lateral context or, if not, how do they differ from the vertical? In the individual's psychic development do they precede or follow? Are they chronologically simultaneous, or does one displace the other? Or, at our most iconoclastic, are we to see all psychoanalytic theory as autobiographical, with the focus of both the writing and clinical practice of the giant creators of psychoanalysis emanating from their inter- and intrapsychic struggles, each locked in his or her own autonomous world, giving virgin birth to faithful followers who can never leave their progenitors?

My contention in this chapter is to demonstrate the interdependence of the vertical with the lateral, while being in constant juxtaposition. My analogy, to which I shall refer throughout the chapter, is to a staircase, with each lateral tread being both preceded and followed by the vertical. Should there be a break in the continuity of the stairs, a precipitous drop will appear, causing retreat to the previous step or, at best, a cessation of further upward movement. The analogy holds whether the stairs are those of the individual's development in his object relationships, or between one generation and the next. My purpose is to show that it is in the unconscious choices and development of *couple* relationships that this staircase of alternate lateral and vertical is theoretically and clinically at its crucial interface.

The main case study I want to explore is not from my own clinical practice, but from Freud's. This is of the famous "Wolf Man", the all too familiar case about whom more words must have been written in the last hundred years than of any other patient. But my own particular focus will not be so familiar. It is on the development of his and his *wife's* relationships from their families of origin, *through their siblings*, to each other. This is the main thrust of the Wolf Man's own invaluable published account of his life and of his analysis with Freud, one which differs markedly from Freud's. I can find no better example of how the individual psychoanalytic practitioner can lead his patient up the vertical marathon of the parent–child relationship, only to leave him stranded on the lateral step of sibling relationships. Here, he contemplates retreat or death, unable to proceed to the qualitative couple relationship; one which could retain its own sexual coupledom, while graduating to the next vertical step of producing a "third", an individuated child.

My conclusion will be to urge the expansion of theoretical and clinical attention to the lateral steps of siblings, leading to the interface of the couple relationship, from which may develop the vertical riser to the next generation, or to some creation that gains independence. This is whether the work is with individual, or with couple, patients. Finally, we might examine the institutional settings of our work as psychoanalytic psychotherapists, where we can become enmeshed in uncreative relationships, based on the personal struggles of our eminent founders, and often failing to advance alternately from one dimension to the other.

The universal validity of the lateral step of sibling relationships

We are indebted to the psychoanalyst Juliet Mitchell for her powerfully original writing through the years, linking hysteria, psychopathy, madness, incest, rape, violence, and murder into the prime focus of the failure to manage the universal human rite of passage that siblings impose on us (Mitchell, 2003). These may be siblings who already exist, come to exist, or have existed and then died. Even the only child, Mitchell asserts, must be beset with the *thought* of their possible existence, or finds their equivalent in a peer group. The trauma that siblings impose on us is that we are not the *sole* person of our genus in existence. *Unique*, yes, but *sole*, no. Not the only Her/His Majesty the Baby, not the only Receiver and Giver of Life. There exist others who are the same as us, but also different and separate. They are not inside us, or we inside them. One is not under the total command of the other, as if it were a linear symbiotic extended limb. Such recognition, Mitchell contends, cannot come lightly. She sees it as involving an inevitable initial hatred and fear of the other, the "either I obliterate him/her or s/he obliterates me", however swiftly that "trauma" might be resolved.

Mitchell asserts that it is only the sibling/peer group relationship that *survives* this trauma and the hatred that accompanies it, that can become a source of mutual respect and enjoyment. Only then can the strong love and attraction develop that we know and can observe growing between siblings, and between friends, often into a lifelong attachment. For children it can include the rivalrous excitement and sexual curiosity of the "you show me yours and I'll show you mine" variety or the "see how much higher I can pee up the playground wall". In this sense it can be a psychologically healthy relationship between brothers and sisters in any combination, extending to peer group attachments irrespective of their gender. These are not the vertical relationships that create babies. When children think of producing babies it is through parthenogenesis, the extension of the self in their own image, not the separate new creation that comes from the sexual intercourse with another of different gender.

Mitchell argues convincingly that, no more than parent–child incest, can *actual* incest between siblings ever be a benign development; despite our culture sometimes seeming to condone it provided no "monstrous" birth results. For this is where gender becomes crucial. The boundaries of the lateral relationship are gender free, only in the sense that it is immaterial which gender is engaged with which when the struggle is about separate *existence*. This replicates the way, in the vertical relationship, that the gender of the baby is immaterial to its problem of mastering attachment–separation anxiety. It is when these boundaries are transgressed in the sibling relationship that it can be turned illicitly, through incest, into the vertical relationship between parents and children. This can only be an attempt to deny those lateral boundaries and to avoid recognizing the difference of the "Other". Sibling incest is as pathologically stuck in the failure to make this recognition in the lateral relationship as parent–child incest fails to recognize the boundaries of the vertical relationship. Oedipus symbolically blinds himself, as his mother–wife hangs herself, in the intolerable recognition that their sons and daughters are also his sisters and brothers

It is only in the non-incestuous heterosexual relationship that the healthy transition can be made from the lateral to the vertical. This is not to say that the homosexual or lesbian relationship is in itself "unhealthy", but it is to underline that such couples are not able *from within themselves* to create a new generation without the outside help, however fleetingly, of a different gender.

But nor, indeed, is it to say that every *heterosexual* couple, whether or not they produce children, has *successfully* resolved the central trauma of the lateral relationship, the "we are the same but different", and can go on as such a couple to the vertical relationship that produces the baby. If truly resolved, this baby will be seen as coming from, but being different from, both its parents, and not becoming stuck in a new couple with either. They can be left to pursue their lateral coupledom in juxtaposition to their vertical parenting of the child. The child is left to gravitate into its own lateral relationships, which may develop in time, through its own adult couple relationship, into the next vertical generation. In the successful resolution of these developmental stages both the children and the parents engage simultaneously in lateral relationships with siblings or their substitutes, and in vertical child–parent (or their substitutes) relationships. But the tread and the riser of the staircase are not the same, and if attempts to make them so through incest go unheeded, the result can only be psychic catastrophe.

The differential factors of the lateral relationship
as seen in couple choice

So how is the benign healthy staircase of alternate yet concurrent vertical and lateral relationships ever to develop? It must indeed be a core universal factor for full human development to have to tolerate the existence of others who are like us, but not symbiotically attached to us. But, of course, the myriad factors that set the scene for our experience of this universal truth will always be unique, even if we are one of monozygotic twins (Lewin, 2004). Nevertheless, many of these factors are in repetitive patterns, the principles of which can be observed and generalized. As couple therapists we often see these patterns, however unconscious they may be, in the same or mirrored form, in the individual members of the couple, as the basis of their mutual attraction. We experience them too, in the countertransference of the clinical work, in a different, often more powerful way than in individual work. But we also see how the couple themselves, often through the proverbial crowded room, can unconsciously sense the same shared–opposite features of their internal world. As therapists our concern is to help couples to become conscious of these factors in a way that enables them to develop, whether together through the relationship, or separately.

I want to look, at this point, at the fascinating minefield of *position in family* as the single factor most likely to determine the development of our lateral relationships and so of our choice of partner. Frank Sulloway's famous research, contained in his seminal work *Born to Rebel* (1996), found position in family to be overwhelmingly the single most influential factor in determining our later development. He delineates how, throughout history, we can discern this pattern of the oldest being the competitive, dominant, conforming conservative, while the later-born, literally "born to rebel", questions the old, creates new paradigms and is responsible for "shocking" innovative discoveries. He is also generally better able than his oldest sibling to accept and adapt to such discoveries when they are made by others. Sulloway invites us to see how each child looks for its unique "niche" in the family, the one that it can appropriate, expand, and protect from other family members. The trauma of not being the only person to exist in this family, in this *world*, as it would seem to be in the child's earliest formative years, can be mitigated by cornering the market in one particular area where the child's supremacy may go unchallenged. That choice of area for its sole occupancy must often seem to dictate itself. The oldest child is the one most likely to be devastated by the paradigm shift required in the face of its traumatic displacement as Her/His Majesty the Baby. Typically, it will capitalize on its position as the strongest and most able in every field of possible competition with the later-born, even if eventually it is outclassed by younger siblings. And into this oldest's repertoire will go the capacity to observe and conform to parental aspirations, thus ensuring their support for its sole occupancy of the self-selected niche.

But for the later-born the obvious niche to select is going to be that of the youngest, the baby. Psychoanalytically we are habituated, since Freud, to thinking of the *father* as being the baby's first encounter with the "third", the one who is not part of the earliest mother–baby pair. So we are presuming with Freud (or indeed with Klein, from an even earlier age) that the baby is innately aware of the sexual couple, of which it is not a part, which was needed to produce its very existence. We seem to have discounted recognition that for a later-born child the first "third" is stereotypically the older sibling, the toddler at the knee of the lap on which the baby lies. And this is likely to be not so much an intrapsychic phenomenon as an ever-present reality in the world of lateral relationships of sibling rivalry. Baby observation studies typically confirm those of the mother that the baby learns at a very early age to anticipate and shrink from the toddler's furtive kick, or "embrace" that threatens strangulation. It becomes bolder in retaliation, as well as in evident enjoyment of the older sibling, only when safely back in protective attachment to the mother. With the later-born child there is seldom such objective evidence of an early intensely ambivalent relationship to the father as the "third". This may, of course, be seen more readily in the first-born, for whom the father is more often literally the first "third" it encounters, the equivalent to the older sibling in the stakes of lateral relationships for the later-born. But even for these first-born children, displacement is generally more likely to be "traumatic" on the lateral tread, with the birth of a younger sibling, than it is in any "oedipal" contest in the vertical relationship.

As long as the later-born remains the youngest it may also maintain and reinforce its niche through life. But with the arrival of yet later born siblings the niche will typically be relinquished to the newcomer, to be replaced perhaps by the niche of peace-maker, valued both by parents and siblings for its capacity to compromise and resolve conflict. Or in the face of its discovery that no such niche is possible in a family where compromise is inaccessible, the in-the-middle child may struggle to find it *outside* the family, or indeed to become alienated in the attempt

If we start with these generalizations of observed commonalties, it leads us to see the many factors that will alter the patterns. *Gender* difference is an obvious candidate. The oldest *girl* can appropriate the niche of gender-specific speciality, as can the oldest *boy*, when the other gender has monopolized the niche of just being the oldest. Or, if sufficiently pushed in his search for a unique niche in the family, the later-born boy can choose the feminine niche or a girl the masculine. When a later-born can see that the oldest, regardless of gender, has failed to fulfil the potential of that niche, s/he can muscle in on it, or even exchange niches with the older.

The dead sibling

Then there is the formidably powerful effect of having a dead sibling, whether before or after the child's own birth. The niche of the dead, as can be evident in the compulsion to suicide, inexorably lends itself to the idealization that need never confront the inevitable failures of reality. But it is these failures that the "replacement" child must struggle to deal with, without ever being in the position to have an open contest as it might with a live sibling. There may be an overlap here with the position of the *only* child, who, as Mitchell points out (Mitchell, 2003), never has to face conflict with a living sibling; but s/he must nevertheless deal with the universal rite of passage of "I am unique, but so are my peers, and my unborn sibling (whom I may have successfully obliterated) maintains an idealized niche which I in my reality can never reach."

The effect of the vertical on lateral relationships

This is to look at sibling conflict, and jostling for special niches in the lateral relationships, as if it could be viewed independently of

the child's experience of its actual parents and of their vertical relationships with their children. In real life circumstances, who are
these parents but the pre-existing gods and self-appointed judges of
the world into which the child is born, even if they have died or
absented themselves. The laws of the child's world are those of the
adult parental figures who govern it. It may be a matter of years
before the child perceives that there are other worlds where the
same laws do not apply, and by this time it can be hard to shake the
belief that this play of the family it was born into is the only play
on stage. Parts in the play may be exchanged, and the child will
often struggle to get into what it perceives as the dominant part, but
not the play itself.

A benign form of this parent-dominated world into which the
fortunate child might be born will come from the parents who have
successfully managed their own lateral relationships of sameness
and difference. They will have reached the point of embarking on
the vertical parent–child relationship that will allow each child to
find its own unique niche in which it can predominate. These are
parents who can ease the trauma of the oldest as it is displaced, so
that it can graduate to another niche that does not involve intolerable conflict with the later-born; the parents who are comfortable
enough in their own gender roles and achievements, however these
may be divided equably between them, not to compete with or try
to live vicariously through their children. These parents can resume
and maintain their own lateral couple relationship physically and
emotionally rather than transfer symbiotic or erotic relationships
from partner to child. They stay alive, stay alive together, and
manage their own conflicts without giving the children parts in
their own parental lateral play. But this may seem an unrealistic
idyll.

In the real world the siblings' choice of niche may seldom be
boundaried by such mature parenting. And the deficiencies of their
actual parents will then be reflected in the degree of pain and
conflict inflicted by the siblings on each other as they jostle for their
own niche; or, indeed, of the only child who tries alone, without the
help of siblings to share the burden, to be the youngest and the
oldest for its parents, all that they require of it, and their only mediator in parental conflicts.

Choice of partner

The general principles of mutual unconscious choice of partner may be markedly similar whether the family of origin has been one that fosters benign mutual respect and gratification, both vertically and laterally, or at the other extreme of corrosive conflict in the face of irresolvable psychic dilemmas. Paradoxically, this means that couples can be seen to "divorce" each other for the very same qualities as those for which they "married" each other. The unconscious choice is made of a partner who seems in some sense to share a similar emotional and familial background, with similar emotional "tasks" left to tackle, but has found a different "niche", often an opposite way of dealing with the shared world. In common parlance, each has "chosen his/her other half", the missing as well as the shared pieces of each partner's internal jigsaw. But where the "self" that is then seen in the mirror of the partnership cannot be owned, its individual members will separate, psychically if not physically, as they accentuate their differences. As psychoanalytic couple psychotherapists we are used to seeing this phenomenon as mutual projective identification. Each partner finds in the other the counterpart of the self; a choice that may be dictated unconsciously more by the sense of the *self* that it is hoped to achieve in the couple than by the sense of the other.

When we come to consider the elements that have been introjected from their pre-existing individual external worlds into their shared internal world, we have become habituated to thinking primarily in terms of the vertical parent–child relationship. We tend too readily to discount the relative importance of the lateral sibling world, even although this can often be seen to be the most immediate forebear of the choice of partner. I have been arguing, in fact, that these two are inseparable, with the quality of the lateral sibling tread being interdependent with that of the vertical parent–child riser that preceded it. To miss out recognition of the lateral step altogether is to lose a vital dimension in our understanding and clinical work, not only with the couple, but also with the individual patient.

To reassert this crucial step, what are the familiar lateral scenarios of mutual couple choice we can observe? In their intricate detail they are as numerous and varied as the unconscious choices made *vis-à-vis* siblings in their search for mutually compatible roles. And just as these have observed commonalties, so do the choices of partner that emanate from them. How frequently, for example, we find a "match", of an oldest marrying a youngest. The eldest child, who has had to relinquish its "baby" position, finds in a youngest one who has been able to exploit that role to the full; while this later-born hopes to unite itself in the oldest with the role of successful dominance. Or, perhaps, rather than to *exchange* with previously desired or relinquished roles, it may be to *perpetuate* the gratification of the original role that the child has already developed in its family of origin. The later-born may be good at admiring and placating an older sibling. The first-born may have developed a capacity for caring for and encouraging a later-born that can readily be transferred to a later-born adult partner. The only child can choose in the partner the missing siblings it has idealized, one who has longed to have the individual space free of siblings. The child with the sick younger/older sibling who had dictated the child's own role, may look for such sickness in the partner who wants to find again the caring sibling. Or there may be the exchange of roles: "Let me try out the longed-for role of the sick, cosseted sibling" in exchange for "Let me be the strong, approved-of sibling who can demonstrate its strength by looking after the sickness of the other". Perhaps the shared experience is to have a sibling who has died, with all the many variations of same/opposite results that these partners can now dovetail in their adult choice. Then there are gender choices: the boy marries his sister, the sister her brother, or the brother *becomes* the sister he longed to be by choosing the sister who longed to be her brother.

Cross-cultural choice of partner

Nina Cohen's research (Cohen, 1982) into cross-cultural couples demonstrated the paradox that the choice of a partner of a different race was often based on the shared experience in the couple of *sameness*, even perhaps in the absence of a common language. Cohen considers that this becomes possible because, in the absence of recognizable features of "this could be a member of my all-too-familiar family of origin", the couple could share an idealization of their at-one-ness, without recognizable bumps or crevices of differ-ence. Often, one or both of the partners would be bi-sexual. Psychoanalytically, we have tended to interpret this choice as based on fear of replicating a relationship with a *parent* that could be incestuous. But why is it that we have been so reluctant to notice the much more commonly acknowledged incestuous feelings between *siblings* than between parents and children, which need to be warded off from our adult choice of partner? Why do we label this as the "split *mother* image" of the man who has to separate his relationship with his "good", non-erotic wife, the mother of his chil-dren, from that of his "bad", erotic partner who must remain child-less, rather than a "split *sister* image"?

The outcome of unconscious choice of partner

There are many more variations on these themes of couple choice. But we must embark on considering the principles of factors likely to lead these couple choices into gratifying partnerships that progress through the sexual couple interface from the lateral to the vertical, with children who can later develop their own productive lateral relationships, leaving the parents to enjoy their coupledom. If these same choices may lead as inexorably to the divorce court, what is the difference in their development? The central determin-ing factor would seem to be the quality of the earlier relationships, internalized and now projected. If the partners have previously been unable to deal with their destructive envy of a sibling whom they wish to displace or to incorporate as an extension of them-selves, then the choice of a partner that repeats or reverses that lateral relationship is likely to fall at the same hurdle. It becomes a compulsive repetition that will magnify, rather than resolve, the problem. To seek to make an intimate partnership with the bearer of a quality from which one has felt excluded will actually sharpen, rather than soften, the difference. Far from being now in control of that quality in the other, the experience is more likely to be one of "nose on the windowpane", looking in on the zone from which one continues to feel excluded. This may be all the more likely an outcome of a mutually projective choice, since the partner will be travelling in the opposite direction, trying to escape the envied quality rather than incorporating a partner into it. So, partnerships will tend to exacerbate differences rather than to ameliorate them, just as siblings will increase the separateness of their respective niches.

But such a negative view of choice of partner would be to ignore that the unconscious wish to tackle the shared unresolved problems of their lateral relationships may in fact make the mutual choice an effective starting place for growth. The individual who is beset by anxiety about a particular outcome of an intimate relationship is more likely to choose a partner who shares that anxiety than one who is oblivious to it, so that together they can tackle it. Relationship problems can generally be seen in terms of dilemmas, of ambivalence, where the pursuit of a goal in one direction will militate against reaching an incompatible opposite goal. When couples have shared dilemmas, threatening each of them intrapsychically, they can divide up their ambivalence so that one holds the entire negative and the other all the positive on the issue. This then becomes a relief to each individually, but can lead all too inevitably to the replacement of intrapsychic conflict with interpsychic. The disowned projected side of the conflict is now out of the partner's control and can be feared and attacked. Instead of remedying old lateral sibling conflict that was once similarly divided, the couple relationship now becomes a repetition of the old. Ironically, one of the most common, and most fundamental, ways in which a couple may split their shared ambivalence can concern the very issue itself of moving from one step of the developmental staircase to another. Once *this* ambivalence is divided between them, each can feel excluded from the step the other is now felt to monopolize.

Partners may indeed find in each other one who would seem to be enabling in their initial "lateral" stage, but when they seek to develop their relationship into the next vertical stage of parenthood they find that this transition interface cannot be successfully negotiated. It can become evident, despite appearances to the contrary, that the couple have not individually managed to accept the trauma of being the same but different. There is no tolerance of there being another to whom they are not symbiotically attached, a couple from which they are the excluded third, or that they themselves are part of a couple from which another is excluded. In the partner they may have found another who has experienced the same dilemma in their family of origin, which has not allowed comfortable differentiation. Together, the couple has created an illusory attachment of sameness, from which difference is excluded into areas of their separate lives that do not overlap. Where there is initially a shared wish for a mutually gratifying parent–child relationship, the couple may well manage this between them. One, not necessarily always the same one, will be the gratifying parent for both, while the other is the gratified child, with each enjoying the other one's role vicariously.

The transition from the sexual to the parental couple

Pregnancy and birth of the actual child can only serve to destroy this illusion. The couple contains two individuals who are different and only one has the baby. If the one who does not have the baby experiences the new mother–baby pair as the couple from which he is excluded, he may well feel the same jealous rage as the older sibling does against the displacing sibling. And it may be part of the couple's shared unconscious fit (as it evidently was for Laius and Jocasta, parents of the hapless Oedipus) to agree that the child is such a threat to the parental couple that it must not be allowed to intrude. Alternatively, the couple's relationship, particularly sexually, may dwindle or atrophy in the face of the new mother–baby vertical relationship. Indeed, the baby may be seen by both parents to have joined the mother in the new symbiotic couple by which she becomes encapsulated, confirming the father's intolerable exclusion. Did she, too, as a child feel excluded from a sibling's relationship with a parent? Was this the shared fear that became part of the couple's unconscious fit in their lateral relationships? Is the shared defence against it no longer sustainable in the face of the birth of the baby? Does the father then react by looking for his own new lateral other, the lover with whom he can be symbiotically entwined to the exclusion of the partner, the new mother? "Your new baby, my new baby." Or "Your new sexual partner, my new sexual partner." Or "Your new symbiotic other who excludes me. My new symbiotic other who excludes you." Or "You have left our symbiotic couple to go on to a new vertical symbiotic couple with your baby; I am returning to a lateral couple in a sexual relationship which will have no baby."

Any of these possible formulations, or others, can underlie this familiar presenting problem of the couple who come into couple therapy. Perhaps the father has reacted with depressed withdrawal in the face of the new threat that the mother seems helpless to alleviate? Or does he become himself the sole parent of the new baby, edging out the mother into the position of the depressed third? Does she dovetail with this "solution" by excluding herself, perhaps by rushing back to work, or into a new/old relationship? A long list of possibilities, but still only a fraction of the permutations that a couple can employ, individually or together, to avoid their coupledom being destroyed by the intrusive third. Many are gender free and as discernible in the struggles of same-gender couples. They can be seen with couples who adopt. Our culture is particularly permissive of many of these permutations. (Laius and Jocasta left their intrusive third to die. In the Ancient Greece of Sophocles, or indeed in Freud's nineteenth century Vienna, it is unlikely that if Oedipus, their first baby, had been a *girl* she would have been envisaged as such a threat.)

Perhaps in another opposite scenario the couple's problem is that they *cannot* produce a child. One or both may be infertile. Shared ambivalence about having children may have led to their putting off the fateful step of transition to the next vertical relationship (seen, perhaps, in the way one or both have aborted or rejected earlier babies, in this or previous relationships). So then the pain and despair is felt about the lack of the now idealized relationship with its third, the baby who is not to be. Again our culture can offer often cruel hope. Can the couple bear to give up the endless quest through the fertility treatments that can so effectively ruin their coupledom *without* resulting in the longed for baby? Will adoption be tried without the couple seeming to have the emotional resources needed to combat the disappointing reality of the child who is not their genetic extension?

Once more I am describing, seemingly only in negative terms, these crucial junctures in which the couple's attempts to traverse the interface between the lateral and the vertical are doomed to failure. But this is not necessarily so. The unconscious mutual choice of each other, the shared dilemmas and mirrored ways of resolving them, may have a fruitful outcome. Our culture's permissiveness may provide an enabling context for the couple's struggle. For some, a reversal of stereotypical roles in their parenting and their sexuality may provide an effective solution to their shared dilemmas. Fertility treatment may produce the child who, in its reality, may actually rescue its parents from the sterile idealization of the child they never had. The lives of childless couples, whether heterosexual or same-sex, may become gratifying again when they adopt, or when at least one of them is able to have his/her own genetic child.

Case example

I worked many years ago as co-therapist with Lily Pincus (co-founder, with Enid Balint, of the Family Discussion Bureau, and writer of several seminal texts in marital therapy), with a couple who had been torn apart by the husband's affair a few months after the birth of their first child.

> He had been an oldest child, who was controlling, particularly to the youngest, of his two younger sisters, when evacuated with them during the war. His wife, born just after the war, had encountered jealous rejection from her six and five years older brother and sister, whom she had learnt to placate when necessary. She could also retreat into closed ranks with her father. He, too, was facing hostility from the older children, as well as from their mother, on his return from war service.

> Before the baby the marriage had been based on a mirroring similarity, with the wife seeming to welcome her five years older husband's domineering devotion, in contrast to her brother's remembered alternate bullying and rejection. The husband was happy to transfer to his wife a similar zealous care to that he had shown his youngest sister, particularly when in the alien environment of their evacuee foster home. After six years of marriage, with the couple alternating positions of ambivalence about having children, the reluctantly conceived baby, a girl, had had the detrimental effect on this harmonious symmetry that had brought them to marital therapy.

> Neither could explain how the husband could have embarked so uncharacteristically on this ill-concealed affair (with his ten years younger secretary), devastating his wife and leaving him profoundly guilty.

As therapists, our shared countertransference was concordant with the husband, to whom we felt protective, and curiously negative to the wife, despite her evident and justifiable distress; one for which I, especially, would usually have had a strong empathic sympathy. I could not readily share Lily Pincus's view that "an affair can often enrich a marriage". We used this initial joint reaction to help us explore the family dynamics with them. We understood how neither had experienced a safe attachment to their mothers; he had reacted to his deprivation by giving his youngest sister the care he wished he had had for himself. Avoiding the competition for her mother who had guiltily sided with the two older siblings, his wife had tried to compensate for this loss by a somewhat forced flirtatious closeness to her father. Both husband and wife had enjoyed, in their first six years of childless marriage, a more gratifying duo than either had found previously with their parents or siblings. But the arrival of their baby had destroyed this harmony, which could not be transposed into a trio. The wife now closed ranks with the baby, to whom she compulsively devoted herself, to the exclusion of her husband, in a way she came to see she wished she had received from her mother. We also saw that this was how she had found her husband attending to *her*, albeit rather compulsively and cackhandedly, as is the familiar experience of those who receive care that is primarily aimed at fulfilling the need of the carer. So, when she switched her role of receiving his care, from which he could get vicarious gratification, to one of obsessively devoted attention to the baby, together with both losing interest in each other sexually, he embarked on his affair. He was, however, at pains to point out that it was not the sex he felt drawn to as much as the closeness and affirmation of his value that the affair gave him.

This is a brief and over-simplistic account with no detail of the vicissitudes of the relationship and the therapy in the ensuing fifteen months; all comprising joint sessions, which left the couple better able to separate psychologically from each other, and from the child, in a way that gave them confidence to continue together without our further intervention.

Transference/countertransference in couple therapy

It will be clear from the above account that it is not one of "working in the transference" as generally understood by the individual psychoanalytic therapist. Rather, it is looking afresh at the work as an example of seeing how the couple's relationship was one of transference *to the couple* of their lateral sibling relationships, the quality of which had been dictated by their experience of their vertical parent–child relationships. As couple therapists we were not then, and I would not now be, seeking to "work in the transference" in the sense of deflecting the focus of the therapy from the couple to the relationship with the therapist(s). In treating the couple as the conjoint patient, we resist being drawn into interpretative work, whether or not in the transference, that addresses only *one* of the couple, even when one partner seems to be in only silent acquiescence, or, indeed, in active opposition to the partner's views. The supposition is that whatever one of the couple is, or is doing, is likely to be on behalf of the other as well, however adamantly disowned by the other. This is particularly so if it seems to express one half of a shared ambivalence, leaving the partner to express (or suppress) the other half, in that most familiar of joint couple defences.

Some years ago my husband and I published a paper about the interpretation of dreams in couple therapy (Morley & Morley, 1986). Of course, only one partner is the actual dreamer, but we noticed how excited the other partner could be and how fruitful their own associations to the dream that would be relevant to the shared internal world of both. We had in therapy a couple, Mr and Mrs B, of whom the husband told us he had had the ability to correctly guess the sibling order of his peers at school. He was aware that it was mutually relevant to the choice of his wife, as an oldest with two troublesome younger brothers, when he was the youngest of his family with a middle brother having died the year before he was born. In a joint session Mrs B referred to her husband's dream since the previous session, and asked him to tell us about it. He did so and it went as follows:

> He dreamt that he saw a light aeroplane crash nearby. It burst into flames and he ran to it to see if he could help. There were two pilots sitting one behind the other. The first had been enveloped by the flames and his features had melted so that he was almost unrecognizable. The other, sitting behind him, was dead but not mutilated in any way and wearing his helmet and goggles. Mr B was unable to rescue either of the airmen.

Neither husband nor wife was aware of the significance of anything in the dream, although both were fascinated by it. We invited them to explore its imagery. Mr B thought about the possibility of the two pilots being his brothers, but was puzzled that *both* should be dead when in real life only one had died. Mrs B commented that there were times when her husband had wondered whether he would have found the one who had died rather easier to get on with than the oldest brother, who had lived. Mr B responded rather sharply that there were times when his wife could have done without either of her two brothers. But Mrs B wanted to move on from their siblings to her association of the badly burned pilot to a foetus with its not yet formed features, reminding her of the very traumatic miscarriage in which their first pregnancy had terminated. Mr B then thought that the second pilot might be a reference to their still-born child, who had resulted from the second pregnancy. We could now see the link between these traumatic losses of their first two babies to the siblings, of whom he had lost one and might have wished he had lost both, since he feared he was always regarded as inferior to both. But he had found in his wife a partner who had had to cope, often *in loco parentis*, with two very much alive, difficult younger brothers. In reciprocation, Mrs B had found in her husband a youngest who had survived both the death of his middle brother and the scornful rejecting behaviour of his successful, favoured, oldest brother. The shared complexity of unconscious identification and rejection of these siblings, living and dead, had made this a good marital fit until it was asked to contain the double loss of their first two infants. What was important about the dream images and their associations was that they allowed the couple to share and discharge some of the mutual grief that they had tended hitherto to keep to themselves.

This therapy was conducted in a mixture of one-hour individual and one-and-a-half-hour joint sessions. (Our practice, in this format, is to get the couple's permission to share details of their individual sessions between therapists, but not with their partner.) The session with Mr B's dream occurred some two weeks before our long summer break. We could have interpreted the dream as referring to the couple's impending loss of ourselves. And, indeed, it could have had that aspect in its unconscious timing. But we regarded it as more effective therapy to keep the focus on the couple themselves and on their individual experiences of their lateral sibling relationships. There we could see how the marriage, unconsciously based on those shared and opposite experiences, had fallen so poignantly at the fence of negotiating the interface with the vertical parent–child relationship. Had we dwelt on some whole-object transference to ourselves, whether as parents, siblings, or children, whom they would be losing temporarily in the break and permanently when the therapy terminated, it would have been to encourage the continued focus on a loss that could only be the shadow of the actual losses they had sustained. They needed our help to become conscious of the meaning and entailments of those losses, real, wished for, or defended against. What they did *not* need was to be left stuck with the focus on the renunciation of therapists and whatever that might mean transferentially, when they were about to have an important break together as a couple in which they could hope to find a new creative sexuality. In this case the couple reported a closer, more intimate holiday than they had previously enjoyed, which we later learned had, despite some setbacks, led to a pregnancy and eventual birth of a live child.

The use of the countertransference in couple therapy

We would expect generally to make greater and more varied use of our *counter*transference with couples than with our individual patients. Working as sole therapist with a couple, one is likely to have less influence on the countertransference that, when working psychoanalytically with individual patients, we are used to experiencing most readily as parental, probably with frequent gender bias of women therapists as maternal and men as paternal. However careful the therapist may be to maintain a neutral stance, the whole setting of therapy lends itself to the individual patient experiencing the therapist as the senior partner in the enterprise. The therapist sets the scene, and makes powerful interventions to which the patient may conform or rebel; just as the child (the *only* child in the therapy) reacts to the parental world in which he finds himself. So, the therapist's countertransference is more likely to mirror that vertical parental transference rather than be experienced as lateral, involving siblings.

The couple, of course, outnumbers the single therapist in the consulting room; and even if they met only recently they know each other, both consciously and unconsciously, better than the therapist knows either. The therapist's countertransference may, of course, be parental, but if so is likely to be that of the parent in the face of *siblings*, be it quarrelling, naughty, conforming, or withholding siblings. Or it may be that a sibling countertransference is that of the older sibling left, perhaps feeling out of one's depth, with the responsibility for younger siblings. Or is the therapist the *younger* sibling, experiencing the older siblings in the patient couple who exclude, dominate, or scorn?

The feelings evoked in the transference–countertransference changes with two therapists working with a couple in a foursome. With a resilient relationship between the therapists, who are able to process their countertransference reactions (evoked differently by every couple they work with), they can feel on sturdier ground, less vulnerable to the couple, particularly those whose anger and frustration is forcibly conveyed in the session. The "container" provided by the foursome is more likely, though certainly not exclusively, to evoke a parental countertransference. The couple may then feel safer to explore their lateral sibling relationships from the past into the present. They may use the therapy to focus on their struggle to make their couple the fulcrum of change. Here their legitimate, non-incestuous sexual relationship with the other, who is the same but different, can develop the capacity to move into the vertical relationship with children (or with other creative activity) with whom the non-sexual intimacy is not allowed to undermine or destroy the sexual parental couple.

However, should the therapist couple themselves be in a relationship with unresolved tensions, they will have difficulty in providing this safe container for the couple in therapy. This problem is sometimes apparent in an asymmetrical therapist couple, such as that of a student with an experienced therapist. But it can also appear in the therapist couple who, particularly if they are personal partners as well as professional, will, of course, have all their own rich mixture of lateral as well as vertical relationships intermingling in their own unconscious choice of the other. But where they are practised in exploring the infinite variety of countertransference reactions that can be evoked by the patient couple, and are able, indeed, at times to do so *in the sessions,* this can be an enabling factor in the work. It can certainly be an easier dimension to explore with a therapist partner rather than to have to rely solely on the *"internal supervisor"* (Casement, 2002) of the individual therapist, or even on the external supervisor who is not actually present in the session.

The psychoanalytic therapist with individual patients can, of course, also be attending to the "internal" couple(s) of the patient. But he may be keeping the focus exclusively on the patient and treating his/her comments about others as unreciprocated projections of intrapsychic elements into the other, and/or into the therapist. The couple therapist, even when working with the individual patient, may attend to, and even ask for, almost as much detail about a patient's actual or potential partner as s/he knows of the patient. S/he will often be able to produce as detailed a genogram with all the related siblings and intergenerational factors of the individual patient's important "others" as s/he would for a couple.

My contention is that wherever a patient has a pre-existing couple relationship, or is forming one in the course of therapy, it is often expedient and enabling to widen the focus of the work to include such a relationship, either literally or at least in the discourse of the individual therapy. Not to do so can be disabling or fruitless. (See my MA thesis, Morley, 1994.) The individual patient who is seeking therapy may have managed, albeit only tenuously, to move from the vertical dyad of a parent–child relationship through the lateral triad of siblings/peers into a couple, one that might be helped to make the next vertical step of creative commitment. It may be that the therapeutic relationship then comes to be in unhelpful competition with the couple. Of course, it may prove *ineffective* competition. If the patient has found in the partner someone who dovetails with the mutual shared projections of their internal worlds, the relationship with the therapist may be only its pale shadow. And the partner, particularly if not in therapy, may hang on tenaciously to the patient, wanting to keep her/him to the original unconscious contract of their mutual choice.

But the scenario for the therapist working with the individual who is in a couple relationship or trying to form one may well be worse than ineffective. It may prove actually destructive, both to the individual patient and to the couple relationship. This can be the case when the therapy is all too well able to set up in direct rivalry to the couple. The individual who is struggling to move up the relationship steps from vertical to lateral, and perhaps on through the couple to the next vertical, now finds in the therapist a seductive dyad again. The therapeutic relationship is essentially asymmetrical, and one in which the patient does not have to be responsible for the therapist, beyond paying his fees; there are no siblings or children to interrupt His/Her Majesty the Patient's attention to his own internal world. This experience may be essential to the patient who has not yet had a good enough dyadic experience to be able to give it up or to gravitate to a triad. But to those who are in a couple, the therapeutic relationship can be enormously gratifying and all-absorbing, with the effect of one taking a lover, leaving the partnership to feel arid and ungratifying in contrast. To work effectively in the individual transference it is, after all, essential that the relationship with the therapist is of central importance. In contrast, the couple therapist focuses on the *couple* as the one in which change can occur, as they are helped to reintroject their mutual projections. The couple therapist is the facilitator and monitor of this process and does not need to invite the transfer of the patient's objects to him/herself for change to occur. The couple relationship may indeed become the stronger and more effective container for the individual's creative development. And in this case it does not have the problem of how it can be given up, in the way that the therapeutic relationship shares with the vertical parent–child relationship, if the "child' is to progress up the alternate lateral–vertical steps.

The sibling/couple relationships of Freud's "Wolf Man' patient

I want now, as I promised in my introduction to this chapter, to look at Freud's work with the "Wolf Man", the young Russian aristocrat whose story is so well known, as considered exhaustively by Freud himself, and with commentaries from other writers too numerous to mention, that I will not repeat it here. I prefer to call the "Wolf Man" by his Christian name, Sergej (Pankejeff), if only to underline that he did have a personal identity beyond that of being Freud's most famous patient. He is unique in being the only one of Freud's patients who published his own detailed account of his life and of his analysis with Freud, which we can examine *alongside the analyst's account*. Muriel Gardiner, a close personal friend and mentor of Sergej's and one to whom he turned particularly after his wife committed suicide, edited his memoirs and published them in 1973, together with Freud's case history, under the title *The Wolf-Man and Sigmund Freud*. I have made the following brief summary of his case history, based on his own account of himself, from my couple therapist's standpoint.

> Sergej, born 1886, wrote his memoirs many years after his analysis, but it is extraordinary how little overlap there is between his own account and Freud's, including even of the famous dream, which gave him his "Wolf Man" label. In so far as he remembers or mentions it, Sergej recalls the dream as relating to his fear of wolves at the age of four, which he attributes in part to his sister Anna, two and a half years older and his only sibling, who included in her sexual teasing a promise to show him a picture of a pretty young girl before confronting him with one of a rapacious wolf standing on its hind legs. There is no mention of the association Freud depicts, of Sergej at the age of eighteen months, at five-o'clock on a summer afternoon, in the oedipal trauma of watching and interrupting the primal scene of his father having sex with his mother three times *a tergo*. [In the publication of her conversations with Sergej in the last few years of his life, the psychoanalyst Karin Obholzer (1982) reports him as saying "It's very farfetched . . . He (Freud) maintains I saw it, but who will guarantee it is not a fantasy of his? . . . I cannot believe everything Freud said, after all . . . I have always thought the memory would come. But it never did."] In the section of the memoirs where he is pleased to be Freud's "favourite patient" and wants to support his interpretations, Sergej's writing becomes oddly wooden and impersonal, as if he is repeating a lesson. Where he comes dramatically to life is when he is describing his own memories, particularly about his sister, who committed suicide when he was twenty-one; but above all in relation to his beloved wife, Therese, from whose suicide thirty years later he claims never to have recovered.
>
> Sergej sees his sister as their father's favourite. She was the defiant, dominant oldest, leaving him no option, he thought, but to be the placatory one, particularly with the servants and tutors to whose care they were left in the frequent absence of their parents. He describes an occasion in their teens when they are invited to a fancy dress party and Anna upsets Mademoiselle, their French governess, by insisting on

going dressed as a boy. Their father took Anna's side so adamantly that the weeping Mlle threatened to leave, but comforted herself with Sergej's easy obedience, which he reluctantly sustained, despite wishing that he too could rebel. When Anna, at twenty-three, was secretly planning to poison herself, she begged him to write to her a week after their emotional parting, and to visit her, at a time when their lives were developing separately. Sergej ruminates sorrowfully that although her female body seemed attractive to him, Anna herself perhaps felt too uncomfortably *male*. Was this why she killed herself?

In that ensuing desolation he saw how his mother was lost in outpouring of (?guilty) grief for Anna, while he and his father (with whom he had always felt alien and humiliated) tried unsuccessfully to get closer to each other in their shared loss. But within a year of Anna's death their father also died, at the age of forty-nine, with the suspicion that this, too, was suicide.

Depression, which Sergej attributes principally to the loss of his sister, took him to a sanitorium, where he met his German future wife, Therese, on the nursing staff and was instantly attracted to her buoyant personality. So, his wife never knew his sister, but she was to tell him later that Anna was *the one member of his family with whom she always felt she had an affinity*. The two fell swiftly into an intense ambivalent relationship in which secret rendezvous were set up and then jettisoned alternately by each of them.

Therese, who was divorced and had one child, a daughter of then eight, explained her dilemma as one of having to choose between Sergej and her daughter. Her background mirrored Sergej's in that she was the younger of two, but with a much older brother, by eight years, who (like Sergej's sister) she told Sergej was the dominant, defiant eldest, and renowned for his profligate sexuality. Unlike Sergei, who loved and admired his sister and wished he could emulate her, Therese disapproved of her brother and had a poor relationship with him. But, like Sergej, she became the "good" one and dutifully succumbed to maternal pressure to marry a "suitable" man, only to divorce him soon after their daughter's birth.

After two or three years of Therese alternating meetings with Sergej with looking after her daughter, Else, Sergej gave up the struggle, saying that he must leave her to look after her child, with the approval of all the doctors and advisers he spoke to. But he could not get Therese out of his mind. Further depression and visits to other sanatoria led to his referral to Freud. Sergej is clear that the *only* reason he allowed himself to enter analysis with Freud, to whom he was referred at this point, was because Freud approved of the relationship with Therese *in principle* because it showed that Sergej was "breaking through to the woman". But this approval was conditional on his having his analysis *first*. His entreaties to be allowed to see her again were of no avail until, he writes, the analysis got so stuck that Freud relented. Sergej needed a detective agency to track Therese down in Munich, where he found her living with Else and so ill with depression at not seeing him that he could barely recognize her. He would have married her instantly but Freud permitted them *only to live together*, which they did in Vienna, unacknowledged socially or by their families and therefore *without the child*, who went to live with Therese's brother. Unusually, this analysis lasted four years, so it was only then in 1914 that Sergej and Therese could marry, with Freud at last now meeting Therese and being agreeably surprised, Sergej writes, that he had "had quite a false picture of her and that actually she looked like a tsarina". (No mention of any of this is in Freud's accounts, which remain exhaustively exploring the supposed oedipal trauma at eighteen months and its aftermath.)

Therese's daughter remained in Germany and never came to live with them, but when there was news of her tuberculosis at sixteen, first her mother journeyed to be with her (and without her mother-in-law) in 1917, followed by Sergej ten months later only a few weeks before his stepdaughter died. (At the end of his life he tells the editor of his memoirs how sad he was that they were never able to have children of their own, the one thing that would cheer the loneliness of old age.) So again this couple seem to have had to demonstrate that they could not maintain their relationship in juxtaposition with either parents or children.

Taking up their story after twenty years, Sergei writes that they were living in Vienna in 1938, where many Jewish people were committing suicide. Therese had become seriously depressed and suggested, to his horrified concern, that they turn on the gas and die together. A year later she gassed herself alone in their flat. Sergej was distraught beyond endurance and never recovered from this loss. One of the few points of agreement between his own account and Freud's is that he could be sexually attracted to peasant girls and servants; but he is clear that they could never be partners; whereas Freud dismisses Therese herself as a mere nurse and therefore a woman of lowly origin, comparable to a peasant girl.

Sergej was at times sycophantically grateful to Freud for giving him his identity as the Wolf Man, Freud's favourite "son", but he also felt bitter

about his unresolved dependency on Freud, from which he could never
be released. The dependency was of course primarily emotional, but
became financial with the Russian Revolution leaving him penniless.
Freud then not only charged no fee, but gave Sergej modest sums of
money for a further six years. Unlike Freud himself, Sergej claims that
Freud was never able to cure him of his symptoms; nor had he ever
been helped by Freud or by anyone to understand his wife or foresee
that she might kill herself and so deprive him of the only person he had
ever truly loved other than his sister Anna.

Looking at Sergej's and Therese's stories, it would seem that
neither of them was effectively able to make the transition to the
sexual couple who can simultaneously sustain having a child from
their lateral relationships with their siblings, which were themselves based on unresolved tensions from their vertical relationships with parents. With *unwitting* help from Freud, they adapted
these potentially incestuous relationships with siblings into the
gratifying sexual intimacy they enjoyed with each other, but could
never either detach it from the vertical relationship with parents/
analyst or go on to a new vertical relationship with children. It
appears not to have been possible for them to go from a dyad to a
triad. Both could alternate their one-to-one relationships with a
parent, a sibling, a child, an analyst, or a partner, but not traverse
the couple's fulcrum of the triad, the couple which leaves both
parents and siblings behind as the non-sexual "third", and retains
its own sexuality as it creates the child.

Freud, it seems, could never *knowingly* reach a point of Oedipal
resolution for this patient. He was interested above all in illustrating
his Oedipal theory of the castration complex. This was at the point
of abandoning his earlier seduction theory, when he realized, as he
writes to Fliess, that he would have to accuse his own father, a year
after his death, of pederasty towards *Sigmund's* younger siblings
(Masson, 1985). So was he unable to help Sergej out of the powerful dyad with himself into a permanently creative couple relationship, rather than an unacknowledged sexual relationship that must
wait subserviently in the shadows of the powerful vertical relationship with himself, the "father". In the power struggle between
them it seems that Freud and his patient never shared an agenda or
a view of what was transpiring in the analysis. But, as the weaker
of the two, with his powerful transference to Freud as the father he

had never had, Sergej needed to placate him and to pursue his own needs under cover in a way that Freud appears not to have recognized.

If Freud could not help his patients to complete the relationship staircase (perhaps because he was himself stuck in the dyad that is only ever a linear extension of the self), what about the mythical Oedipus? It is interesting that Freud chooses *this* myth to illustrate the universal paradigm of the *son* who murders his father to marry his mother, as if the *parents* have nothing to do with it. Oedipus is the only one of the three who does not know of this relationship to his natural parents (although Laius did not tell Jocasta the Oracular warning), while they thought they had murdered their only child. Is this an identification for Freud with the abused child who prefers to embrace powerful guilt than to suffer helpless innocent shame?

Are psychoanalytic institutions limited in their lateral relationships by their adherence to their founders?

Juliet Mitchell argues that the microcosm of the failure to give up autonomy and to embrace the lateral sharing of siblings, real or imagined, lies at the root of the global phenomenon of human conflict in all cultures, races, and institutions (Mitchell, 2003). So, indeed, may it be for the conflict in the world of psychoanalytic institutions. The profession of psychoanalytically informed couple therapy is certainly itself a later-born sibling in the world of psychoanalysis. It has its ethos firmly entrenched in the great creators of psychoanalytic theory and practice, and in their current professional followers. But it is also differentiating itself creatively from older siblings in developing its own growing body of research into the theory and practice of psychoanalytic *couple* therapy. The history of that family suggests that it would do well to avoid enclosing itself in the claustrum of an institutional requirement to go through an intensive individual psychoanalysis. This may indeed be the proper requirement made of older "siblings" who specialize in intensive individual therapy, particularly for those who are not able to make gratifying creative couple relationships. The couple therapist, the professionally later-born, is different, and training requirements may also appropriately be different.

Straying out of the psychoanalytic "family" there are also important links for couple therapists with other therapies, particularly the systemic and psychosexual therapies. Old assumptions die hard that the non-directive work of the psychoanalytic therapist would prove incompatible with the "behavioural" techniques incorporated into the psychosexual and systemic therapies, but increasingly these are seen as providing a valuable and sometimes essential dimension. They can be helpfully integrated with the professional skill of the psychoanalytical couple therapist, who is standing at the junction of lateral and vertical relationships, the essential catalyst of transition from family to non-family, from forbidden incest to the necessary sexual intercourse that produces the next generation.

References

Casement, P. (2002). *Learning from our Mistakes*. London: Brunner/ Routledge.

Cohen, N. (1982). Same or different? A problem of identity in cross-cultural marriages. *Journal of Family Therapy*, 4: 177–199.

Coles, P. (2003). *The Importance of Sibling Relationships in Psychoanalysis*. London: Karnac.

Gardiner, M. (1973). *The Wolf-Man and Sigmund Freud*. Harmondsworth: Penguin.

Lewin, V. (2004). *The Twin in the Transference*. London: Whurr.

Masson, J. M. (1985). *The Complete Letters of Sigmund Freud to Wilhelm Fliess, 1887–1904*. Cambridge, MA: Harvard University (Belknap) Press.

Mitchell, J. (2003). *Siblings: Sex and Violence*. Cambridge: Polity.

Morley, E. (1994). Using the focus of couple psychotherapy in work with the individual patient. Unpublished MA thesis; University of Hertfordshire.

Obholzer, K. (1982). *The Wolf Man Sixty Years Later: Conversations with Freud's Patient*. London: Routledge & Kegan Paul

Sulloway, F. J. (1996). *Born to Rebel*. London: Little, Brown and Co.

CHAPTER NINE

Siblings

Jennifer Silverstone

Introduction

This paper is about siblings, how siblings find each other, use each other, and sustain each other.[1] I am going to suggest that siblings can hold the family narrative for each other, and become the containers for each other of a history of their childhood. This is particularly true in the cases where there has been a lack of the capacity for maternal ambivalence, by which I mean acknowledgment that mothering contains love and hate as a healthy state of affairs, and where there is a lack of the ability of the mother to keep her child in mind. Siblings can also play an important role where there is an idealization or denigration of a child, or a negative view of the child, or where for other reasons there is an absence of mind in the mother.[2]

In other cases, where the family carries a trauma, siblings can become central to the internal world. I shall take a brief look at the passing on of trauma through families and into the next generation of siblings. This will include taking note of the whole family, its structure, and a consideration of the role of maternal function, for I believe that part of the maternal function is in creating and re-creating

the narrative of a child's life. We shall see that in the face of early failures of containment of various kinds, and where siblings have had
to become caretakers, the sibling transference can become central in
the therapeutic work. When these states of mind are revealed the
focus of work usually shifts away from the Oedipal constellation. I
shall also make some reference to the only child.

In every text to which I refer, barring the two seminal texts on
siblings, those of Coles (2003), Mitchell (2003), and that of Lewin
(2004) on twins, there are few direct references to siblings. Siblings
are rarely written about, as significant internal objects. For instance,
Bollas (1987, 1995) writes extensively about internal objects. He
states that:

> Each person who is characterologically disturbed needs to exter-
> nalize his pathological object relations, to re-create in the transfer-
> ence the atmosphere that prevailed in his family and, in some
> limited and necessary manner, to force the analyst into the analyst's
> own private experiencing of the family atmosphere . . . I only take
> up objects that are fundamentally representation of true external
> others, such as mother and father. [Bollas, 1987, p. 253]

It is my view that in some instances siblings are just such objects,
who take up such positions of significance in the internal world of
some patients.

To illustrate my thinking about the complex place siblings can
hold in the internal world, I shall use clinical material from the
work I have done with three of my patients and use brief references
to other cases. In all the cases I refer to, the psychic structure has
been tempered by an attachment to an internal object, which has
pushed the maternal transference into the background. In only one
case was an attachment to a sibling clear early on in the work and
consciously expressed by the patient. In the other cases the maternal transference receded over time and the sibling position became
more focused and enabled us to think more broadly around the
internal sibling object.

I am going to suggest that when mothers are not the primary
care-givers, there is a lack of lived experience, and along with it a
diminished sense of going on being; but that this can be mediated
by the sibling relationship. In two of the cases the sibling relationships have become central to the patient and, therefore, the sibling

has become a lively part of the transference. Both these patients have had their lived experience with, and among, siblings, and both have differing manifestations of an absent mother. In the first case the patient was a replacement child for a dead sibling and became himself a carer of one of the other siblings. It is not uncommon for siblings to mother each other (see Coles, 2003). This is not a gendered activity. Though little girls may play at being little mothers, boys are sometimes in the position of having to, or wanting to, take up maternal function, different to, and separate from, a paternal function. The second patient's primary relationship was with her elder sister; and the third discussion is of an only child. Having no sibling does not mean an absence of an internal world configuration in which a phantasy sibling lives. After all, in all of this discussion I am referring both to external reality and to internal phantasy.

Mother

The backdrop to my consideration of the nature of sibling relationships is primarily the mother. We instinctively think we know that what are embedded in the first and earliest moments, and, indeed, months and years, are the blueprints for future developments. This is the most significant period for a future healthy relationship for mother and baby alike. The maternal relationship, and the therapeutic one, need to have the capacity to tolerate ambivalence. By this I mean that all states of mind of the infant or patient need to be tolerated in order that a space can be provided for a robust and useful internal object. It is the denial of ambivalence, or love and hate, that diminishes this possibility.

> Maternal ambivalence signifies the mother's capacity to know herself and to tolerate traits in herself she may consider less than admirable—and to hold a more complete image of her baby. Accordingly, idealization and/or denigration of self, and by extension, her baby, diminish. But the sense of loss and sorrow that accompanies maternal ambivalence cannot be avoided. Acknowledging that she hates what she loves is acutely painful for a mother. [Parker, 1995, p. 17]

Roszika Parker quotes a moving letter a mother writes to her fourth, as yet unborn, child. This letter describes the mother's feelings of love and hate as she comes to terms with this unwanted and unplanned child. Parker suggests that it is this ambivalence, so clearly expressed, that allows the mother to respond to the newborn with authentic feelings of love at the birth: "I think the extent of her ambivalence during the pregnancy broke through her defences, compelling her to abandon the check she held on her emotions as a mother" (Parker, 1995, p. 204). This freedom of expression enabled the intensity of love and joy at the sight of the baby to outweigh her hate.

In order for a mother to be a good enough mother, she need not be too good. She will inevitably fail her baby, and she will hate her baby when she fails him.[3] She will fail him in the space she leaves for creativity and exploration, she will not always anticipate the danger the baby encounters, both in his unprocessed thoughts and in the real, unexplored world. But, because she also loves her baby, she will love him after her failure, and wish to make him better and repair the damage that she believes she has done in her phantasy, as well as in the real world, and restore him to equilibrium. He will become whole in body, and a whole object replaced as such in her mind, though as I have said, she will berate herself in her own mind for her failure to guard him, or from letting go of him in her mind, or in reality.

It is inevitable that the therapist will fail the patient and hate the patient for the failure, while loving the patient for recovering from the failure and reaching a mutuality of understanding. In preparation for a new patient the therapist will need to acknowledge her ambivalence, and this may be expressed in the reluctance to take on an open-ended commitment. A new patient, like a new baby, demands great swathes of time set aside for someone not yet known. There will be the anticipation of the possible lack of movement in the work as well as the development of the transference, positive and negative, and anticipated failures of understanding. But these will be counterbalanced by the joys of seeing, and being part of, change. It is a privilege to watch someone grow and find a sense of fulfilment where there was only a vestige of self-worth present before treatment. There is an excitement, too, in being experienced differently as the therapy develops, both in the therapist and in the patient; these feelings enable psychotherapeutic treatment to flourish. I am linking these complex emotions with the therapist's ability to acknowledge ambivalent feelings about her patients: I hate this patient, I love this same patient, and saying this to oneself enables the transference to flourish unencumbered by guilt or a steady flow of too much pleasure.

To return to Parker's (1995) case of the mother facing her fourth unplanned child, I am suggesting that the three children born previously to this woman might not have been the recipients of a resolved state of maternal ambivalence. An unresolved ambivalence hinders the maternal relationship, as it does the therapeutic one, and hinders the development of a rugged transference. In the face of maternal and paternal ambivalence there is a greater potential for health, but with idealization or denigration, preoccupation or trauma, there is the potential for failure to thrive. It is in these cases of parental preoccupation or trauma, where the children are idealized or denigrated, that the presence of a sibling relationship can act as a lively and constructive mediator.[4] And so, we can expect to find in the therapeutic work a sibling transference where there has been a lack of ambivalence, or other difficulties in the parental relationship.

D's case illustrates how the birth order in the patient's history became the focus of the work. This young man had spoken of his family, his siblings as a lively and intelligent bunch, and his rather special relationship with his mother. In exploring his wish to stay special to his mother, to amuse her and entertain her as a child, and in adulthood, it slowly came into focus that he was entertaining her in order both to keep her attention and ensure that he was lively and alive for her. The patient, enthusiastic and appreciative in every way, worked hard and well on the problems of his inner world, readily falling, it seemed, into a positive maternal transference in which I basked. However, it lacked some depth, and the key to its lack of grip was that I was basking and amused and flattered in some way by the attention I was getting. All this was rather intangible, but nevertheless unsettling. Out of the shadows came a dead sibling whom in fact the patient had been conceived to replace. This ghostly sibling came into the work slowly but shaped many of the subsequent sessions: a dead child, silently mourned and never spoken about.

D gradually came to the understanding that he was in part a replacement child. His consciously concerned mother was not, he felt, deeply attached to him, but rather to a lost object. He unconsciously compensated for her lack of mothering by mothering himself, another sick sibling, therefore identifying with his mother's albeit failed attempt to keep one of her children alive. Mother's lack of engagement with my patient, the son she said she loved, was possibly to protect her from the terrible pain of any further loss. Her unconscious ambivalence left the patient always feeling unwanted but cared for. He approached relationships with enthusiasm but never followed them through, never feeling that his presence would be sufficient, never feeling his friends really wanted him. His defence against these feelings of not being wanted was to develop an endearing raffishness, a forgetful and boyish charm on which he unconsciously traded: his absence would be put down to forgetfulness, his charm would ward off anger. This was the nature of the transference and it took some years for him to be able to telephone if a session was to be missed, or a break taken, somehow hoping that we would play the game of not noticing together, like two naughty children. However, he cared about me in a way that bypassed the maternal transference, and at a deeper level he was desperately intent to maintain with me the companionability of a fraternal lateral transference.

In a maternal projective identification he had found himself the caregiver and protector of an older but ill sibling. He had devoted his early adulthood to caring for this sibling who was pathologically depressed and with whom he felt in a kind of symbiotic tangle. He became the maternal caregiver and succeeded in warding off his own depression by caring for his sibling. Maternal caretaking has dogged his adult relationships: too much caring, like mother cared for him, and not enough space to be himself and therefore to be known for who he really is. He was never deeply available in his adult relationships, but tantalizingly present, always doing something for someone else, frightened of his own natural dependent needs. Slowly, he has become more aware of the unconscious absence in his relationship with his mother, less punitive in his feelings towards his father, and slightly freer to be himself in his relationship to his siblings. In his dawning realization that being is as important as doing, he has experienced that he is more of a companion when he allows himself to have needs. These needs can be, and indeed are, met. This enables him to touch a deeper sense of his own feelings. He can now become more realistic in his valued role as a father to his own children, more free to relate to them without too much emphasis on caregiving, on keeping them alive. All of this affects the transference, where I am now a more complex figure for him, neither a sibling nor an idealized mother. I have my faults, so there is the possibility of a livelier negative transference, and he cannot entertain me in order to banish his own negative feelings. This patient's partner became pregnant during our work and therefore his ability to have needs, to tolerate his own ambivalence in the face of fatherhood, became urgent matters of understanding.

This patient's father was potent, successful, and absent through commitments to work. His children, therefore, had little to model themselves on other than hard work and material success. The siblings turned away prematurely to the external world and searched for success. Their mother, devoted but grieving, was there for them, but absent in some ways to her most loved child. Each of the siblings has had difficulties in their adult relationships but it is striking that in the last few years there is a renewed interest in, and care for, each other. They are, in a way, creating a new, lively, extended family in which they talk more frankly to each other than they could tolerate throughout their childhood. Sibling rivalry is more conscious, needs are openly expressed, and the disillusion of not having these needs met is tolerated.

The father

Fathers, of course, also come into the picture. They, too, need to hold the maternal couple in mind, and in so doing they support the space so necessary for maternal preoccupation. The capacity to father is as complex as the capacity to mother. A father has to reach into his internal resources to find the model of fathering that rests within his internal world before he can achieve some of the complex joys and sorrows that parenthood inevitably brings.

> The degree of anxiety, for example, which infantile emotions and behaviour arouse, will vary from parent to parent. Mothers have

different abilities to contain distress and anxiety and to be aware of
the areas of similarity and difference between their own needs and
that of their baby. Likewise, fathers have different capacities to
contain the baby's mental state, and their own ability to support the
intensity of the relationship between mother and child will be
tested for the first time. Feelings of exclusion may be re-evoked,
either as sensed or as actual, as well as resentment about being left
out of what has now become, if only temporarily, the primary
couple. It may be some time, even years, before an unresolved difficulty in these early relationships makes its appearance in the
family, usually under the impact of some kind of renewed stress.
[Waddell, 1998, p. 113]

I do not wish to enter the lively debate around gender and
notions of femininity and masculinity, but I want to point to the role
of the father in the family. Fathers are there, too, for ruthless use by
the object, available for love and hate, or preoccupied and unavailable. Fathers can also be aligned with the mother, protecting and
nurturing but not fathering. Or they can father using a distant or
authoritarian stance, failing to contain the necessary ambivalence of
their own inner world. When faced with the state of infancy, or
later, at any point in the child's development, fathers can face deep
rivalries and envy with their own child. In order to defend against
this state of affairs, they may set up a false sibling alignment, enter-
ing the fray on the side of the child rather than facing their own
adult maturity and the pain of disillusion.

It is at the time of weaning—of the infant's first major experience of
loss—that the father will often be most naturally the object called
upon to help the child process the attendant feelings. When his own
losses are unresolved he will probably lack the necessary emotional
resources for this task. On the other hand, when things go well, he
may be an invaluable resource to his infant. [Barrows & Barrows,
2002, p. 170]

When parents fail in some or all of these tasks, the child has
many defences against the idea of failure. The most common
defence is to turn against dependence and become reliant upon the
self, or to turn to the sibling for comfort and care.

Siblings may turn to each other in the face of loss of the father.
It is not unusual for children to have absent fathers, for men can be

disturbed by the creation of a family and abandon their partner when a child is born. Furthermore, "In clinical practice the impression gained is that most fathers who leave a marriage do so after the birth of the second child, closely followed by the birth of the first child' (Emanuel, 2002, p. 135). And so we can take it that many mothers are left holding one or two babies in the face of the loss of a partner and that the deserted sibling couple may well turn to each other as well as to the mother for solace.

The family envelope

Didier Houzel (1996) calls the family of the present and its interconnected generational members collectively *the family envelope*, and says of it, "This construction is sometimes impeded by the weight of the past not only the child's own past but also that of the entire family, sometimes extending over several generations". When the family envelope becomes strained by too many conflicts it becomes torn and fails in its primary task of containment. When it is intact it contains and supports the constantly shifting positions within it; it enables family members to acknowledge and internalize in different ways its members, all of whom will be at different stages of development; even if a role, mothering for example, is being repeated.

> The child's psychic reality is constructed by complex processes, to the elucidation of which psychoanalysis has made a substantial contribution. This construction is sometimes impeded by the weight of the past, not only the child's own past but also that of the entire family, sometimes extending over several generations. Where such trans-generational transmission takes place, it freezes all or part of the child's personality in a preformed stereotyped role, which he is compelled to play over and over again. [Houzel, 1996, p. 910]

I have described the role of maternal ambivalence in the mental health of the infant and the containing function of the father. I have added Houzel's concept of the family envelope to add a further dimension to the complexity of family life and the way that transgenerational trauma can impact upon parents and siblings. We can look to those who have written about the Holocaust. Here, the often unnamed and unmentionable trauma of the parents courses like an underground river through the lives of the first- and second-generation survivors.

> Difficulties in the process of separation–individuation as a result of pathological symbiosis and a special type of identification are characteristic of Holocaust survivors' offspring. The psychoanalytic literature about children of survivors describes the mechanisms employed in the transmission of the Holocaust to them as early, unconscious identifications which carry in their wake the parents' perception of an everlasting life-threatening inner and outer reality. [Kogan, 1995, p. 820]

It is not surprising that some of the first- and second-generation children find themselves turning to each other for comfort and identification and turning away from the un-named terror that seems apparent in the parents. These children may well look to each other and to the groups that exist for the children of survivors for a wider sense of containment, feeling that their parents have already had too much to deal with and cannot bear further psychic pain.

Pines, working with Holocaust survivors, points out that survivors who are mothers are further challenged when their children reach adolescence. The mother, who has survived an early traumatic separation, may not be robust enough to withstand the adolescent fight for individuation. These adolescent children of survivors may turn to their siblings for support rather than challenge an already damaged parent (Pines, 1986, p. 304). Coles (2003, p. 75) discusses the paper written by Freud with Dann (1951) on the capacity of children to create sibling bonds of profound meaning in the face of extreme deprivation with no living parents. The extreme circumstances of this group of Holocaust survivors, who were brought up with no parents or parental involvement, tells us more about the capacity to survive than about object relations. Nevertheless, these children found meaning among themselves and managed, to a degree, to value and care for each other with an amazing consistency. Siblings can and do sustain each other when maternal function fails, as this moving study of children of the Holocaust illustrates. Though the members of this group were neither blood siblings nor stepsiblings, they shared a narrative, and therefore a history. No other living adult contained their story, and containing the narrative is a key parental function. Their responses to external and internal events were similar and recognizable to each other even if they were not to their carers. They were like siblings excluding their parents from their shared language or secrets.

Eva Hoffman (2004), writing in her book *After Such Knowledge*, speaks of herself and her sister's visit to the home their parents fled from, and their shared experience. Her book is dedicated "To my sister Alina, fellow inheritor of the legacy". What is striking about so much of the writing around the notions of transgenerational trauma is that siblings are curiously absent. Yet, in the psychic turmoil of intergenerational change it is often the case that siblings contain for each other the vital and lively history of their childhood narrative: without a story it is hard to move forward and simultaneously glance back.[5]

Siblings and the sibling transference

When a woman conceives a child she is both beginning something new and repeating a process, a process in which her mother conceived her and in which she in turn has conceived another. The relationship between the newly pregnant woman and her mother undergoes a period of change throughout pregnancy and brings, amongst other phenomena, a shift in identification. Although it is now not uncommon for conception to be medically assisted it is also not uncommon for a woman to find that she has conceived a child when she reaches the age that her mother conceived her or another sibling. This unconscious repetition sets up, or reinforces, identification with mother, both in the internal world and in external reality.

Patterns of mothering are sometimes avoided by the false and defensive creation of sibling status between mother and daughter, or father and son. A mother who mothered her child as if she were a sibling may respond similarly when she becomes a grandmother. A patient who was mothered as if a sibling may well herself find the relationship with her own infant very difficult until the time comes when a sibling bond can be established and the demand to internalize the maternal transference has diminished. This is but one of many ways a mother may have of avoiding the state of absolute dependence in the infant, by unconsciously denying the existence of such a dependent state. It is possible that these mothers respond well to putting their child in the care of others.

The conflict of mothering, or who might be mothering whom, is something we need to be aware of especially when a patient has been mothered by, or seems to mother, their siblings. In other words, when we think of the mother of the baby we also need to be aware that the mother has to work from her internalized mother, the phantasy mother, even if it does not seem to correspond to the mother of her external reality. All this upheaval is not the prerogative of mothers of daughters; sons too bring to the mother and father questions of potency and sexuality. Men need to make the shift into protector and caregiver, while their repeated need to be mothered when their partner may be maternally concerned and psychically unavailable, can disrupt the relationship, as I have already suggested. All these vicissitudes and the huge shifts in relationships, in generational order, in regression, and within the family, however haphazardly we define family, are seen and experienced in the consulting room while working with pregnant patients or with men who are about to become new fathers, and others who are to become grandparents. It is not uncommon for the strains of these shifts to create splitting and antagonism between all those involved in the early days of pregnancy or in the early months of the new infant's life as readjusting to these primitive emotional states takes its toll. Mothers mother as mother mothered, sometimes consciously emulating, sometimes consciously rejecting, their own conscious maternal pattern; but unconsciously the internal mother shapes and forms the struggle to become a maternal object.

As it will now be clear, when I am discussing siblings and how they affect the transference I am not taking the sibling relationships on their own. I believe the transference evolves around the family constellation, as I have argued, and we need to get a feel of the family in the internal world of the individual patient. For instance, a mother brings to her baby her own imaginative sense of what being a mother might be, and if she herself has not been adequately mothered her internal deficit may affect the baby and future babies.

In preliminary interviews, or diagnostic work, I am in the habit of asking for a narrative from the patient. It is in this first attempt to tell their story that a sibling relationship may be either owned or denied. It is a moment when I am free to ask questions in a way that I might not be again, and to construct for myself the spaces where a sibling might or might not be. Sometimes, where each sibling is described as problematic, I get the feel of parental function being consistent in its absence of thought or containment. Sometimes the patient describes the siblings as leading full, perhaps enviably settled lives, free from their own haunting pain. As often as not, prospective patients do not remember what they may have known in childhood about the vicissitudes of their life with their siblings. It is sometimes the case that repairing sibling relationships is part of what the patients find themselves engaged in as work progresses.

Ms F, a young woman brought up and nurtured by her elder sibling; she has scant attachment to her maternal internal object and therefore to the maternal transference, which takes second place. This has brought in its wake a lack of Oedipal struggle and concomitant difficulties in individuation.

What is it about her that makes me struggle even as I write this to find her name; she is nameless in my internal world, and faceless when she rings the consulting room bell. I have not yet ever anticipated her arrival, so I have to deal with my momentary lack of mental recognition, but I have never forgotten her, the young woman that she is. There is never a sense of the familiar or indeed a sense of anticipation in our meeting; we share this as a counter-transference harmony. She has often described the journey to the session in which she is either full of thoughts that she leaves behind her as she approaches the street, or a journey in which a kind of reverie takes over until she finds herself on my doorstep empty of thoughts. There is in me an absence of a sense of knowing this patient. She is a lively young woman who brought with her, at our first meeting, a typed history of all the major events in her life. She gave this list of dates and places to me as she left her first session and as if, somehow, she must have known that what was missing was a story, and the only form of narrative she could imagine was an external record of the lost events of her childhood. She could not construct this history alone; her past was a muddle of blurred events. Ms F achieved the task of creating an inventory of her past by getting her caretaker sister to do it with her; it was her sibling's function to contain the family narrative, as neither parent could or would do it. Though her early life was marked with family turmoil, the birth of siblings, endless changes of home and school, all of which were difficult, she talked about the events with a highly defended and brittle laugh.

As the work wore on, what became apparent was that when these disruptive events occurred, such as accidents or serious illness in the other siblings, she could never remember where her mother was, or indeed if she had been present. Together we would worry over this absence. "Where was she?" Ms F would ask me. "Where was she?" I would counter back, not knowing and not having any sense of finding mother in the drama. I was curious, but not worried by the absence, curious but not concerned. Events that might have moved me deeply only ruffled me in a strange way. Slowly but surely it emerged that the mother was absent not just in mind but also not in reality available. Similarly, accidents, of which there were many among the siblings, and which necessitated hospitalization, were mutually shrugged off, as if they still had not succeeded as moments of dangerous seeking for an object.

The main caretaker for this young woman was the eldest child in the family, a sister some years older than her, who had been, was, and, indeed, still is, the maternal object to the other four children. Understanding the transference reaction, our kind of mutual indifference to each other began to illuminate the futility of our task. How could I respond to her as a preoccupied and absent mother, and how could she have feelings about a mother who had never mothered her? We reached an impasse. I could not reach her, nor her me; and as we began to piece her world together I had to become either this indifferent mother, short on memory concerned for my own well-being, or a sister, barely old enough to be maternal, but concerned enough to be watchful and indeed central in patient's internal world. It is to her sister she refers for the history of the family, for her solace for her advice and for her, however limited care.

She has held herself together by using her body in sporting activity: she used the trampoline until she weakened her ankles and uses the gym as solace. Her friendships, though strong, are experienced by her as one-sided. That is, she is the listener, or rather the silent one. She is predominantly watchful, as she was as a child, taking her place always second, always a step behind, leaving a space to attempt to gauge the situation and retreat when necessary. She is, in the family configuration, the second child of five, the first three siblings close in age and born when the family was at the height of its dysfunction, the last two siblings being close in age but born a decade later to a parental couple who were in some sense attempting to start again.

Her concerns are for her younger siblings, now old enough to look after themselves. In some sense her interest in them and her concern for them are misplaced, but with her eldest sister's departure from the scene she takes on the mantle of caretaker mother as well as a sibling. She is, after all, literally the next sibling in line. Her attachment is to her sister, her elder sibling; they share a common past and between them have shaped a bearable narrative out of the chaos of the family history. She had no choice as an infant but to look to her sister and no choice as she grew up but to cling on to her sister at all costs, as the preoccupied parental couple neglected the family they were busy producing.

I would like to suggest that this configuration will shape, and has shaped, her attachments to others, and her struggle towards individuation has been severely hampered by the lack of an attachment to mother or an adult caregiver. As a consequence of the lack of attachment she has not, in some senses, developmentally moved on; there has been no struggle for true individuation and an absence of an Oedipal conflict. In her relationships with men, where she has looked for a relationship of mutuality, she has failed because she has to stay in the present, watchful and empty of affect in preparedness for flight or uncontainable emotion. She cannot look to the future, or reflect on the past. It has not occurred to her to take her boyfriends home, for the parental couple is not internalized in a way that would enable her to identify with them in the real world as a couple; and in the internal world her siblings are the family, and her elder sister the significant caretaker. Her history is not contained by mother but rests still on typewritten sheets that she left in the consulting room.[6] She has no idea of how a couple might behave, so she cannot share and enable a two-person relationship. She is watchful and interested in others and yet so involved in the projective process around the idea that she must, in order to survive, know what is going on in the mind of the other she is attempting to relate to, that she literally cannot think.

In working with this patient it is the sibling transference that dominates and needs interpretation. Without this the work lacks vitality. The family of siblings dominates the internal world and the parental couple are, of course, present but deeply fragmented. This is not to say that mother and father, first separate and then representing the idea of the couple, the cornerstone of the transference, will not be worked with, but this case study illustrates a need for putting the siblings first and facing them out in the transference: taking into account the birth order and understanding that the sibling dynamic has a lively and important place in the internal world. Mother will take time to come into focus, and she comes in the form of the negative transference expressed as indifference, but the risks involved of her coming to a depth of negativity are still experienced as too high for the patient.

Some patients carry strong and vital relationships with their siblings in their internal world and in external reality. Others have lost their internal connectedness to siblings and merely speak of seeing them in the external world. The relationship can take different forms: a sibling can be too present or completely absent in the psychic structure of the patient's mind. We learn about these psychic structures in the consulting room in two ways, consciously, as I have already said, through history taking, but primarily unconsciously, through the transference. A sibling transference has a different quality to a parental transference. In some cases it does not feel authentic, and it leaves the therapist wondering about the quality of the depth of the interaction taking place within the session. Here it is the countertransference that often holds the clue. The alliance between the patient and therapist may feel too even-handed, and the analytic work becomes slow and mutually unsatisfying. Alternatively, the transference may not be particularly specific, and the countertransference hard to grasp. The relationships between siblings, friends, or peers are defined as lateral by Juliet Mitchell (2003). She asks:

> Why should there be only one set of relationships which provide for the structure of our mind, or why should one be dominant in all

times and places? Even if there will be fewer full siblings in the world, there will still be lateral relationships—those relationships which take place on a horizontal axis starting with siblings, going on to peers and affinal kin. [Mitchell, 2003, p. 2]

These lateral relationships move into the transference when these relationships have become central to the patient's psychic structure. They do not represent the vertical relationships we define as those between siblings and their parents and it is these sibling relationships or lateral connections that can dominate clinical work and put the Oedipal transference albeit temporarily to one side. It is sometimes the case that sibling transferences are Oedipal in nature and attention in the transference needs to be given to this constellation. [Sharpe & Rosenblatt, 1994][7]

For the most part, sibling transferences can fall in and out of focus in the therapy as they do throughout a person's life, perhaps coming to the fore when the siblings begin to create a family of their own and begin to feel discomforted at the deep echo of a repetition. When therapists are caught up in the sibling transference they may have to wait and worry about the maternal/paternal transference and whether it will reappear. Or there may be other cases where one is forced to wonder whether the parents have ever been central to the patient's identity. For instance, those cases where there has been a lack of maternal containment and where the maternal function has been handed on to a sibling, then we may expect that the most significant transference may be the sibling one. A mother to several children may feel briefly attached to her baby but not to her developing child, and the transference may stay with the older siblings. A patient, the first-born of seven children, said, "I do not want to have children, I have done that since I was seven until I was kicked out of home at fifteen." This patient felt that her mother's interest and engagement with all the infants, including her, was brief, and as soon as she could mother handed over the feeding and nappy-changing and caretaking to her daughter. This patient suffered from a fear of vomiting, but she was only actually sick once about every fourteen months, with the same regularity that her mother had become pregnant. When a child is made to mother an infant sibling the strain of picking up maternal function prematurely may deepen the propensity for the formation of a false self, or overburden the child, curtailing vital aspects of the capacity to play, and therefore to thrive. This is what one may be working with in the therapy.

The only child

Only children often have a story about their single status and, indeed, some of them have internalized siblings of their own creation. Only children may carry guilt or dread of the long-held phantasy of being usurped and this suggests hostility toward an internal object. Alternatively, they may have unconsciously created an ally in the struggle around the Oedipal triangle, or, under the constraint of being alone, created an imaginary friend or twin.[8] In the external world an only child may turn to another family member or friend, or to their mother or father, to form a sibling alliance. The only child with an absent mother is forced into a similar position as the child with siblings, except all is phantasy, either in the form of an imaginary friend, or twin, or in the dread of a sibling coming to get what little is on offer and take it away. This dreaded non-sibling could be just as lively an internal identification as any other. However, there is a difference between the imaginary trauma and a real and repressed event, and there is a difference between the phantasy in the internal world of a sibling relationship and the reality of having a real life sibling. In playing together siblings have the opportunity to enact violent and hateful feelings as well as loving and protective ones. Children with siblings are faced with the shifting maternal object, the diminishing lap, the preoccupied mother; these affective states are real and take real external negotiating as well as demanding massive internal upheaval. But with the only child, the phantasy of a dreaded intruder, the rival or companion, can be conjured up or put in abeyance, more or less at will.

M is an only child, with a detached and alcoholic mother and an ineffective father. Here the transference was skin deep and masked by an attachment to a young inexperienced nanny figure that could just about hold the most basic boundaries. In all the patients I mention it was the case that the mother was herself inadequately mothered. Though I am not trying to draw conclusions, but rather point out ways of responding to family history, I have far less experience of working clinically with only children than I have with patients who are siblings.[9]

In my long-term work with this only child there is a sibling phantasy and a sibling transference to mother. Her history pertinent to this discussion was that she was born to a mother who longed for a child and had tried over many years to conceive. This birth followed a series of miscarriages. This longed-for child came too late for mother and she responded with fear to her demanding infant, spoiling her by feeding her to a steady obesity. Mother was unable to mother. She could not work with any of her infant's projections and cannot now metabolize any of her only child's adult concerns. Primitive terror was placated and not processed, subtle anxiety was greeted with maternal alarm, every emotion was rejected and left to wreak damage, and damage was done, the rivalry between them was that of siblings.

The patient lived with a steady dread of a sibling who might come and steal something that was hers. The lack of maternal containment and the inability to create any transitional space has meant that the transference has been stretched like a skin too thin for real containment. In the mother–daughter relationship rivalry was the cornerstone. Mother behaved like the beautiful spoilt sister and no maternal feelings were authentically expressed. This leaves this patient with no sense of the maternal, no idea of how to mother, and for years she carried a dread of children who may speak out of turn and shame her. She does not want, and will not have, a child, and her intimate relationships are starved of real sibling experience where love and hate can be worked through; she had no concept yet of the robustness acquired through nursery play. She finds it hard to understand why people do not behave as she does, or how she would like them to, there has been no other to watch and learn from. A mother who has become a rivalrous sibling fails to be truly loved or hated in a useful internal world way. The psychic stakes are too high, the possibility of loss too great. The sense of dread my patient had of being displaced by a sibling has diminished, but she has not yet gained a maternal internal object.

Conclusion

Siblings have each other in reality or in mind. In the face of early loss, in the search for containment and care, siblings can nurture and care for each other in a lively and vital way. Sometimes siblings slip away into the background of the therapeutic work, disguised in hostilities and rivalries that emerge unexpectedly in the workplace or in the relationship with partners. Sometimes siblings emerge as central to the patient's internal world. Siblings have the capacity to mother and father each other; they provided a space for the exploration of early murderous and rivalrous phantasy. By and large, siblings withstand ruthless use. They may be indifferent to each other, but they can provide love and sustenance. They enable the boundaries of love and hate to be tested and incestuous wishes to be grappled with. Adults stay in relation to their siblings throughout their lives; others who have lost siblings search for them, feel incomplete without them, or may feel contentment with them. Others lose their siblings, in phantasy or in reality, with relief or with pain, but sibling relationships form a vital and lively part of the internal world and provide a blueprint in which an individual thinks about, creates, and sustains relationships; in the search for later adult companionship siblings may be the model that potential partners may always be measured against.

Siblings may also provide stability, continuity, and love, companionship, and mirroring. Where, for a variety of real or internal world reasons, there is disturbance in the couple, siblings can and do mediate. Siblings can create order for each other, can support and encourage emotional growth and ease the pains of separation and loss. Where there has been a loss of continuity, a loss of history of containment of the family narrative, siblings can compensate by containing their history for each other. It is a necessary part of psychotherapeutic clinical work to think around the individual and to become immersed in their internal world. I am suggesting that the wider context of family and family culture must be taken into account, that there are times when the individual adult has to be seen in the full context of his lived experience, and where that includes siblings it may necessitate the exploration and analysis of a sibling transference and that can be both productive and useful.

Notes

1.   I am indebted to Prophecy Coles, both for stimulating my thinking with her book *The Importance of Sibling Relationships in Psychoanalysis* and for her patient editing of this chapter.

2. For further discussion of absence of mind, see Jennifer Silverstone (2002).
3. See Winnicott (1975), the chapter "Hate in the countertransference", for a discussion of the good enough mother.
4. Full discussion of maternal ambivalence, see Parker (1995), especially the chapter "Like child", for a discussion of Winnicott and infant observation.
5. See also Anne Karpf (1996).
6. See Daniel Stern (1985, p. 174) on the creating of a narrative and the use of language:

> The advent of language ultimately brings about the ability to narrate one's life story with all the potential that holds for changing how we view oneself ... It involves thinking in terms of persons who act as agents with intentions and goals ... This is a new and exciting area of research in which it is not clear how, why or when children construct (or construct with a parent) narratives that begin to form the autobiographical history that ultimately evolves into the life story a patient may first present to a therapist.

7. There is a full discussion of Oedipal sibling triangles in Sharpe & Rosenblatt (1994, p. 502).
8. See Vivienne Lewin (2004).
9. I have done 102 psychotherapy consultations over the last decade, and only six have been with only children.

References

Barrows, P., & Barrows, K. (2002). Fathers and the impact of loss. In: J. Trowell & A. Etchegoyen (Eds.), *The Importance of Fathers: A Psychoanalytic Re-evaluation* (pp. 161–171). London: Routledge.

Bollas, C. (1987). *The Shadow of the Object: Psychoanalysis of the Unthought Known*. London: Free Association Books.

Bollas, C. (1995). *Cracking Up: The Work of Unconscious Experience*. London: Routledge.

Coles, P. (2003). *The Importance of Sibling Relationships in Psychoanalysis*. London: Karnac.

Emanuel, R. (2002). Becoming a father. In: J. Trowell & A. Etchegoyen (Eds.), *The Importance of Fathers: A Psychoanalytic Re-evaluation* (pp. 131–146). London: Routledge.

Freud, A., & Dann, S. (1951). An experiment in upbringing. *Psychoanalytic Studies of the Child, 6*: 127–168.

Hoffman, E. (2004). *After Such Knowledge: A Meditation on the Aftermath of the Holocaust*. London: Secker and Warburg.

Houzel, D (1996). The family envelope and what happens when it is torn. *International Journal of Psychoanalysis, 77*(5): 901–912.

Karpf, A. (1996). *The War After*. London: Minerva.

Kogan, I. (1995). Love and the heritage of the past. *International Journal of Psychoanalysis, 76*(4): 805–823.

Lewin, V. (2004). *The Twin in the Transference*. London: Whurr.

Mitchell, J. (2003). *Siblings: Sex and Violence*. Cambridge: Polity.

Parker, R. (1995). *Torn in Two: The Experience of Maternal Ambivalence*. London: Virago.

Pines, D. (1986). Working with women survivors of the holocaust: affective experiences in transference and countertransference. *International Journal of Psychoanalysis, 67*(3): 295–307.

Sharpe, S. A., & Rosenblatt, A. D. (1994). Oedipal sibling triangles. *Journal of the American Psychoanalytic Association, 42*: 491–523.

Silverstone, J. (2002). An absence of mind. In: B. Bishop, A. Foster, J. Klein, & V. O'Connell (Eds.), *Ideas in Practice* (pp. 87–102). Practice of Psychotherapy Series: Book 2, London: Karnac.

Stern, D. N. (1985). *The Interpersonal World of the Infant: A View from Psychoanalysis and Developmental Psychology*. New York: Basic Books.

Waddell, M. (1998). *Inside Lives: Psychoanalysis and the Growth of Personality*. London: Duckworth.

Winnicott, D. W. (1975). *Through Paediatrics to Psycho-analysis*. London: Hogarth.

INDEX